HOW TO OPERATE YOUR HOME

Standard Edition

Tom Feiza
Mr. Fix-It

**Published
by
Mr. Fix-It Press**

N8 W28892 Shepherds Way
Waukesha, WI 53188
Phone: (262) 303-4884
Fax: (262) 303-4883
E-mail:Tom@misterfix-it.com
www.howtooperateyourhome.com
or www.htoyh.com

NOTICE:

This book is available at special discounts for bulk purchases, sales promotions, premiums, fund-raising, or educational use. For details, contact the publisher.

ISBN 978-0-9832018-3-0

Printed in the United States of America

Be Safe

The information in this book has been carefully assembled to ensure that it is as accurate as possible. However, the book provides general information only, and it is sold with the understanding that the publisher and author are not rendering legal or professional services.

This book does not provide product-specific information, and you should consult the manufacturer of the product or equipment for specific information. Operation and maintenance information is provided for general understanding only. For information specific to your home, consult with local contractors and professionals.

When attempting a home repair project, always consult professionals and follow label directions. Companies that manufacture equipment and home repair products are the ultimate authorities. Follow their instructions.

Many home repair, operation, and maintenance projects involve a certain degree of risk and should be approached with care. You should only attempt repairs if you have read and understood the instructions for the product, equipment, or tool that you are using. If questions or problems arise, consult a professional or the manufacturer.

Due to the variability of local conditions, construction materials, and personal skills, neither the author nor the publisher assumes responsibility for any injuries suffered or for damages or other losses that may result from the information presented.

Dedication

Who made me Mr. Fix-It?

I owe a lot to Uncle Nick and Uncle Joe in Virgil, Illinois, who put me on the road to being a real fix-it guy. I worked at their dairy farms, racetrack and motorcycle shop and on their many construction projects.

I was nine years old when Uncle Nick began paying me 50 cents a day to work on his farm. When I graduated from Marquette University's engineering school, I was still working for and learning from Nick and Joe and their crews.

They taught me that you "learn by doing" and that the real education takes place working in the trade. From Uncle Nick and Uncle Joe, I learned the value of hard and honest effort.

My mom was also a great fix-it lady who taught me a lot about painting and refinishing.

What is my house like?

Ask Gayle, my wife and best friend. She will tell you we have a lot of fix-it projects waiting for me. Just like every other couple, we operate with a "honey-do" list—you know, "Honey, you need to do this." And when the list gets too long, we talk about hiring a contractor. Our home is just like every other home.

So, this book is dedicated to:

My wife, Gayle, and my kids, Lindsay and Tom III, for putting up with all my fix-it projects and my basement full of stuff; and to my mom, Uncle Nick, and Uncle Joe.

Tom Feiza – "Mr. Fix-It"

Acknowledgements

Special thanks go to all the people who listen to my radio show, watch my television appearances, attend my seminars, use my home inspection service, and read my newspaper column. Your questions, answers, and tips made this book possible.

Many manufacturers have provided me with excellent technical information, and I value their help.

My editor, Leah Carson, took my rough copy and made the information much more useful and user-friendly. Lynn Eckstein designed my Mr. Fix-It logo years ago, and she is responsible for the original cover design. Tom Feiza III created the cover revisions and the wonderful interior layout.

Graphic artist (now architect) Justin Racinowski took my rough drawings and produced the easy-to-understand computer-generated drawings for the first edition. Lindsay Mefford (Feiza) created the artwork for this revised edition from our originals and my rough sketches.

Most importantly, I owe a lot to my wife, Gayle, and our kids, Lindsay and Tom. They helped me keep things in proper perspective by dragging me out of the office for vacations and family time.

Please enjoy my book and have a great fix-It day!

Tom Feiza – "Mr. Fix-It"

Author..Tom Feiza, a.k.a. Mr. Fix-It

Editor........Leah Carson, Excellent Words, LLC (Leah@excellentwords.com)

Artwork ....Justin Racinowski, Lindsay Mefford, Tom Feiza

Layout ....Tom Feiza III (tomfeiza@gmail.com)

Cover Art..Tom Feiza III, original by Lynn Eckstein

About the Author

Tom Feiza, Mr. Fix-It, is a "recovering" mechanical engineer and a real life fix-it guy. He personally tests home-related products and evaluates home construction problems.

Tom worked on a dairy farm through grade school, high school and college. After graduating from Marquette University as a mechanical engineer, Tom became licensed as a professional engineer and later as a home inspector. After college, Tom worked for over 20 years in the construction, maintenance and operation of large facilities. He shifted from engineering to become Mr. Fix-It, helping people with their home operation, maintenance and repair problems.

Tom now combines his hobby, his passion and his profession into his unique enterprise—Tom Feiza, Mr. Fix-It, Inc.

Tom hosts a live radio call-in show on AM 620 WTMJ in Milwaukee, Wisconsin. He writes books and magazine articles, and he helps provide useful illustrations. Watch for his information all over the Internet.

Tom presents unique and entertaining how-to seminars at home shows, association meetings, and retail events. He also gives entertaining keynotes at dinner meetings and professional conventions.

In another venture that helps him stay in touch with homes, people, and their related problems, Tom provides home inspection services and engineering investigations and evaluations for residential construction.

Contents

Introduction

So you have a new home—and no idea what to do next. It's like bringing your first baby home from the hospital. Throughout the pregnancy, everyone was helpful and encouraging. You read all the books and went to all the classes. But now you are home alone with the baby. What do you do next?

Sure, you have that home improvement "Honey Do" list for the painting and decorating tasks that will make the house your home. But what about the furnace, the roof, the garage door opener, the hose bibs, the everything? A home is the most complicated thing you have ever bought. It has more than 5,000 parts and components. Now you own it, and you need to run it.

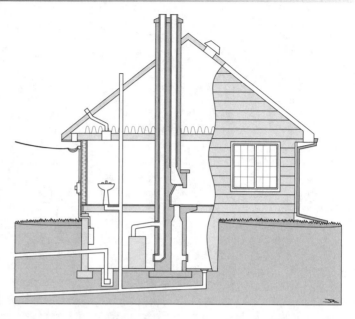

So where is that operating manual? You didn't get one?! You got one with the new car—and driving a car isn't complicated. For a new home, you're lucky if you get instruction manuals for major systems. For a used home, don't plan on receiving any instructions.

Everyone who owns a home has faced all the same questions and concerns. We never had an operating manual. Most of us just muddled through and eventually got things right. We learned through trial and error and corrected our mistakes. Lucky buyers had a dad, mom or Uncle Nick who was a great resource and would explain what to do and how things work. This book fills the void. It's an operating manual for your new or older home. It won't replace Uncle Nick—but it will come close. The book shares my 35 years of experience around homes, fixing or breaking the complicated stuff that fills them up.

You see, I am a mechanical engineering graduate of Marquette University and a registered professional engineer. I have over 25 years of experience working as an engineer on the maintenance and construction of buildings and equipment. Big deal! Actually, I know stuff about houses because I'm a hands-on guy. My Uncle Nick took me under his wing when I was 9 years old. He was a great teacher with the patience of a saint. Since Uncle Nick, I've regarded homes as a great learning experience.

I have not included all the answers. That is impossible. But all the basic information is here.

Enjoy your home. It is the biggest and best investment you have ever made. This book will certainly make your home a little easier to understand, operate and enjoy. Congratulations on your purchase!

Tom Feiza

"Mr. Fix-It"

Chapter 1 – Start It Up and Take That First Spin

Walk Through Before Closing

Just before closing, walk through your new home to observe its condition and contents. This will help avoid surprises and misunderstandings. Your real estate broker may arrange the walk-through and help you make sure everything is in order. Bring your purchase agreement and any related documentation so you can refer to all items that are included in your home purchase.

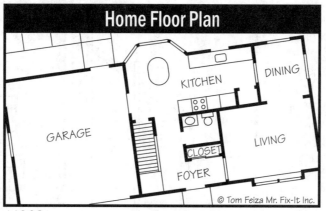

Home Floor Plan

KITCHEN DINING
GARAGE LIVING
CLOSET
FOYER

© Tom Feiza Mr. Fix-It Inc.

M002

In addition to the home purchase agreements, check the following:

- Documentation on equipment and utility systems: instruction books, service information, contractor information

- Appliances

- Heating and air conditioning operation

- Potential water leaks in ceilings, basement, water heater, plumbing

- Garage door opener operation and controls

- Home construction documents, if available

- Warrantees or guarantees that may transfer with your home

- Any natural gas smells or sewer odors

- Any physical damage inside and out

- Septic and well maintenance information

- Instruction manuals for equipment and appliances

Have the owner explain all the features of the home and its systems. Only he or she will know about that special key for the basement storage.....the interior switch that turns off the power to the garage....the emergency release for the garage door.

Utility Services

Prior to closing, arrange a transfer of all utility services to your name. Be ready to answer questions about budget payment or monthly payments. Ask about special electrical controls on air conditioning and water heaters that save you money and reduce utility demands. This is a good time to ask the utility companies for any home operating tips or instructions they may have.

Also, ask the utilities for emergency procedures and phone numbers. Often, they will mail you this information.

Most telephone companies now connect their lines to a junction box at the exterior of your home. This will usually activate the internal jacks that the owner had connected. Any changes inside your home will be your responsibility, and you can hire either the phone company or private contractors to set up the inside wiring.

Garbage, Recycling

In some municipalities, garbage and trash removal is provided by private companies. Arrange this in advance. Your new neighbors will be your best resource for information on private trash contractors that service the area.

You will also need to learn local rules on recycling paper, metal, cardboard, plastic, aerosol cans, and glass. Ask about separation of trash and requirements for containers. Your local municipality and neighbors will be a big help. Also ask about rules on disposal of hazardous materials such as paint, solvents, chemicals, and oil.

Insurance

Prior to closing on your home, you will need a homeowner's insurance policy in force. Your mortgage company will require this, and you should understand all the details of the policy. When you set up this policy, be ready to answer questions about the size of the home, type of construction, security and fire alarm systems, local fire department, wood-burning appliances and other details.

Post Office / Phone Numbers

Remember to plan in advance for a change of address and phone number(s). A quick note to family and friends will take care of the important people. File a change of address form with your current post office.

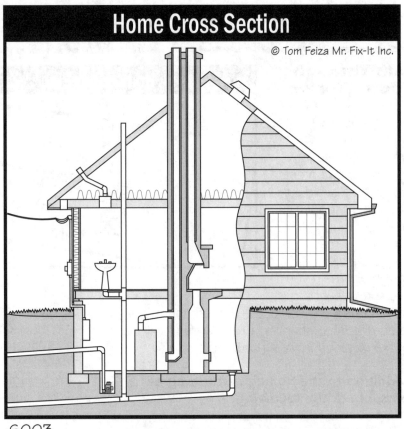

Home Cross Section

© Tom Feiza Mr. Fix-It Inc.

S003

Keys and Locks

When you take occupancy of your new home, you should receive all keys and security codes. Plan on re-keying all locks. Consider keying all exterior door locks to the same key. Find a trusted neighbor or friend who can keep a spare key for an emergency, but don't put your name and address on the key; use a code, first name, or initials only.

For your garage door opener, change the security code on the transmitters and receiver. Most door openers installed in the past 20 years have a security code that can be changed easily; check the instruction manual.

Welcome Wagon / Local Government and Service Groups

Take time to contact your local government office for information on the community. Also, contact the Welcome Wagon and any other local service organizations. They can provide useful information about your new neighborhood.

Safety and Security– Your First Priority

Local Fire, Police and Emergency Numbers

By your first day in your new home, have on hand all local emergency phone numbers for fire, police, ambulance, family physician, poison control center, hospital, eye doctor, utility companies, Mom and Dad at work, schools, and relatives. Keep these listed next to your phone, and make sure your kids know where to find this information. Also, carry a copy of the list with you. Accidents and problems can occur in new and unfamiliar places, so be ready.

Kids—Safety Information and Practice

Take some time with the kids to identify emergency telephone numbers. Walk through the exits and make sure everyone knows how to operate all locks and doors. Test your carbon monoxide, smoke and fire alarms so you all know where they are, how they work, and what they sound like.

It is wise to place smoke and fire detectors on all levels, in sleeping areas, in utility rooms, and at the top of stairs. Test smoke detectors periodically after you move in.

Add carbon monoxide alarms on every level of your home, and specifically in sleeping areas. Maintain batteries, and test them on a routine basis.

Smoke Detector / Alarm

Test once per month. Replace batteries yearly. Replace battery if "chirping." Replace unit before 10 years of age.

© Tom Feiza Mr. Fix-It Inc.

M011

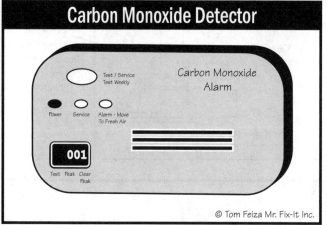

Carbon Monoxide Detector

Test / Service
Test Weekly

Carbon Monoxide Alarm

Power   Service   Alarm - Move To Fresh Air

001

Test Peak Clear Peak

© Tom Feiza Mr. Fix-It Inc.

M020

Establish an escape plan. All family members should know how to exit your home in an emergency and where to meet outside. Be sure your kids know that they must leave immediately and not return for pets or possessions. Use a sketch of your home's floor plan to identify all escape routes, utility shutoffs, and meeting points. Include your emergency numbers with the plan.

In some homes, a window may be the alternate exit from a second story or lower level. Identify such windows, and practice opening and using them.

Consider adding some battery-powered lights that come on during a power outage. Always have a few flashlights available.

Practice your escape plan with your kids. Activating an alarm helps the kids take a drill seriously. When practicing, keep in mind that emergencies can occur in the night, during a storm, when you are sound asleep, and/or when the power is off.

Fire Extinguishers

Equip your home with a fire extinguisher on each level and in the garage, basement and kitchen. Fire extinguisher have different ratings; select one that's rated "ABC," which means it's good for all common household fires. Contact your local fire department for more information.

Flammable Storage

The best advice for storing flammable materials is "just don't do it." When such storage is necessary, keep it to a minimum. Of course, we all need to store some gasoline for the lawnmower and solvents for household chores, so learn to store and use flammables safely. Use the original container or a container designed for that purpose. Keep flammable materials away from open flames and sources of combustion.

When using flammable solvents or cleaners, follow all safety precautions on the container. Never use a solvent cleaner or finish in a closed area without ventilation or near a source of combustion such as a gas furnace, gas water heater, or electric heater.

Use a spillproof container when storing gasoline. Gasoline should never be stored indoors. Vapors from gasoline are extremely flammable and must never be allowed to accumulate. If gasoline is stored in your garage, the entrance into your home should be up at least one step. Since gasoline vapors are heavier than air, they will settle in low areas. If you have a gas-fired heater or a water heater in the garage, do not store gasoline there.

Tags for Main Utility Valves and Shutoffs

In the event of an emergency, you may need to turn off a utility service to your home. It is important to identify the main shutoffs with tags telling how to turn them off. Make sure everyone in your family knows where to find and how to operate these shutoffs.

Identify the following:

- Main electrical disconnect: fuse block, breaker or switch

- Main water valve

- Main gas valve or propane valve

In addition, identify shutoffs for individual parts of systems:

- Furnace disconnect switch (electrical)

- Furnace gas or fuel valves

- Air conditioning disconnect switch

- Gas valves for appliances

- Hot water shutoff

- Individual breakers or fuses for branch circuits

- Plumbing valves for appliances and main distribution connections

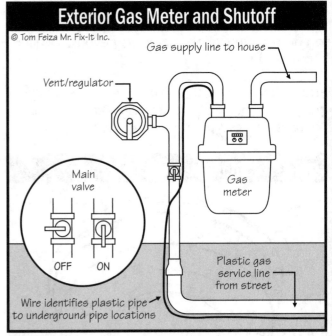

Exterior Gas Meter and Shutoff

© Tom Feiza Mr. Fix-It Inc.

Gas supply line to house

Vent/regulator

Main valve

Gas meter

OFF   ON

Plastic gas service line from street

Wire identifies plastic pipe to underground pipe locations

P002

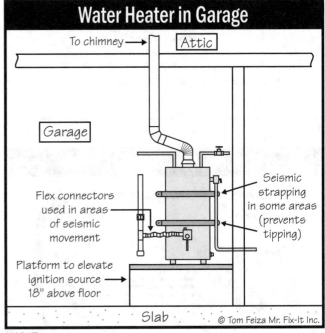

Water Heater in Garage

To chimney   Attic

Garage

Flex connectors used in areas of seismic movement

Seismic strapping in some areas (prevents tipping)

Platform to elevate ignition source 18" above floor

Slab   © Tom Feiza Mr. Fix-It Inc.

W013

Garage Door Safety

All garage door openers should have an automatic reverse that stops the door's downward motion if there is an obstruction in its path. This feature helps prevent injury to people or pets beneath the door.

The first day in your home, test the garage door reverse. After that, test it once a month. **(For testing instructions, see Chapter 6.)**

If your garage door opener does not reverse, take it out of service until it is repaired or adjusted. Look for adjustment instructions on the housing of the opener or in the instruction manual. If you are confused or unsure about how to make these adjustments, consult a professional.

Check the location of the garage door operator button(s). The button should be located at least 5 feet above the floor so children can't reach it. Since these control buttons are low voltage, you can easily relocate them as needed.

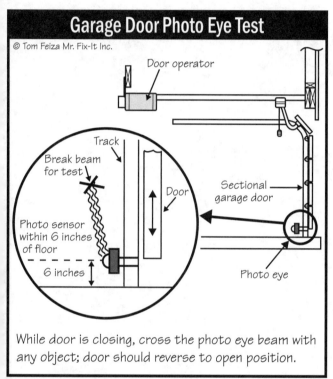

Garage Door Photo Eye Test

© Tom Feiza Mr. Fix-It Inc.

While door is closing, cross the photo eye beam with any object; door should reverse to open position.

M017

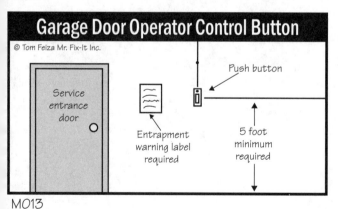

Garage Door Operator Control Button

© Tom Feiza Mr. Fix-It Inc.

M013

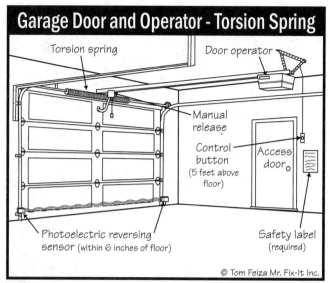

Garage Door and Operator - Torsion Spring

© Tom Feiza Mr. Fix-It Inc.

M012

Lighting Controls and Exterior Security

A brightly lit entrance is always a welcome sight on a dark evening. Consider adding motion sensor lights to entrances and garage door areas. These inexpensive fixtures replace the existing light fixtures. When anyone drives up or walks up, the unit senses motion and turns on the light.

For further information: Your local fire and police departments can be excellent sources of safety information. You could also contact the National Safety Council, the National Fire Protection Association (NFPA), and/or Underwriters Laboratories (UL).

Chapter 2 – Environmental and Safety Concerns

Lead

Starting in 1996, federal regulations required landlords and sellers of single family homes built before 1978 to notify renters and buyers about potential lead hazards. This requirement has raised concerns for everyone.

The regulation affects homes built before 1978 because that is when the manufacture of lead-based paint was banned. Lead-based paint was used almost universally in homes until the 1950s and was used to a lesser degrees in the 1960s and 1970s. If you buy a home built before 1978, you will be given an excellent booklet, "Protect Your Family from Lead in Your Home."

The main concern with lead is that exposure can harm young children, babies, and even unborn children. People can get lead in their bodies by breathing or swallowing lead dust or by eating soil or paint chips with lead in them. If you think your home may have lead hazards, call the National Lead Information Center at 1-800-424-LEAD to obtain free information.

Lead-based paint that is in good condition is usually not a hazard, but peeling, chipping, chalking or cracking lead-based paint is a hazard that needs immediate attention. Friction and rubbing points on windows and doors raise the biggest concern. Remodeling and paint removal can increase the risk if the lead-based paint is not handled properly.

Good housekeeping techniques can help reduce the risks of existing lead-based paint surfaces. Clean up paint chips immediately. Clean floors, window frames, windowsills and other surfaces weekly. Use a mop or sponge with warm water and a general all-purpose cleaner or a cleaner made specifically for lead. Thoroughly rinse sponges and mop heads after cleaning.

Wash children's hands often, especially before they eat and before naps and bedtime. Keep children from chewing windowsills or other painted surfaces.

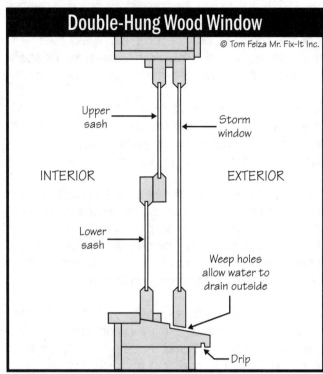

DOO1

Lead can also be present in drinking water. Call your local health department or water supplier to find out about testing your water. If your water supply does have lead, follow the recommendation of the local water supplier.

For more information, contact:

- The National Lead Information Center

- Your local health department

- The Consumer Product Safety Commission

- The Environmental Protection Agency (EPA)

Asbestos

Asbestos was often used in building materials until the 1970s. However, the mere presence of asbestos in your home is not hazardous. The danger is that asbestos materials may become damaged over time; damaged asbestos may release asbestos fibers that present a health hazard.

Studies show that people exposed to high levels of asbestos fibers have an increased risk of cancer and asbestosis. The risk increases with the number of fibers inhaled. Smokers are also at increased risk.

You may find asbestos fibers in pipe and duct insulation, resilient floor tiles, cement sheeting and shingles, soundproofing, joint compounds, and many fireproof or fire-resistant materials. The only way to determine whether a building material contains asbestos is to have it sampled and tested by a qualified lab.

If you think you have asbestos in your home, don't panic. Usually the best thing you can do with asbestos materials in good shape is to leave them alone. Repairs or remodeling must be done properly to avoid disturbing these materials. Do not sweep, dust or vacuum debris that may contain asbestos; these steps may release asbestos fibers into the air.

For more information, contact:

- Consumer Product Safety Commission

- Environmental Protection Agency

- American Lung Association

- Your state and local health departments

Radon

Radon is a radioactive gas that has been found in homes all over the U.S. It comes from the natural breakdown of uranium in soil, rock and water, and it gets into the air we breathe. Typically, radon moves up through the ground and enters a home's foundation through cracks and holes. Your home can trap this radon.

Testing is the only way to know whether you and your family are at risk from radon. You cannot see, smell or taste it. Breathing air containing radon increases your risk of getting lung cancer. If you smoke and your home has high radon levels, your risk of lung cancer is especially high.

You can conduct a radon test using a small charcoal canister or alpha-track detector. Test kits are available through hardware stores, and the cost usually includes lab analysis. The most accurate testing procedure follows EPA testing requirements. You can also hire a professional testing firm, but make sure it is registered with the EPA and that it follows EPA guidelines. A professional test will cost about $150.

A short-term test over two to four days provides only a quick snapshot of the radon levels in your home. A much better test is a long-term test conducted over more than 90 days.

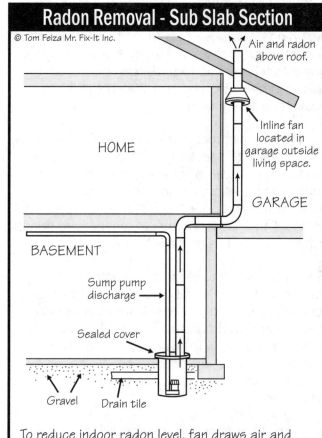

Radon Removal - Sub Slab Section

© Tom Feiza Mr. Fix-It Inc.

Air and radon above roof.

Inline fan located in garage outside living space.

HOME

GARAGE

BASEMENT

Sump pump discharge

Sealed cover

Gravel   Drain tile

To reduce indoor radon level, fan draws air and radon from below floor slab where radon originates in the soil. Fan operates continuously.

V034

If excessive radon is present, a common solution for a home with a drain-tile system is a sub-slab depressurization system. It removes radon from below the slab.

Radon can also be present in your drinking water. Contact your water supplier for specific information. You can receive more information on radon from several local and federal sources.

For more information, contact:

- The Environmental Protection Agency

- State or local health departments

- The American Lung Association

Carbon Monoxide

Carbon monoxide (CO) should be a concern for all homeowners. The government estimates that 300 people are killed by CO in their homes each year. CO is called a silent killer because it has no taste, color or odor. Almost all CO problems are caused by poor maintenance or improper use of fuel-burning equipment.

You can take simple precautions to protect your family by understanding CO and by properly maintaining combustion equipment in your home.

CO is produced when fuel is burned. Fuel-burning appliances such as your furnace are potential sources. Properly maintained appliances produce very little CO and will not cause a problem. However, improperly operating appliances, your auto, or any non-vented indoor fire can cause CO poisoning.

Proper maintenance of fuel-burning appliances is essential. This includes the furnace, water heater, gas clothes dryer, fireplace, and even a gas range or space heater. All of these appliances should be used as designed, and all need periodic servicing.

Pay particular attention to furnaces and water heaters. Have them serviced regularly, and routinely inspect the flue connections and chimney. Flue pipes should not have holes, rust or soft areas. Flues should not show signs of water streaking or sooting; this indicates that combustion gas is not flowing up the flue into the chimney.

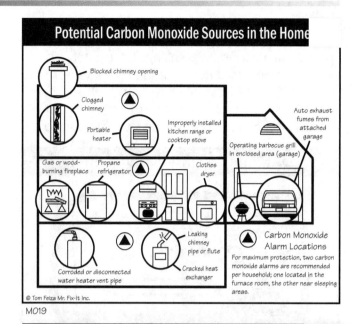

Potential Carbon Monoxide Sources in the Home

Blocked chimney opening

Clogged chimney

Portable heater

Improperly installed kitchen range or cooktop stove

Auto exhaust fumes from attached garage

Operating barbecue grill in enclosed area (garage)

Gas or wood-burning fireplace

Propane refrigerator

Clothes dryer

Leaking chimney pipe or flue

Corroded or disconnected water heater vent pipe

Cracked heat exchanger

Carbon Monoxide Alarm Locations
For maximum protection, two carbon monoxide alarms are recommended per household; one located in the furnace room, the other near sleeping areas.

© Tom Feiza Mr. Fix-It Inc.

M019

Water Heater Signs of Backdrafting

Rust, white stains, drip marks

Rust, burn marks

Melted foam insulation

Rust falling out of metal flue

Gas water heater

Combustion gas

When the combustion products of a gas water heater are not moving up a chimney vent, you may see melted insulation, burn marks, rust, white stains, and drip marks. This is a dangerous problem.

© Tom Feiza Mr. Fix-It Inc.

V033

Also, know the symptoms of CO poisoning. Initial symptoms are similar to the flu without fever: dizziness, nausea, fatigue, headache and irregular breathing. If you have these symptoms at home and then feel better when you go outside your home, suspect a problem. If all the members of your family have similar symptoms at similar times, suspect a problem.

You can also help protect your family with a CO detector. Buy one similar to a smoke detector. It should have a loud audio alarm. Do not rely on detectors with small dots that turn black when exposed to CO—how often will you look at the dots? Select a top-of-the-line alarm with a digital CO readout so you can monitor the level in your home.

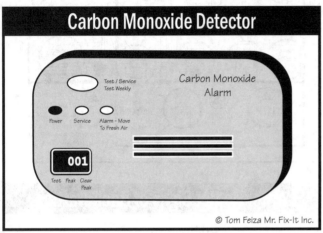

M020

The best location for a CO detector is on a wall in your sleeping area, about 5 feet from the floor. Place it where you will see it every night before you go to bed so you will remember to check the level.

Mold and Mildew

Since about 1990, mold has become a serious concern for homeowners. The news media present graphic stories of sick homeowners and homes that must be torn down because of mold contamination. In recent years that message has been reinforced by more and more stories. Some people are even concerned with the small black dots that may appear from time to time in caulk around the bathtub.

Is mold a real problem? Every homeowner needs to think through this issue relative to his or her own home. Mold has been around forever, but recently it has become a big issue. Why? Is it really an important issue?

Recent government and scientific studies have found that mold poses a threat to those who have breathing problems, allergies, or weakened immune systems. Government studies also show that mold does not normally affect healthy people.

We certainly don't want to be exposed to mold and risk our health. So, what do we do? Avoid the conditions that cause mold to grow: moisture, warmer temperatures, and a food source.

Mold is everywhere—inside and outside your home. Mold helps turn leaves and grass back into soil. The green growth on the north side of the tree trunk is—you guessed it—mold.

What has changed? Why is it a problem now?

Older homes are big energy wasters. Air and heat move easily though old homes. Air movement and heat easily dry out old homes if they become wet. (Want to dry your hair? Blow hot air on it.)

Newer homes are tight—wrapped in air barriers and moisture retarders with tight insulation. We have stopped the air movement and heat loss, but now these homes don't dry out. If new homes get wet and don't dry out, there is the potential for mold.

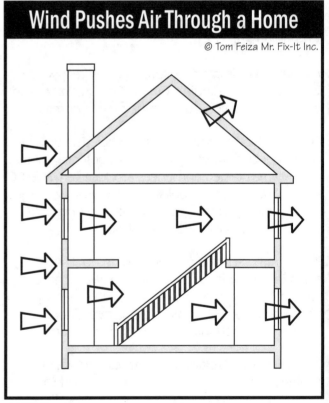

V038

Our First Defense

Our first defense is to keep our homes dry. Without moisture, mold will not grow. This means we can't allow excessive condensation, roof leaks, or plumbing leaks; and if surfaces do get wet, we need to dry them as soon as possible. If soft materials become wet, they should be removed.

What to do if you suspect mold

Look for visible mold growth. Search for areas with a noticeable mold odor. Look for signs of water stains, leaks, standing water, or condensation. Eliminate the water and stop the mold. Most government agencies don't recommend more extensive testing because a simple visual inspection can confirm whether there is a mold or moisture problem. There are no accepted standards for testing and exposure levels for mold. There are no standards relating health issues to levels of exposure. Your best bet is to find the moisture problem, eliminate the moisture, and clean up any mold.

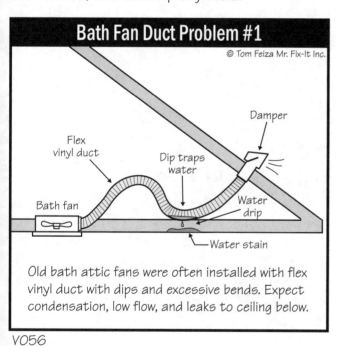

Bath Fan Duct Problem #1

© Tom Feiza Mr. Fix-It Inc.

Damper

Flex vinyl duct

Dip traps water

Bath fan

Water drip

Water stain

Old bath attic fans were often installed with flex vinyl duct with dips and excessive bends. Expect condensation, low flow, and leaks to ceiling below.

V056

Mold Information – Resources

For good information on investigation, testing, and mold removal, I suggest the following resources:

Minnesota Department of Health

www.health.state.mn.us

Building Science Corporation

www.buildingscience.com

The New York City Health Department

www.nyc.gov/health

Forest Products Laboratory

www.fpl.fs.fed.us

Environmental Protection Agency

www.epa.gov

State of Wisconsin – Department of Health and Family Services – Mold Information

www.dhfs.wisconsin.gov/eh/HlthHaz/fs/moldindx.htm

Chapter 3 – Utility Systems – Heating and Air Conditioning

Utility and General System Notes

This is where your homework starts. Take time to read these chapters. They contain important information about the many systems in your home. The explanation of each system includes operating information, terminology, sketches, main shutoffs, and part names.

Since some systems are very complicated, they need to be serviced routinely by contractors. You can do simple maintenance yourself; this information is provided in utility systems chapters and in Chapter 8 on Service Requirements by the Calendar.

Your home will not have all of the systems shown in this book. For instance, you may have a warm air furnace or a hot water furnace, but not both. You may have either a central air conditioner or a heat pump. As you read, walk around your home to determine the type of equipment you have and identify important valves and switches. If some systems or parts are confusing, ask a professional service contractor or a knowledgeable friend to walk you through the system.

The chapters on emergencies will help you solve problems and perhaps avoid a service call. I have attempted to include all common problems.

Heating and Air Conditioning

Most homes are heated with a warm air furnace (also called a forced air furnace) because this type of system provides heating and cooling through the same air distribution ducts. A warm air system requires supply grills in most rooms. Some homes are heated with a hydronic (warm water) system that uses radiators, baseboard (convector) elements, or heating pipes buried in walls or floors.

The energy source for heating can be natural gas, propane, or oil. In warmer climates, electrical resistance heating elements may be used in a warm air furnace. Usually, the energy source for air conditioning is electricity, but gas-powered engine systems can also provide cooling.

Some homes have separate heating and cooling systems. One common system combines hydronic heating with ducted air conditioning.

As you review the information on heating and air conditioning, identify the system used in your home.

As with all systems in your home, you must understand the basics of heating and air conditioning so you can perform basic maintenance and operate the system properly and efficiently.

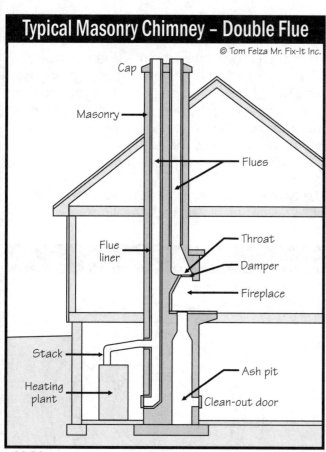

Typical Masonry Chimney – Double Flue

© Tom Feiza Mr. Fix-It Inc.

- Cap
- Masonry
- Flues
- Flue liner
- Throat
- Damper
- Fireplace
- Stack
- Ash pit
- Heating plant
- Clean-out door

F002

Gas Warm Air Furnace

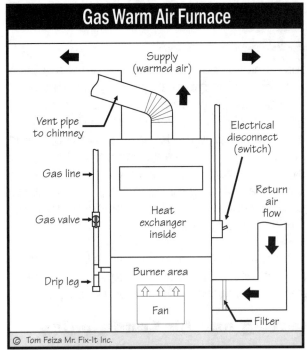

H001

Must Know / Must Do
Heating and Air Conditioning

- Understand how your heating and cooling system works and who you can call for service.

- Understand the control (thermostat) for the heating and cooling system.

- Perform basic maintenance: filter changes and perhaps lubrication.

- Schedule yearly maintenance by a professional.

- Identify and know how to use emergency shutoffs for electricity, gas, oil, and so on.

Thermostat

The thermostat provides automatic control for heating and cooling systems. You set it to the temperature you want to maintain. The thermostat, located in the conditioned (heated and/or cooled) space, senses room temperature, and when the room temperature varies from your setpoint, the thermostat activates the heating or cooling system.

A dual heating/cooling thermostat will have switches that let you change the system from heating to cooling and operate the fan separately. Some thermostats also allow you to turn off the heating and cooling systems.

All heating and cooling thermostats operate with similar buttons and controls. The basic and common controls are as follows:

HEAT – OFF – COOL

This switch will put the system in the heating mode (HEAT), turn the system off (OFF), or switch the system to cooling (COOL) if there is an air conditioning system. Once the system is set to HEAT or COOL, the thermostat temperature setting controls the system based on the room temperature.

FAN – ON – AUTO

This switch allows operation of the fan manually (ON), independent of the heating and cooling system. This allows you to circulate air in your home without operating the heating or cooling system. In the automatic (AUTO) setting the fan will cycle on and off as needed by the heating or cooling system. AUTO is the setting normally used.

The typical home system is either fully on or fully off; it doesn't provide variable heating/cooling.

Heat Only Thermostat

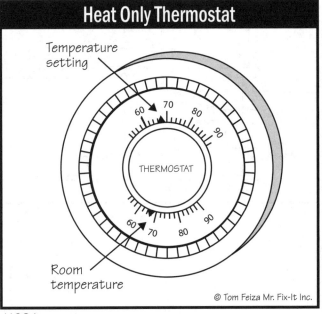

H024

Heat - Cool Thermostat

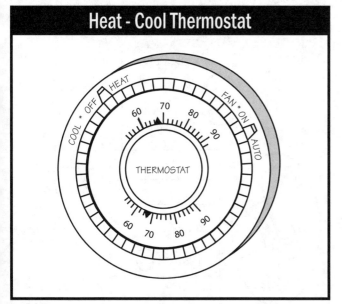

H023

When the thermostat calls for heat, the furnace reacts at 100 percent capacity until the room temperature reaches the setpoint; then the furnace shuts off. Turning the thermostat up higher will not heat the room any faster. When you switch the system to cooling, turning the thermostat lower will not cool the room any faster. (A few homes do have complicated systems in which the furnace is capable of variable heating/cooling, but these are the exception.)

Electronic (or digital) thermostats can be programmed for automatic adjustment of the setpoint temperature based on time of day and day of week. These help conserve energy; they can lower the temperature during sleeping hours or when your home is not occupied.

Thermostats should be installed and maintained by professionals. Special anticipator settings on the thermostat match its operation with the operation of the furnace. If you replace a thermostat, make sure that this anticipator setting is done properly.

Thermostats are very sensitive. Your thermostat should be level, out of direct sunlight, and away from direct heat sources. If a thermostat develops a major problem, the usual recommendation is replacement rather than repair, because much better electronic thermostats with modern setback capabilities are readily available at reasonable prices.

Digital Thermostat

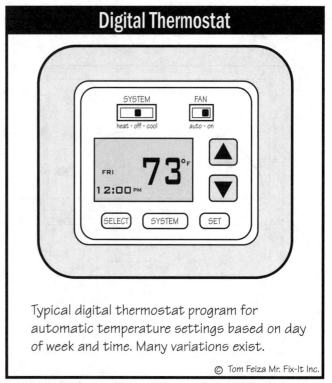

Typical digital thermostat program for automatic temperature settings based on day of week and time. Many variations exist.

© Tom Feiza Mr. Fix-It Inc.

H025

Warm Air Furnace

The most common type of warm air (forced air) furnace provides heat by burning a fossil fuel to warm air and then distributing the warm air inside your home. The heat source is confined within a heat exchanger inside the furnace housing. For gas, propane, and oil systems, the fuel is burned inside or below a heat exchanger. The hot products of combustion flow through the heat exchanger and up a chimney or are drawn out through a vent pipe.

The hot products of combustion warm the metal of the heat exchanger. After a minute or so, when the heat exchanger's metal is warm, the circulating (furnace) fan starts. This fan circulates air across the hot metal on the outside of the heat exchanger. The heated air warms your home.

For homes without basements or crawl spaces, warm air furnaces can be located in attics or closet spaces. The typical warm air furnace located in an attic or crawl space uses the same components as a basement (upflow type) furnace but the furnace is often designed to operate horizontally to save space.

Warm Air Furnace and Distribution Ducts

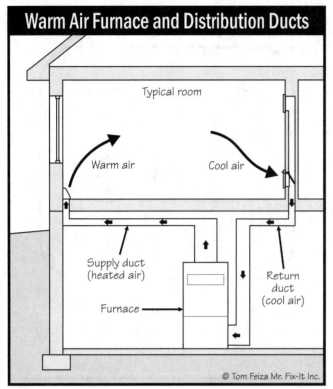

Typical room

Warm air

Cool air

Supply duct
(heated air)

Return
duct
(cool air)

Furnace

© Tom Feiza Mr. Fix-It Inc.

HO10

Furnaces for homes built on a concrete slab are located in the attic or in a closet. For the closet installations, a downflow warm air furnace may be used. These furnaces are similar to the upflow furnace, but the components are reversed. The heat supply ducts are in the floor slab. Homes on slabs can also have a warm air furnace in a closet using a typical upflow furnace – the supply ducts will be in the attic and the return will be through the walls or in the floor slab.

The efficiency of gas furnaces has improved dramatically in recent years. Standard (65%) warm air furnaces have been improved with electronic ignition devices to eliminate the standing pilot light and prevent this heat loss. These furnaces have also been improved with a motor-operated flue damper in the pipe that goes to the chimney. When the burner is on, the damper is open. When the burner is off, the damper closes and eliminates the draft up the chimney, saving energy. These improvements will make a 65% furnace operate at about 70 to 75% efficiency.

You will find 80% efficiency furnaces that use a draft fan to force the products of combustion up the chimney. You will find 90%+ efficiency furnaces that vent with plastic PVC pipe. These higher efficiency furnaces squeeze so much energy out of the

Warm Air Furnace with Damper & Igniter

To chimney

Supply

Electrical
Ignitor
(at burner)

Hot
surface

Damper
(open)

Return

Gear
Motor

A standard (65% efficiency) warm air furnace can be improved to 70 or 75% with a power-operated flue damper and igniter. The damper closes when the flame is off and the ignitor eliminates the standing pilot light.

© Tom Feiza Mr. Fix-It Inc.

HO41

Warm Air Furnace – Horizontal Flow

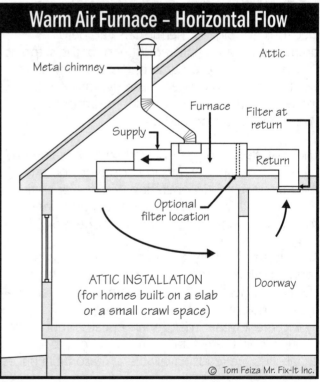

Attic

Metal chimney

Furnace

Filter at
return

Supply

Return

Optional
filter location

ATTIC INSTALLATION
(for homes built on a slab
or a small crawl space)

Doorway

© Tom Feiza Mr. Fix-It Inc.

HO11

products of combustion that they need special fans to help remove the products of combustion; the combustion gas is not hot enough to naturally draft up the chimney.

In an electric warm air furnace, air circulates directly over an electrical resistance-heating element.

A propane gas furnace is similar to a natural gas furnace but uses a different burner and control system designed for propane.

Oil warm air furnaces have a special oil burner and combustion chamber. The burner pressurizes the oil and sprays it through a small nozzle, forming a mist. The burner also provides an air supply and a high-voltage spark. This results in a very hot flame that is contained in a ceramic combustion chamber. From the combustion chamber, the hot combustion gas flows up through the heat exchanger, just as in a gas furnace.

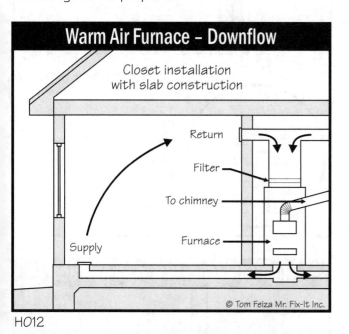

Warm Air Furnace – Downflow

Closet installation with slab construction

Return
Filter
To chimney
Furnace
Supply

© Tom Feiza Mr. Fix-It Inc.

H012

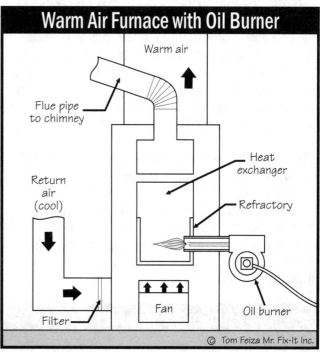

Warm Air Furnace with Oil Burner

Warm air
Flue pipe to chimney
Heat exchanger
Refractory
Return air (cool)
Fan
Oil burner
Filter

© Tom Feiza Mr. Fix-It Inc.

H013

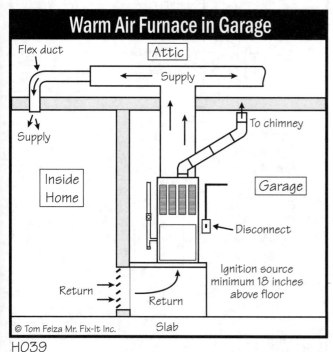

Warm Air Furnace in Garage

Flex duct
Attic
Supply
Supply
To chimney
Inside Home
Garage
Disconnect
Return
Return
Ignition source minimum 18 inches above floor
Slab

© Tom Feiza Mr. Fix-It Inc.

H039

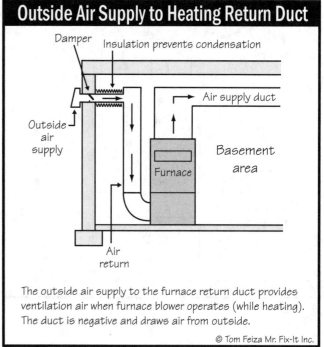

Outside Air Supply to Heating Return Duct

Damper
Insulation prevents condensation
Air supply duct
Outside air supply
Basement area
Furnace
Air return

The outside air supply to the furnace return duct provides ventilation air when furnace blower operates (while heating). The duct is negative and draws air from outside.

© Tom Feiza Mr. Fix-It Inc.

V028

A warm air furnace recirculates air in your home. It does not draw in outside air unless there are special provisions for an outside air supply (which is not common). The fan circulates the air, which is drawn from the return grills and ducts inside your home and discharged through the supply grills. There will be a furnace air filter located near the fan; you must maintain this filter.

Systems for air supply and ducting have changed through the years. The early "gravity" warm air furnace system (commonly called an octopus) did not use a circulating fan. The air was said to move by "gravity"—that is, warm air simply rose up into the rooms. This type of system often has warm supply grills in the center of the home and the cold returns along outside walls.

When furnaces were improved with circulating fans (the forced air/warm air furnace), heating ducts made a transition to the upper portion of the center wall; return ducts were still located along the outer walls. In an older home, you may find a strange combination of supply and return grills, since they were added as heating systems were upgraded or replaced.

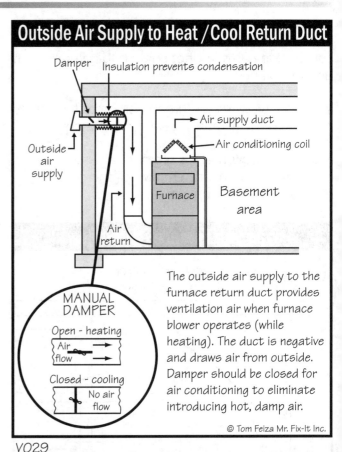

Outside Air Supply to Heat /Cool Return Duct

The outside air supply to the furnace return duct provides ventilation air when furnace blower operates (while heating). The duct is negative and draws air from outside. Damper should be closed for air conditioning to eliminate introducing hot, damp air.

© Tom Feiza Mr. Fix-It Inc.

V029

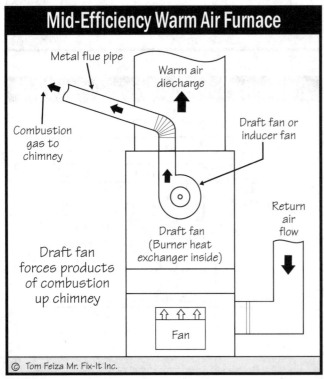

Mid-Efficiency Warm Air Furnace

© Tom Feiza Mr. Fix-It Inc.

H002

High-Efficiency Warm Air Furnace

© Tom Feiza Mr. Fix-It Inc.

H003

Warm air or forced air furnaces have a circulating fan or blower located near the heat exchanger. This fan circulates the house air over the warm metal of the heat exchanger inside the furnace. The fan may be powered directly by a fan motor mounted inside the fan housing. A motor through a belt and pulley arrangement may also power the fan.

Warm Air Furnace Fan and Motor

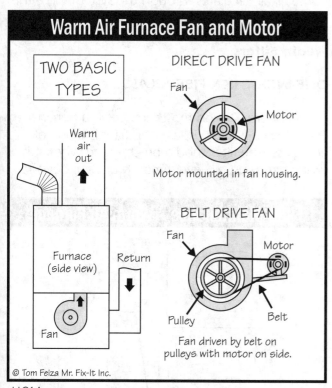

TWO BASIC TYPES

DIRECT DRIVE FAN

Fan

Motor

Motor mounted in fan housing.

Warm air out

Furnace (side view)   Return

Fan

BELT DRIVE FAN

Fan   Motor

Pulley   Belt

Fan driven by belt on pulleys with motor on side.

© Tom Feiza Mr. Fix-It Inc.

H014

For a belt drive fan, you must maintain the belt and belt alignment. Turn off power to the unit before you open the fan chamber. The belt should not be cracked or frayed. If the belt is very hard and shiny on the driving "v" sides, it is old and needs to be replaced. The pulleys should align so the belt runs straight between each pulley.

Proper tension on the belt is required to transmit power. With moderate hand pressure applied on the belt halfway between the pulleys, the belt should deflect about 1/2 to 3/4 inch. The motor mounting brackets are often adjustable to change the belt tension.

Many older furnaces require lubrication of the bearings on the fan and fan motor. On newer furnaces, bearings may be lubricated for life and will not need additional lubrication. Check your owner's manual or consult with a heating contractor for the specific requirements for your furnace. You can also

Warm Air Furnace Belt Drive Maintenance

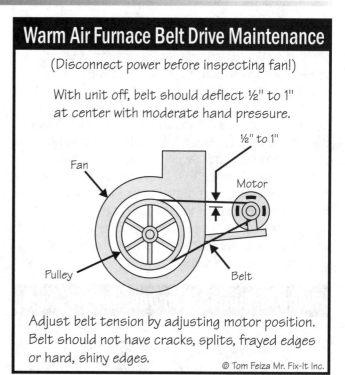

(Disconnect power before inspecting fan!)

With unit off, belt should deflect ½" to 1" at center with moderate hand pressure.

½" to 1"

Fan

Motor

Pulley

Belt

Adjust belt tension by adjusting motor position. Belt should not have cracks, splits, frayed edges or hard, shiny edges.

© Tom Feiza Mr. Fix-It Inc.

H015

Warm Air Furnace: Lubrication for Furnace Motor and Fan

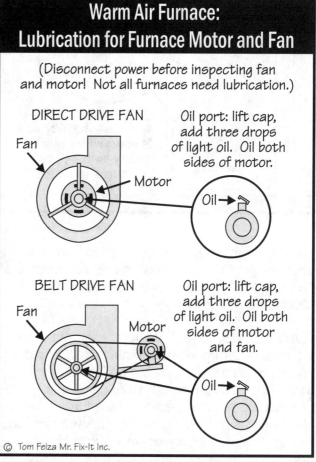

(Disconnect power before inspecting fan and motor! Not all furnaces need lubrication.)

DIRECT DRIVE FAN

Fan

Motor

Oil port: lift cap, add three drops of light oil. Oil both sides of motor.

Oil →

BELT DRIVE FAN

Fan

Motor

Oil port: lift cap, add three drops of light oil. Oil both sides of motor and fan.

Oil →

© Tom Feiza Mr. Fix-It Inc.

H016

look at the ends of the fan and the motor; you may see little (1/4-inch) caps over little tubes. These are ports in which to add oil for lubrication. Generally these bearings should be lubricated with a few drops of light oil every few months.

Newer furnaces will also have a safety switch built into the fan access door. When the fan chamber door is removed, this switch shuts the furnace off. This is a safety device that prevents accidental injury from the moving part of the fan system. If you ever have a situation with no heat or no air conditioning, you should check this access door and safety switch. A loose fan access door can inadvertently shut the system down.

Warm Air Furnace Fan Door Safety Switch

Switch (side view)

Spring loaded button

Control wire

Fan chamber door

When fan chamber door is removed (or ajar), safety switch pops out and turns furnace off.

© Tom Feiza Mr. Fix-It Inc.

H017

An older home may also have a supply grill without a return grill. This is common in the second story of Cape Cod style houses. Often this works well for heating but not for proper air conditioning.

With modern systems, heat ducts are located on the floor or ceiling near the outside walls, windows and doors. Returns are placed on interior walls. If the furnace is in the basement or crawl space, supply grills will be near the floor; if the furnace or supply ducting is in the attic, supply grills will be in the ceiling. This modern arrangement provides for good air distribution and greater comfort. Most modern systems have a return grill in every room except the bathrooms.

Air Filters

Air filters are provided on all forced air furnaces to remove dirt and lint from heated air.

This keeps the fan, heat exchanger and air conditioning coil clean. It also helps clean the air of your home as air circulates through the system (note the direction of the air flow).

Media Filters

ONE-INCH-THICK FIBERGLASS

The standard filter on most furnaces is a nominal 1"-thick media filter. Usually, this filter is made of fiberglass. The filter should be changed when it is visibly dirty—usually every month or two, depend-

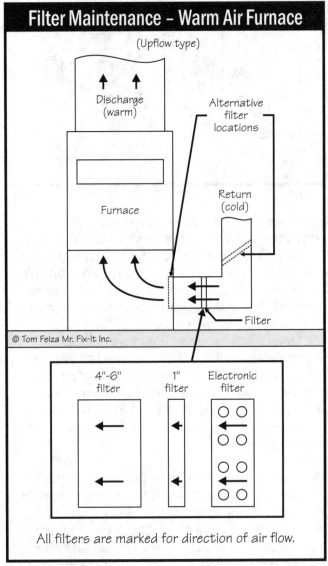

Filter Maintenance – Warm Air Furnace

(Upflow type)

Discharge (warm)

Alternative filter locations

Furnace

Return (cold)

Filter

© Tom Feiza Mr. Fix-It Inc.

4"-6" filter | 1" filter | Electronic filter

All filters are marked for direction of air flow.

H009

ing on the quality of the filter and the amount of dirt in your home's air. Children, pets, plants, and activity tend to produce more dirt that finds its way into the heating system.

Be careful about the direction of the air flow through the filter. Filters are designed to be installed with one particular side facing the air stream. Most filters have directions or an arrow telling you which side should be installed toward the furnace. The arrow is the direction of the air flow and should be toward the base or the fan of the furnace.

Remember: the furnace filter is also used when you operate the fan and/or central air conditioning, so you should check on the filter during the summer, too.

PAPER

I recommend that you try one of the pleated paper filters. These catch more dirt than inexpensive fiberglass filters. Some even have a static charge to attract dirt. Others have a carbon filter content. Paper filters cost between $3 and $15 and can be found in most hardware stores. You will need to change this type of filter more often because it collects more dirt.

WASHABLE

Washable filters can be made of foam or woven synthetic fiber. They are about as effective as inexpensive fiberglass filters. You can improve the efficiency of a foam filter by spraying it with a special filter coating; this oily/waxy spray helps the filter hold dirt better.

PLEATED, 4- TO 6-INCH THICK

A big improvement over the standard 1"-thick filter is a pleated fiberglass or paper filter.

Fiberglass Filter - Flow Direction

Air flow direction

Arrow on filter frame indicates air flow direction

16•20•1

© Tom Feiza Mr. Fix-It Inc.

H026

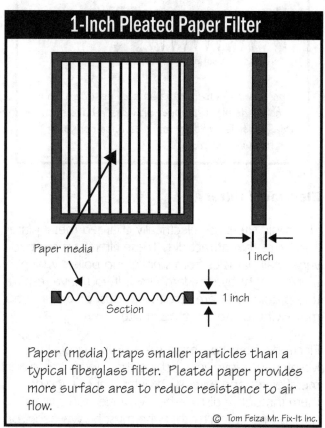

1-Inch Pleated Paper Filter

Paper media

1 inch

Section

1 inch

Paper (media) traps smaller particles than a typical fiberglass filter. Pleated paper provides more surface area to reduce resistance to air flow.

© Tom Feiza Mr. Fix-It Inc.

H027

Must Know / Must Do

Routinely Maintain the Furnace Filter

Maintenance is based on the type of filter, how often the unit is running (heating and cooling), and how you use your home. The three basic types of filters are media, electronic, and electrostatic.

Often, the pleated paper filter is housed in a 6"-thick frame. The paper filter is very fine, and it catches smaller particles of dirt and dust. This type of filter is normally changed once per year, and you replace only the paper element.

A pleated fiberglass filter often is mounted in a throwaway paper frame. The entire unit is replaced about once a year.

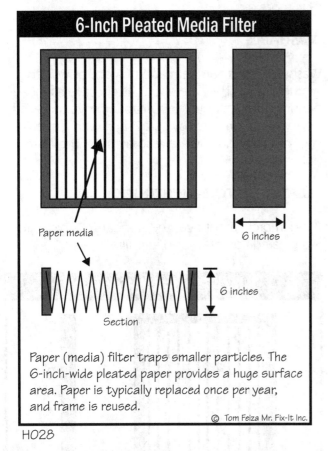

6-Inch Pleated Media Filter

Paper media

6 inches

Section

6 inches

Paper (media) filter traps smaller particles. The 6-inch-wide pleated paper provides a huge surface area. Paper is typically replaced once per year, and frame is reused.

© Tom Feiza Mr. Fix-It Inc.

H028

Electronic Filters

Electronic filters use electrically charged metal plates and wires that attract dirt. These filters can remove very small particles from smoke and pollen which aren't caught by standard filters. If you have respiratory problems or are sensitive to dust or pollen, you may want to use this type of filter.

Electronic filters cost more than $600 to install. Maintenance involves washing the interior frame and metal plates and wires with detergent or running them through a dishwasher. Most electronic filters have a metal pre-filter that also must be washed. For more specific cleaning instructions, contact a heating contractor or the filter manufacturer.

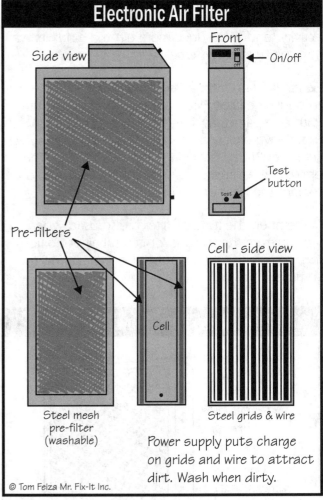

Electronic Air Filter

Side view

Front

On/off

Test button

Pre-filters

Cell - side view

Cell

Steel mesh pre-filter (washable)

Steel grids & wire

Power supply puts charge on grids and wire to attract dirt. Wash when dirty.

© Tom Feiza Mr. Fix-It Inc.

H029

Electrostatic and Electronic Filters

Many types of washable filters have multiple layers of filtering material; vendors claim these layers contain an electrostatic charge that attracts and traps dirt more effectively than a standard media filter.

Several companies also make a 1"-thick electrostatic/electronic filter as a direct replacement for throwaway filters. This filter may have an electronic power supply and may require particular maintenance procedures.

Warm Air Furnace— Maintenance Requirements

All heating equipment should be routinely checked by a qualified service technician. Most furnace manufacturers recommend yearly maintenance.

ROUTINE MAINTENANCE A HOMEOWNER SHOULD PERFORM

Note: Turn off power to the unit before inspection or maintenance.

- Maintain records. Have a professional service the unit yearly. Proper maintenance keeps equipment operating efficiently and ensures safety. Contact the manufacturer of your furnace for specific maintenance requirements.

- Change the filter as required—often every other month.

- Switch high/low returns at the start and end of the heating season. For complete instructions, check the section on "Heating and Cooling Distribution" later in this chapter.

- Check all flue pipes and vents for rust, water leaks, and loose connections.

- Lubricate the fan motor and fan bearing with a few drops of oil twice per year. (This is only required on certain units.)

- Check the belt to make sure it's not cracked or loose. (This is only required with belt-driven fans.)

- Listen to the furnace operate. Follow up on any strange sounds.

- Check drain lines to make sure they are clear and draining properly.

- Look for water leaks or changes in the system.

ROUTINE MAINTENANCE A PROFESSIONAL SHOULD PERFORM

During a routine service call, the service technician should perform the following general maintenance measures. The technician may perform other checks, too, depending on the type of furnace.

- Check and clean burner.

- Check flue pipes, draft diverter, heat exchanger, and chimney.

- Remove burners to clean burners and heat exchanger if necessary.

- Check electrical wiring and connections.

- Check and clean circulating fan. Lubricate fan and motor if necessary.

- For belt drive fans: check for tension, wear and alignment.

- Check supply and returns ducts for air leakage, water stains, rust.

- Check and maintain filter.

- Perform an operational check of furnace and safety controls.

- Test for carbon monoxide in the flue gas and in the air around the furnace.

- Check for gas leaks.

- Check, clean, and adjust pilot light if necessary.

For a high-efficiency furnace, the technician should also:

- Check for water leaks (condensation from combustion).

- Check flue pipes and connections.

- Check for condensation on metal pipes and parts.

- Check for a clean condensate drain line.

- Check operation and condition of draft fan.

You may want to make a photocopy of the professional's list and send it to the service company when you arrange service and/or review the list with the technician at the beginning of the service call.

Hydronic (Hot Water) Heat

Hot water or hydronic systems provide heat by warming water and circulating it through piping to heating devices: radiators, baseboard convectors, radiant pipes in the floors or walls, or even coils with a fan. Older system typically use cast iron radiators; newer systems typically use baseboard convectors (finned tubes).

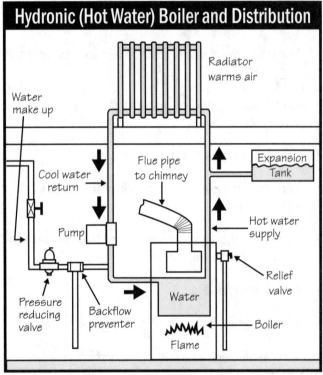

Hydronic (Hot Water) Boiler and Distribution

Radiator warms air

Water make up

Cool water return

Flue pipe to chimney

Expansion Tank

Pump

Hot water supply

Pressure reducing valve

Backflow preventer

Water

Relief valve

Flame

Boiler

H005

Hydronic systems usually burn oil, gas, or propane below a cast iron container or coil that holds water. The warmed water is then distributed to the radiators through a network of supply and return piping. Older systems use gravity to move the water—warm water rises, cool water falls. Newer systems use a small circulation pump to move the water.

The distribution system is sealed and should not leak, but water expands as it warms, so there will be an expansion tank to hold the increased volume. Most systems have an automated fill valve and backflow prevention.

The system automatically responds to a thermostat located in the heated space. When the thermostat calls for heat, the boiler and the pump start. Warm water is delivered to the radiators. When the thermostat is satisfied, the boiler is turned off.

There are many variations to hydronic systems: multiple zones provided by thermostat and zone control valves or multiple pumps...boiler temperature water resets based on outside temperature....many control options...and variations in piping systems, to name a few. If you have a complicated system, ask a service technician to explain it to you.

Hydronic Heating— Maintenance Requirements

All heating equipment should be routinely checked by a qualified service technician. Most hydronic boiler manufacturers recommend yearly maintenance to keep equipment operating efficiently and to ensure safety.

Contact the manufacturer of your furnace for specific maintenance requirements.

ROUTINE MAINTENANCE A HOMEOWNER SHOULD PERFORM

Note: Turn off power to the unit before inspection or maintenance.

- Maintain records, and have a professional service the unit yearly.

- Check all flue pipes and vents for rust, water leaks, loose connections.

- Listen to the boiler operate. Follow up on any strange noises.

- Check drain lines to make sure they are clear and draining properly. (This is required only for high-efficiency condensing units.)

- Look for water leaks or changes in the system.

- Oil the circulating pump twice per year. (Use just a few drops.)

- Check that the temperature/pressure gauge is in the operating range identified by a professional service technician. Mark the proper range on the gauge.

ROUTINE MAINTENANCE A PROFESSIONAL SHOULD PERFORM

A service technician should perform the following general maintenance measures. The service technician may also perform additional checks, depending on the type of furnace.

- Check and clean burner.

- Vent the system at the high points as necessary.

- Check all flue pipes, draft diverter, boiler housing, and chimney.

- Remove burners to clean burners and heat exchanger if necessary.

- Check electrical wiring and connections.

- Check and lubricate circulating pump(s).

- Check for water leaks.

- Check temperature and pressure relief valve.

- Check water supply system and backflow preventer.

- Add backflow preventer if none is present.

- Check expansion tank for proper water level.

- Perform an operational check of controls for temperature, pressure, and safety.

- Test for carbon monoxide in the flue gas and in the air around the furnace.

- Check for gas leaks.

- Check, clean, and (if necessary) adjust pilot light.

Additional checks for a high-efficiency boiler with a draft fan:

- Check draft fan for condensation and rust.

- Check flue pipe for condensation.

- Check condensate drain lines.

You may want to make a photocopy of the professional's list and send it to the service company when you arrange service and/or review the list with the technician at the beginning of the service call.

Steam Heating

A steam heating system is similar to a hydronic boiler system except that it produces steam at low pressure. Because they require more maintenance than hydronic systems, steam systems are rarely installed in newer homes, and older steam systems often are converted to hydronic systems.

Steam systems can use oil, natural gas or propane as an energy source. The burning fuel heats water in the boiler, turning it to steam. The steam, under pressure, rises through the system to the radiators. Vents in the radiators release heated air. The steam condenses back into water as it releases energy in the radiator, and the water flows back to the boiler to be reheated.

While there are variations in the piping systems, almost all residential systems are "one-pipe" systems as described above. You can identify a one-pipe system because it will have only one pipe connected to the radiators.

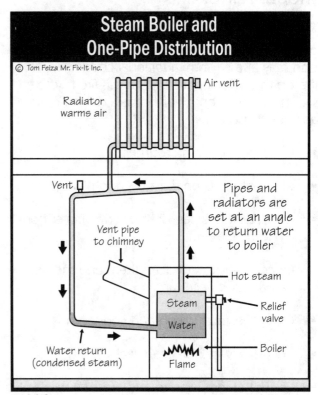

Steam Boiler and One-Pipe Distribution

© Tom Feiza Mr. Fix-It Inc.

Air vent

Radiator warms air

Vent

Vent pipe to chimney

Pipes and radiators are set at an angle to return water to boiler

Hot steam

Steam

Water

Relief valve

Water return (condensed steam)

Flame

Boiler

H006

Steam systems should have professional maintenance at least once per year, perhaps more often. Much of the maintenance required by a steam system is too complicated for most homeowners to perform.

ROUTINE MAINTENANCE A HOMEOWNER SHOULD PERFORM

- Maintain records.

- Check all flue pipes and vents for leaks, rust, and loose connections.

- Check the system for any leaks.

- Check the steam gauge. Have your contractor mark the normal range.

- Check the water level every month. The normal range should be marked on a sight glass.

- Make the sure the radiators slope slightly toward the steam inlet pipe. This will help keep the pipe from knocking or pounding.

- Make sure the vents on the radiators are operating; otherwise, radiators may be cold.

ROUTINE MAINTENANCE A PROFESSIONAL SHOULD PERFORM

A service technician should perform the following general maintenance measures. The service technician may also perform additional checks, depending on the type of boiler. (For a gas-fired system, see the information on oil burners, which require additional checks.)

- Check and clean the burner.

- Check all vents on radiators and piping.

- Check all flue pipes, draft diverter, boiler housing and chimney.

- Remove burners to clean them and the heat exchanger if necessary.

- Check electrical wiring and connections.

- Check for water or steam leaks.

- Check the temperature and pressure relief valve.

- Add a backflow preventer if none is present.

- Perform an operational check of controls for temperature, pressure and safety.

- Test for carbon monoxide in the flue gas and the air around the boiler.

- Check for gas leaks.

- Check, clean and if necessary adjust the pilot light.

You may want to make a photocopy of the professional's list and send it to the service company when you arrange service and/or review the list with the technician at the beginning of the service call.

Oil Burner

An oil burner can be used just like a gas burner in warm air furnaces, hydronic systems or even water heaters. All oil burners are essentially the same except for some very old style vaporizing or pot-type burners. Here we will only cover modern pressure burners or gun-type burners.

A modern oil burner pressurizes oil and sprays it through a small nozzle, forming a mist. At the same time, the burner provides an air supply and a high-voltage spark. This results in a very hot flame that is contained in a ceramic combustion chamber. From the combustion chamber, the hot combustion gas flows up through the heat exchanger, just as in a gas-fired appliance.

Oil Heat—Maintenance Requirements

Oil burners can be quite efficient, comparable to gas units. Oil burners require yearly maintenance. Also, never let your oil system run out of fuel. This can cause major problems with the burner, requiring a service call.

Most homeowners find it convenient to arrange for an oil delivery and burner service company to provide automatic oil tank filling and yearly service. This is the best way to ensure that the system is operating properly. You will also be placed at the top of the service call list if you are an established customer.

Warm Air Furnace with Oil Burner

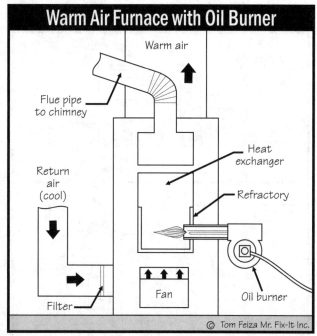

H013

Fuel Oil Burner

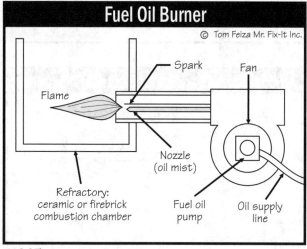

H007

ROUTINE MAINTENANCE A HOMEOWNER SHOULD PERFORM

Note: Turn off power to the unit before attempting inspection or maintenance.

- Follow the maintenance requirements listed above for warm air or hydronic boiler systems.

- Schedule routine maintenance yearly.

- Lubricate the burner motor if it has oil ports (ask your service technician).

- Make sure the system never, never runs out of fuel oil.

ROUTINE MAINTENANCE A PROFESSIONAL SHOULD PERFORM

A service technician should perform the following general maintenance measures. The service technician may also perform additional checks, depending on the type of furnace.

- Follow applicable maintenance requirements listed above for a hydronic boiler or warm air furnace.

- Remove and clean burner, clean blower blades, replace or clean filter and/or strainer, replace the nozzle, clean flame and heat sensors, check and clean or replace electrodes.

- Lubricate the burner motor.

- Check flue and barometric damper.

- Check for oil leaks.

- Check and clean oil pump.

- Clean and test stack control.

- Check and adjust draft regulator.

- Test for efficiency and make proper adjustments.

You may want to make a photocopy of the professional's list and send it to the service company when you arrange service and/or review the list with the technician at the beginning of the service call.

Central Air Conditioning

Central air conditioning uses a warm air furnace system to cool air and distribute it throughout the home. The air conditioning system uses the fan, filter, thermostat and ducts; the heating portion of the system remains turned off.

When a home has hydronic heat, central air conditioning may be provided by a separate system. In this case, there is no heating equipment in the standard furnace housing; it has only a fan and cooling coil.

A central air system includes an interior coil (in the furnace housing) that removes heat from the interior air and an exterior coil that rejects heat into air outside the house.

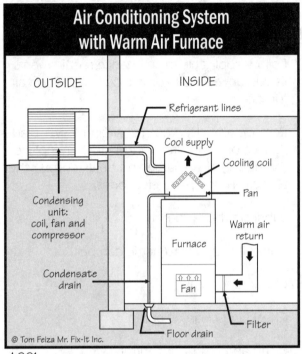

A001

When the thermostat signals for cooling, this starts up the exterior refrigeration compressor, exterior fan and furnace fan. The exterior compressor moves refrigerant through the closed system of coils and valves to produce a cool coil inside.The furnace fan moves air across this coil. The air cools, and moisture condenses on the coil's surface. This moisture is caught in a pan below the coil and drains away through a hose.

It is not necessary to cover the exterior unit during the winter, since these units are designed to withstand the weather. If you do cover the unit for some reason (for instance, if the unit is located where debris might accumulate on it), it's best to cover only the top of the unit. If you were to securely wrap the sides, moisture could condense in the unit. Also, a wrapped unit provides a perfect winter home for animals that may chew wiring and cause other problems.

When it's time for the winter shutdown, turn off power to the unit to prevent accidental operation. The power disconnect could be the breaker or fuse at the main panel. Or the disconnect may be at the exterior unit, usually as a switch or a fuse block or plug that you pull out to disconnect the power.

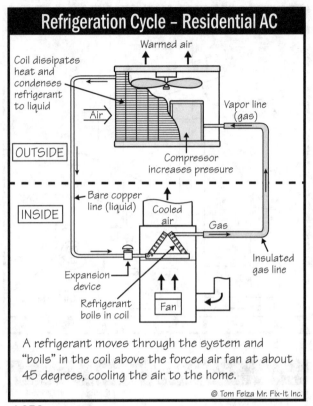

A refrigerant moves through the system and "boils" in the coil above the forced air fan at about 45 degrees, cooling the air to the home.

A032

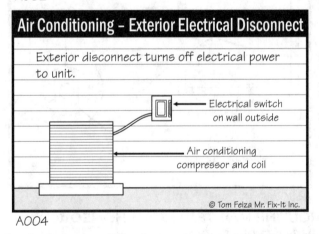

A004

Central air conditioning systems should never be operated in cold weather. This can cause serious damage.

Don't start the central air conditioner unless the outdoor temperature has been above 60 degrees for at least 24 hours. Remember to uncover the unit if you added a cover for the winter.

At the start of the cooling season, when you're about to turn on power to the unit, make sure that the thermostat is switched off, and leave the thermostat off for 24 hours before operating the unit. If the unit has a crankcase heater, this procedure allows the heater to warm the unit.

Central Air Conditioning– Maintenance Requirements

Proper maintenance will keep the unit operating properly and save you energy costs. Have your air conditioning system checked yearly by a professional service contractor.

You should also perform basic maintenance. Contact the manufacturer of your furnace/AC unit for specific maintenance requirements.

ROUTINE MAINTENANCE A HOMEOWNER SHOULD PERFORM

Note: Turn off all power and disconnect switches before performing inspections/maintenance.

- Maintain records, and have a professional service the unit yearly.

- Change the filter as often as required (in some cases, every month).

- Switch high/low returns (and adjust ductwork if necessary) at the start and end of the cooling season. For complete instructions, check the section on "Heating and Cooling Distribution" later in this chapter.

- Listen to the air conditioner operate. Follow up on any strange noises.

- Check drain lines from the furnace to make sure they are clear and draining properly.

- Look for water leaks or changes in the system.

- Keep plants and obstructions away from the exterior coil and fan. Allow 3 feet of clearance at the air discharge and 1 foot all around the unit.

- Keep the exterior coil clean.

- Keep the exterior unit level and away from soil or landscape materials.

- Make sure that supply and return registers inside your home are not blocked.

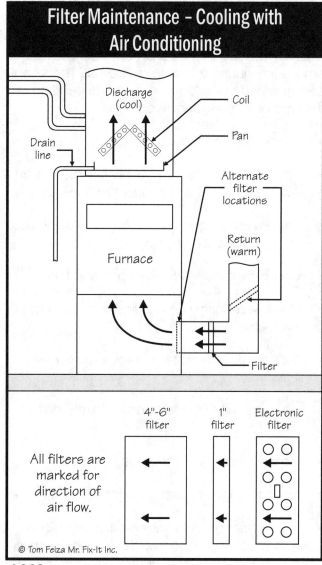

Filter Maintenance – Cooling with Air Conditioning

Discharge (cool)
Coil
Pan
Drain line
Alternate filter locations
Return (warm)
Furnace
Filter

4"-6" filter
1" filter
Electronic filter

All filters are marked for direction of air flow.

© Tom Feiza Mr. Fix-It Inc.

A002

FALL MAINTENANCE

1. Disconnect power to the unit to prevent accidental use.

2. (Optional)—Cover the top of the unit.

SPRING MAINTENANCE

1. Uncover the unit.

2. Turn the power on 24 hours before operation. Keep the thermostat off.

3. Perform the maintenance listed above and arrange for professional service.

ROUTINE MAINTENANCE A PROFESSIONAL SHOULD PERFORM

A service technician should perform the following procedures during a routine service call. The technician may perform additional checks, depending on the type of air conditioner you have.

- Check filter and replace as needed.

- Check exterior unit for level conditions, a clean coil, clearances, and adequate air flow.

- Check interior temperature drop across the cooling coil (15 to 22 degrees F).

- Check the condensate drain pan and line.

- Check secondary pan and line if unit is located in an attic.

- Look for signs of water leaks or excessive air leaks.

- Lubricate the fan motor and check the belt if required.

- Inspect electrical connections.

- Inspect refrigerant lines for signs of leaks.

- If performance problems exist, the technician may check for amp draw, clean the coils, check the refrigerant charge, and/or complete general performance tests.

You may want to make a photocopy of the professional's list and send it to the service company when you arrange service and/or review the list with the technician at the beginning of the service call.

Central Air Cooling – Evaporative Cooler

Evaporative coolers, commonly called "swamp coolers," are used for cooling in climates where air temperatures are high and relative humidity is very low. The outside air must be hot and dry for the units to function, so they are only used in hot, arid places like the American Southwest. This type of cooling will not work in humid climates.

The evaporative cooler works because hot outside air can be cooled as it absorbs moisture. As hot outside air is drawn across a pad full of water, the water evaporates into the air and the air is cooled as much as 20 degrees. The energy required to change the water into invisible vapor in the air makes the temperature drop.

In the process, the air is also humidified, but because it was so dry to begin with, this additional moisture is not objectionable. The cooled air is circulated through the home and to the outdoors.

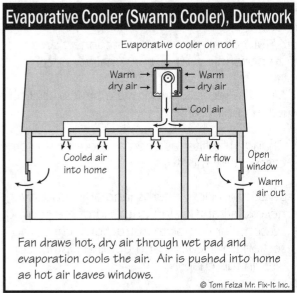

Evaporative Cooler (Swamp Cooler), Ductwork

Evaporative cooler on roof

Warm → dry air → ← Warm ← dry air

← Cool air

Cooled air into home

Air flow

Open window

Warm air out

Fan draws hot, dry air through wet pad and evaporation cools the air. Air is pushed into home as hot air leaves windows.

© Tom Feiza Mr. Fix-It Inc.

V048

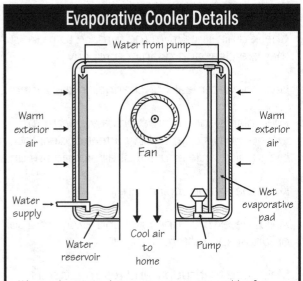

Evaporative Cooler Details

Water from pump

Warm exterior air

Warm exterior air

Fan

Water supply

Wet evaporative pad

Water reservoir

Cool air to home

Pump

Warm, dry air is drawn across a wet pad by fan. Water evaporates from the pad and cools the air. The pump wets the pads and a water supply fills the reservoir pans with a float for control.

© Tom Feiza Mr. Fix-It Inc.

V049

The evaporative cooler is typically located on the roof; cooled air is ducted into rooms and out the windows. A cooler can also be mounted in a window or on a concrete pad outside the home.

Evaporative cooling is what cools our bodies in hot climates. As sweat evaporates, it takes heat from our skin. We can speed the cooling process by wetting our skin with a water mist and blowing air across our skin. That is why we feel cooler when we leave a swimming pool and the wind is blowing—we are experiencing evaporative cooling.

The basic evaporative cooler operates as follows:

1. A water pan on the unit is automatically filled by a float, fill valve, and water supply.

2. A small pump in the pan lifts water and distributes it over evaporative pads on the sides of the unit. The excess water drains back into the pan.

3. A large fan draws hot, dry exterior air across the saturated pads.

4. As dry air is drawn across the wet pads, it gains moisture and is cooled. The energy needed to change water into vapor cools the air.

5. The cooler air is pushed into the home and out the windows.

6. In the process, humidity is added to interior air.

7. Since the pads filter the air and trap particles, the systems may flush out deposits through a drain line in the bottom of the water pan.

Evaporative coolers are less expensive to install and operate than refrigerant-based central air conditioning systems, but they must be maintained, and leaks must be prevented to limit any damage to a home.

Evaporative Cooler – Maintenance Requirements

Proper maintenance will keep the unit operating properly and prevent water leaks and contamination. Because the pads filter outside air, pad and pans must be maintained.

Heat Pumps

A heat pump provides heating and cooling. Simply put, a heat pump is a central air conditioner that can cycle in reverse to provide heating.

Local conditions will dictate whether a heat pump is an efficient alternative for heating your home.

A heat pump transfers heat from an exterior coil to an interior coil in the warm air heating system. A heat pump provides efficient heating in areas where exterior temperatures are moderate. In cold winter weather, though, a heat pump is no more efficient than electrical resistance heating, which costs more to operate than a natural gas or oil furnace.

Before you use your heat pump, have a professional explain its operation. Unfortunately, it's easy to accidentally operate the system with emergency electrical heat; in this mode, the heat pump is turned off and electrical resistance heating coils turn on. This method works fine, and you may not observe any problems—until you get your electric bill.

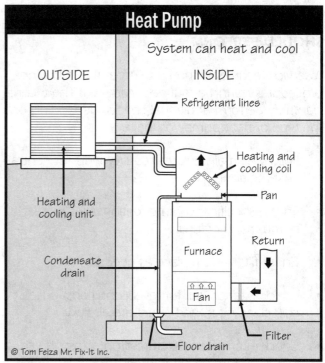

Heat Pump

System can heat and cool

OUTSIDE   INSIDE

Refrigerant lines

Heating and cooling coil

Pan

Heating and cooling unit

Return

Furnace

Condensate drain

Fan

Filter

Floor drain

© Tom Feiza Mr. Fix-It Inc.

A003

The emergency (electrical resistance) system should only be used when (1) the heat pump is not working, or (2) the outside temperature is so cold (about 30 degrees or lower) that the heat pump would be less efficient than electric resistance heating. When the outside temperature gets this low, emergency resistance heating turns on automatically. You do not need to adjust the controls.

Heat Pump—Maintenance Requirements

Maintenance for a heat pump is similar to that for central air conditioning systems, but because a heat pump is operated winter and summer, it will require more maintenance.

ROUTINE MAINTENANCE A HOMEOWNER SHOULD PERFORM

Note: Turn off all power and disconnect switches before performing inspections/maintenance.

- Schedule professional service yearly.

- Watch for ice forming on the exterior unit. This is a serious problem indicating that the unit needs service.

- Follow all the maintenance recommendations for central air conditioning.

ROUTINE MAINTENANCE A PROFESSIONAL SHOULD PERFORM

A service technician should perform the following procedures during a routine service call. The technician may perform additional checks, depending on the type of heat pump you have.

- Follow all maintenance requirements for central air conditioning.

- Follow specific recommendations by the heat pump manufacturer.

- Check filter and replace as needed.

- Check exterior unit for level conditions, a clean coil, clearances, and adequate air flow.

- Check interior temperature drop across the cooling coil (15 to 22 degrees F).

- Check the condensate drain pan and line.

- Check secondary pan and line if unit is located in an attic.

- Look for signs of water leaks or excessive air leaks.

- Lubricate the fan motor and check the belt if required.

- Inspect electrical connections.

- Inspect refrigerant lines for signs of leaks.

- If performance problems exist, the technician may check for amp draw, clean the coils, check the refrigerant charge, and/or complete general performance tests.

- Follow any specific recommendations by the heat pump manufacturer.

You may want to make a photocopy of the professional's list and send it to the service company when you arrange service and/or review the list with the technician at the beginning of the service call.

Heating and Cooling Distribution: Ducts and Dampers

Warm air heating (and central air conditioning) is distributed throughout your home by a system of ducts, dampers and grills. Supply grills provide conditioned air, and return grills provide a route for the air to return to the central heating/cooling unit. The central fan circulates air through these ducts and grills.

These ducts may be metal, fiberglass or even flexible plastic. When there is a basement or crawl space, the ducts are often located just below the first floor. When the furnace is in the attic, distribution is routed through the attic. Often, framing in joist or stud spaces forms return ducts. For homes with slab foundations, the ducts may be buried in the foundation slab.

In warmer climates, for homes with slab construction, the furnace is often located in the attached garage with supply ductwork in the attic and a return in the central hall.

This distribution system often has adjustable dampers that control the air flow to certain points in your home. Frequently, these dampers are adjusted during installation and are never re-adjusted later. At times, though, dampers should be adjusted when switching from heating to cooling or to accommodate a central humidifier that is turned on in winter and off in the summer.

mer, warm air still rises, and the hot attic adds more heat, so you'll need more cooling (air flow) to the second floor than the first.

High and Low Return - Heating

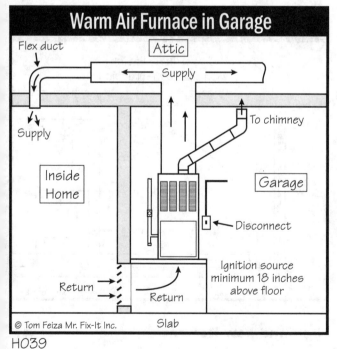

WINTER (heating on)

High return blocked by open lower register damper

Air flow

Hot air

Low return register (damper fully open)

Supply

Return

Furnace

Damper open

With low return open, cool air is drawn from the floor back to the furnace.

© Tom Feiza Mr. Fix-It Inc.

H050

Warm Air Furnace – Horizontal Flow

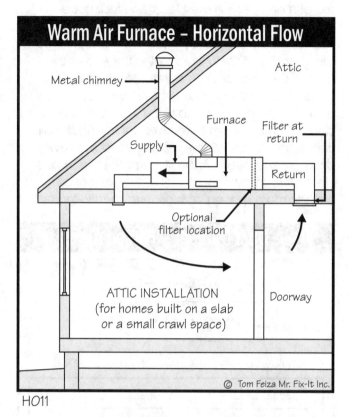

Attic

Metal chimney

Furnace

Filter at return

Supply

Return

Optional filter location

ATTIC INSTALLATION
(for homes built on a slab or a small crawl space)

Doorway

© Tom Feiza Mr. Fix-It Inc.

H011

Warm Air Furnace in Garage

Flex duct

Attic

Supply

Supply

To chimney

Inside Home

Garage

Disconnect

Ignition source minimum 18 inches above floor

Return

Return

Slab

© Tom Feiza Mr. Fix-It Inc.

H039

For a two-story home, you may need to make air flow adjustments for winter and summer. In the winter, warm air rises to the second floor, and you don't need as much heating up there. In the sum-

Must Know / Must Do Ductwork and Dampers

- Never allow openings or holes in ductwork. This wastes energy and makes living spaces uncomfortable.

- You may need to adjust ductwork dampers when switching from heating to cooling or vice versa.

- If your furnace has a damper on the humidifier, you may need to adjust it. Turn it off during summer.

- Ask your service technician if your warm air furnace has a damper for a winter/summer switch.

- Ductwork in attics and crawl spaces should be well insulated to prevent loss of energy.

Dampers are located inside the ducting system. Often, you'll find dampers where round supply ducts connect to the main rectangular ducts. All you will see of a damper is a small lever and lock nut or a small shaft and a wing nut. You can determine the position of the damper by checking the direction of the lever or the screwdriver slot in the end of the shaft. If the lever or slot is parallel to the duct, this means the damper is open. If the lever/slot is perpendicular (at a right angle) to the duct, the damper is closed. Some systems have levers indicating the direction of the damper. Some rectangular ducts have dampers and levers. You can adjust these dampers to close off rooms you don't want to heat/cool or to provide more heating or cooling to specific rooms.

Duct Damper – Forced Air

© Tom Feiza Mr. Fix-It Inc.

Flow

Damper
(open halfway)

Section → Main Duct

Duct damper position indicates air flow

Open – Flow	Closed – No Flow
Lever parallel	Lever perpendicular — Lever

(Wing nut does not indicate damper position.)

Slot in rod parallel	Slot in rod perpendicular
	Slot in rod / Wing nut

Two types of duct dampers: one with slot in rod and wing nut, and one with handle or lever.

H042

At the start of hot summer weather, you may need to direct more cool air to the second story. Start by fully opening all second-floor dampers. Next, partially close dampers to first floor rooms that are cold and receiving lots of air. The dampers often fit loosely in the ducts, so you may find that closing the damper 50% (turning the shaft 45 degrees) will only partially slow the air flow. Sometimes air will flow through a fully closed damper.

However, don't close off more than one-quarter of all the dampers; operation can be hindered if too little air flows through the system. If you need to make major changes to the system, consult a professional.

Once you've found a desirable balance, mark the damper settings for winter and summer.

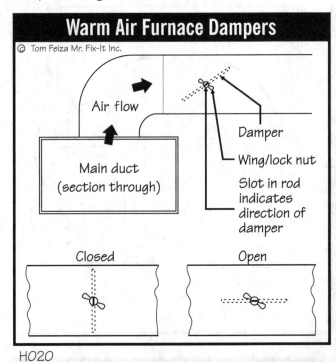

Warm Air Furnace Dampers

© Tom Feiza Mr. Fix-It Inc.

Air flow

Damper

Wing/lock nut

Slot in rod indicates direction of damper

Main duct (section through)

Closed   Open

H020

Warm Air Furnace – Downflow

Closet installation with slab construction

Return

Filter

To chimney

Furnace

Supply

© Tom Feiza Mr. Fix-It Inc.

H012

High and Low Returns

Some distribution systems have "high" and "low" return grills on interior walls. These grills are located one above the other. They aid in air distribution and comfort.

High returns should be opened for cooling. Remember that warm air rises, and you want to return the warm air to the air conditioning coil in the furnace.

During the heating season, the low returns should be open to return cold air at floor level to the furnace.

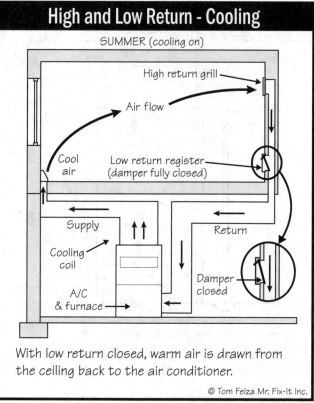

High and Low Return - Cooling

SUMMER (cooling on)

High return grill
Air flow
Cool air
Low return register (damper fully closed)
Supply
Cooling coil
Return
A/C & furnace
Damper closed

With low return closed, warm air is drawn from the ceiling back to the air conditioner.

© Tom Feiza Mr. Fix-It Inc.

H051

Outside Air Supply

Since the mid 1990s, the concept of adding an outside air supply to a forced air duct system has become more popular and has been required by some code officials. This involves installing a duct between the home's exterior and the return duct on the forced air system. When the furnace fan operates, it draws a small amount of air from the outside. This outside air duct may have a damper that can be closed in the summer when the unit is used as an air conditioner. The duct is usually insulated to prevent condensation on a cold surface in the winter.

The goal of the outside air supply duct is to provide some ventilation air. Since this air is cold and dry during the heating season, it will help dry the home's interior air. As air is introduced into the sys-

tem, an equal amount of warm damp air leaks out of the home. This also tends to remove moisture from the home.

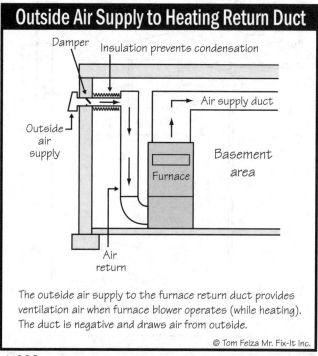

Outside Air Supply to Heating Return Duct

Damper
Insulation prevents condensation
Outside air supply
Air supply duct
Furnace
Basement area
Air return

The outside air supply to the furnace return duct provides ventilation air when furnace blower operates (while heating). The duct is negative and draws air from outside.

© Tom Feiza Mr. Fix-It Inc.

V028

Humidifier Controls and Settings

In northern heating climates, homes can become very dry in the winter. As warm air leaks out of our homes, it is replaced with cold, dry air. This is less severe if we have tightened up our homes for energy conservation, but it still can be a problem. Excessive dryness can damage furniture and harm your physical well-being.

The simple way to add moisture to the air of your home is with a central humidifier on your warm air furnace. A modern system is easy to maintain and should not leak. Modern systems have automatic controls that sense humidity level and operate automatically.

Older systems are not the best, but some are serviceable. Do not use the type that employs a water pan with an automatic fill valve. These are hard to maintain, may harbor disease-causing bacteria, and can leak water and ruin a furnace by rusting it out.

Humidifier on Gas Warm Air Furnace

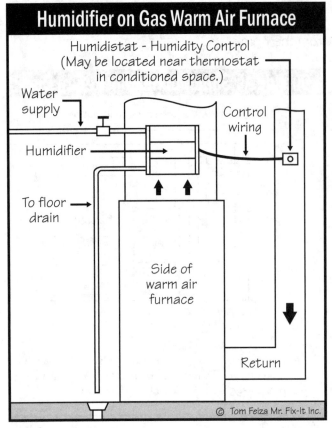

Humidistat - Humidity Control
(May be located near thermostat
in conditioned space.)

Water supply

Control wiring

Humidifier

To floor drain

Side of warm air furnace

Return

© Tom Feiza Mr. Fix-It Inc.

H018

The type with a water panel and drain (Aprilaire is a common brand) works well if you maintain it. This system slowly flushes water across a perforated metal panel, where the air picks up moisture. Excessive water drains through a pan and hose. In general, maintenance requires changing the water panel yearly and cleaning the pan and drain lines. Routinely check for water leaks, and keep the drain line clear.

You must also adjust the humidistat to compensate for the outside air temperature. The humidistat looks like a thermostat and is located next to the thermostat or on the ductwork of the furnace. The colder the outside temperature, the lower the interior humidity level should be. Your windows provide a great humidity indicator. If moisture condenses on the windows, the interior humidity level is too high.

Aprilaire offers a humidistat that automatically compensates for outside air temperature.

Humidifier System and Controls

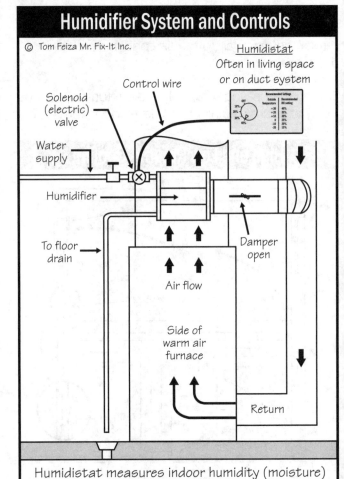

© Tom Feiza Mr. Fix-It Inc.

Humidistat
Often in living space
or on duct system

Solenoid (electric) valve

Control wire

Water supply

Humidifier

To floor drain

Air flow

Damper open

Side of warm air furnace

Return

Humidistat measures indoor humidity (moisture) level and operates humidifier when level is low. Humidified air is distributed by the forced air furnace.

H034

Humidifier Without Transfer Duct

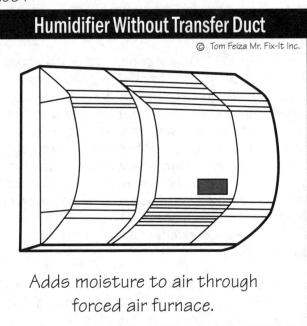

© Tom Feiza Mr. Fix-It Inc.

Adds moisture to air through forced air furnace.

H030

Must Know / Must Do
Central Humidifier

- Routinely check for leaks in the humidifier. Leaks will ruin the furnace.

- Routinely clean and service the unit to prevent bacteria that endanger the health of those in your home.

- Check that the drain line is clear and draining.

- Turn off the unit and its water supply in the summer.

- Adjust the duct damper on the unit if necessary: off for summer, on for winter.

- If condensation forms on your windows in the winter, lower the humidity setting.

- Newer, tighter homes rarely need a humidifier.

Humidifier - Automatic Controls

Typical Humidistat
Located in living space or return duct.

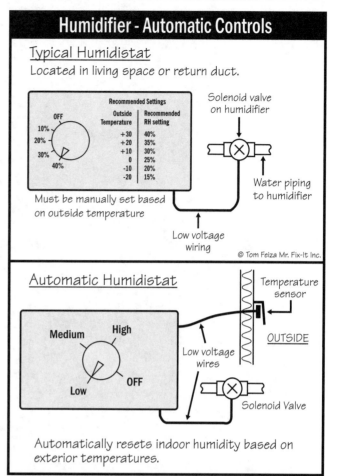

Recommended Settings		
	Outside Temperature	Recommended RH setting
	+30	40%
	+20	35%
	+10	30%
	0	25%
	-10	20%
	-20	15%

Must be manually set based on outside temperature

Solenoid valve on humidifier

Water piping to humidifier

Low voltage wiring

© Tom Feiza Mr. Fix-It Inc.

Automatic Humidistat

Temperature sensor

OUTSIDE

Low voltage wires

Solenoid Valve

Automatically resets indoor humidity based on exterior temperatures.

H035

Humidifier Problems

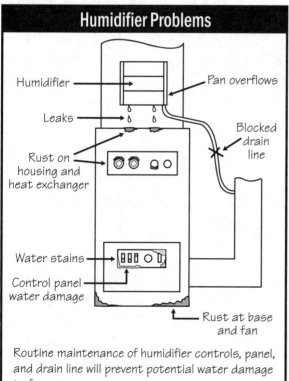

Humidifier

Pan overflows

Leaks

Blocked drain line

Rust on housing and heat exchanger

Water stains

Control panel water damage

Rust at base and fan

Routine maintenance of humidifier controls, panel, and drain line will prevent potential water damage to furnace.

© Tom Feiza Mr. Fix-It Inc.

H031

Humidifier - Fan Powered

© Tom Feiza Mr. Fix-It Inc.

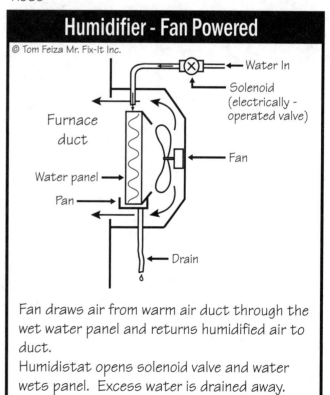

Water In

Solenoid (electrically - operated valve)

Furnace duct

Fan

Water panel

Pan

Drain

Fan draws air from warm air duct through the wet water panel and returns humidified air to duct.
Humidistat opens solenoid valve and water wets panel. Excess water is drained away.

H037

Chapter 4 – Utility Systems – Electrical

Utility Systems—Electrical

The electrical supply to your home begins outside, where you will see either an overhead feed and piping down the side of your home or (if you have underground service) a metal box near the ground.

The overhead service wire should be clear of trees and other wires. It should be at least 10 feet above any surface you can walk on.

With underground service, you will see a meter mounted on the metal box. This box hides the entrance of the service wire into your home.

In cold, wet climates, the main electrical panel will be located in the basement or utility room. In dry climates, the electrical panel may be outside. From this panel, electricity is divided into circuits through individual breakers or fuses and is fed through the wiring system, outlets and cords to various electrical devices.

Most modern homes have 220/240-volt systems with a minimum of 100 amps of power. Older houses may have fuses and can have 60-amp systems. Very old houses can have 110-volt, 30-amp systems, but these are rare.

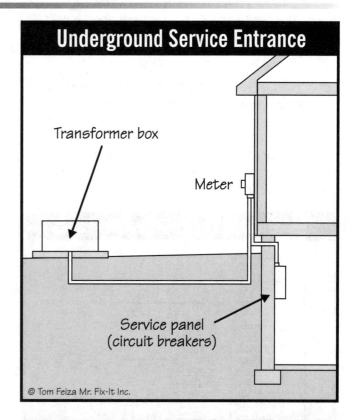

Underground Service Entrance

Transformer box

Meter

Service panel
(circuit breakers)

© Tom Feiza Mr. Fix-It Inc.

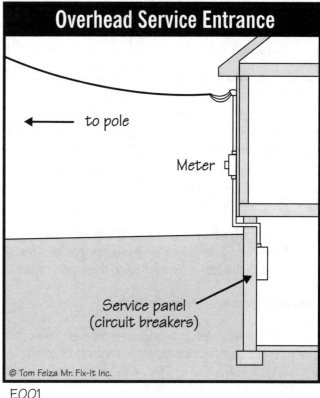

Overhead Service Entrance

← to pole

Meter

Service panel
(circuit breakers)

© Tom Feiza Mr. Fix-It Inc.

E001

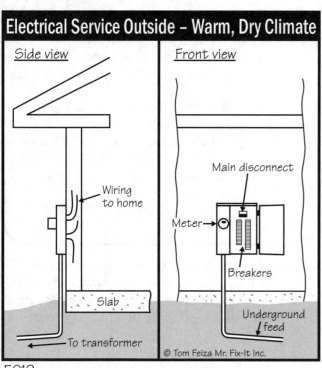

Electrical Service Outside – Warm, Dry Climate

Side view   Front view

Wiring to home

Main disconnect

Meter →

Breakers

Slab

Underground feed

To transformer

© Tom Feiza Mr. Fix-It Inc.

E019

Main Panel

Take a tour of your main electrical panel. Do this with a professional or an experienced friend if you are confused or if you have particular questions or concerns.

During this tour, identify the main disconnects so you can turn off power in an emergency. Also, determine how to reset a breaker and/or replace a fuse.

To begin, locate the main panel and open the door. Do not remove the metal cover beneath, since that would expose bare wires.

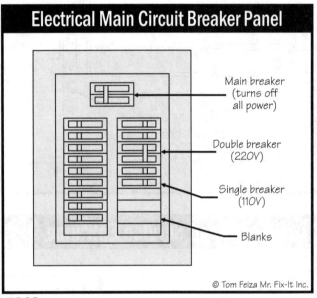

Electrical Main Circuit Breaker Panel

Main breaker (turns off all power)

Double breaker (220V)

Single breaker (110V)

Blanks

© Tom Feiza Mr. Fix-It Inc.

E002

You will find fuses or breakers but not bare wires or exposed connectors. Breakers look like switches that can be moved from "on" to "off." Fuses will be either a round screw-in type or the larger cartridge type mounted in a fuse block that can be pulled from the main panel.

Other configuration are possible. There may be a combination of fuse panels and breaker panels. There may be "sub-panels" located next to the main panel.

Breaker Panel—Main Switch

On most panels, you will find one breaker marked "main." This breaker will be near the top of the box and will be 100, 150 or 200 amp. If you switch this breaker off, all power in your home will be disconnected, and you will be in the dark. I don't suggest turning off the power.

Must Know / Must Do—Electrical

Properly installed electrical systems are very safe and efficient. To prevent safety problems, though, you should understand the basics.

- Know where the main electrical disconnect is located and how to use it.

- To prevent shocks, any outlets near water (such as next to a sink) and all exterior outlets should have GFCI protection installed. (These outlets are explained later.)

- Know which outlets are GFCI protected. Test GFCI outlets and breakers monthly.

- Avoid using extension cords.

- Never attempt an electrical repair unless you know exactly what you are doing.

- Never perform wiring or re-wiring work. Use a professional.

- Identify which breakers/fuses control which outlets.

- If you replace a fuse, always use the same size—20 amp for 20 amp, 15 amp for 15 amp. Have a few spare fuses on hand.

- Know how to reset a breaker. The usual procedure is to turn it off, then on. Some systems use red indicators or an "off" indicator to show that a breaker has been tripped.

- Never cut or modify electrical plugs or outlets.

An older breaker panel may have several breakers marked as main disconnects. Some may be marked "lighting" or "air conditioning." There may also be a fused main with breakers for distribution circuits.

Breaker Panel–Reset a Breaker

Modern circuit breaker panels are convenient because you can "reset" a breaker if it trips and you don't need to search for a replacement fuse. You do need to use common sense and caution when resetting a breaker. If a breaker trips, there may be an overload on the circuit. Before you switch a breaker back on, check for devices that may be causing the overload: hair dryers, electrical resistance heaters, power tools or other devices that use a lot of power. Remove the device before you reset the breaker. If the breaker trips a second time, consult a professional.

There are several types of breakers and methods to reset breakers. Most breakers flip to an "off" position when an overload occurs. For these breakers, you flip the switch back to the "on" position. Some breakers also have a little window that shows a red "flag" when the breaker is tripped.

Other breakers flip to a center position when tripped. The handle will be halfway between "on" and "off." You will need to look carefully to find this type of tripped breaker. This type of breaker often requires you to move the breaker handle to the "off" position and then back to the "on" position to reset the breaker.

Fuse Panel—Main Switch

You will see a main fuse block, about 4" x 3", with a small handle. Turning off ("pulling") this main turns off all power to your home.

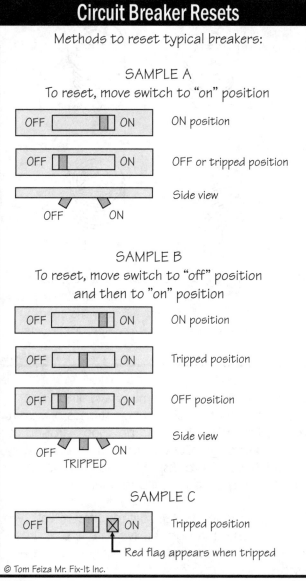

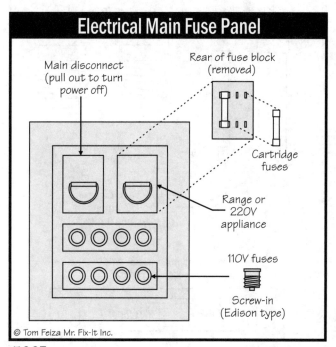

E003

Some older systems have multiple main disconnects—instead of pulling one main, you must pull multiple fuse blocks to turn off all power. Main disconnects should be clearly identified at the fuse blocks or on the cover of the panel. They may be marked "lighting main," "range," "dryer," "air conditioner," and so on. Usually, each 220-volt appliance has its own main.

If this sounds confusing, review the sketches I've provided. If you still don't understand your system, or if it's not well-marked, go over the panel with a professional and rewrite the markings.

Fuses and Replacement

Typical screw-in type fuses are called Edison base fuses. They fit into a threaded socket just like a light bulb. If a fuse "blows," it will appear dark or burned in the cover window. To replace a fuse, you unscrew the old fuse and screw in a new fuse of a matching amperage rating. The "blown" fuse is discarded. You should always match the amperage rating and never put a larger fuse in the socket. For example, a 15-amp fuse must be replaced with a 15-amp fuse, *not* a 20-amp fuse.

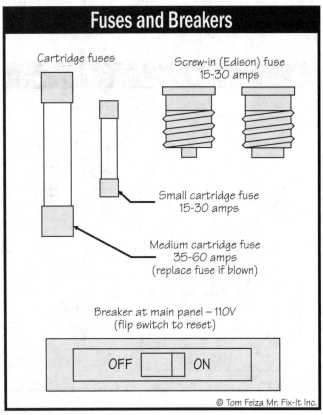

EO11

You can improve the safety of your fuse system by adding S-Type fuse bases. This base is a special socket that is threaded into the standard size Edison socket. Once in place, it will only accept the correct size fuse. Each S-Type fuse has a unique threaded base. Safety is ensured because a 20-amp fuse will not fit in a 15-amp S-Type fuse socket.

Wiring and Flow of Electricity

Distribution wiring is what routes electrical power to lights, outlets and appliances. Most of this wiring is buried in walls and attics, but some will be visible near the main panel and in basements and crawl spaces. Since the 1970s, plastic shielded wiring (Romex is a common brand) has been used in residential construction. Older homes may have cloth-shielded wiring, BX or flexible metal-shielded wiring, or even conduit (metal pipe). There are many variations and exceptions.

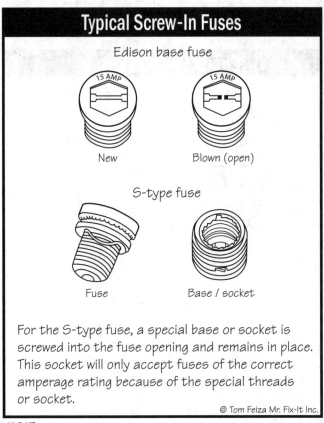

EO15

Homes built around 1910 may have "knob and tube" wiring that consists of two strands of wire run parallel. This wiring is strung on knobs, around corners, and through tubes in framing. It should only be modified by a professional. If your home has this type of wiring, plan for an upgrade.

Electricity flows like water, so it requires at least two wires: it pushes through the live wire and returns through the neutral wire. This is why all electrical devices have plugs with at least two prongs. Modern systems add a third (ground) wire for safety.

Types of Wire

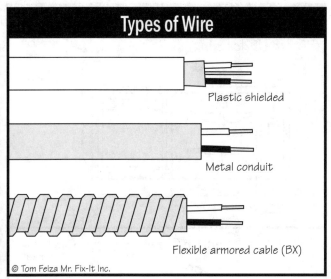

Plastic shielded

Metal conduit

Flexible armored cable (BX)

© Tom Feiza Mr. Fix-It Inc.

E004

Devices like electric ranges run on 220/240 volts and require two power wires (110v plus 110v) plus the neutral wire. Some 220/240-volt appliances have four wires: two power, one neutral, and one ground. All newer 240v appliances are now four-wire.

Sound complicated? It is. Don't modify or tamper with the system. Consult a professional when repairs are needed. Experience and knowledge are necessary when working with electricity. Electricians spend at least six years in school and training just to learn the basics of their trade.

Outlets, Cords, 110 vs. 220/240

220 volt—what? Is that 110, 220, 240 or 90210? Terminology used with electrical systems is confusing, but you really don't need to sweat it. In fact, electric utility companies don't provide an exact voltage. Just remember this:

Electricity is provided to your home with a nominal (approximate) voltage of 110 to 120 volts per wire. When you connect between the two live wire feeds, you double the voltage to about 220 or 240 volts. So you can call it 110 or 120 volts for smaller appliances and 220 or 240 volts for large appliances.

How can you tell the difference? 110 volt is provided to all convenience outlets, light switches, and lighting fixtures in your home. The standard electrical outlet is 110 volt.

Large appliances like stoves and electric clothes dryers use 220/240-volt outlets. These are the big clunky outlets. Electric water heaters, central air conditioners, and heat pumps are directly connected to 220/240-volt power without a plug. Some large electric appliances may also be directly wired.

Electrical code changes implemented around 2002 require all 240-volt dryer and range outlets to be four-wire, so they use a grounded 240-volt outlet. This will require re-wiring the outlet and appliance to provide a ground on new installations.

Types of Outlets

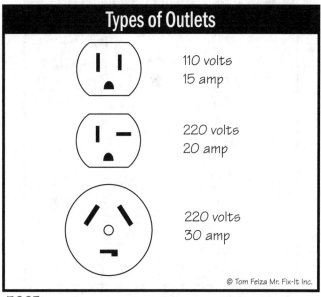

110 volts
15 amp

220 volts
20 amp

220 volts
30 amp

© Tom Feiza Mr. Fix-It Inc.

E005

Just to confuse you, you may find a funny looking small outlet and plug that is the same size but a different shape than a standard 110-volt outlet. These are 20 amp, 220/240-volt outlets. These are not common but they may be found for large window air conditioners, woodworking equipment, and shop air compressors. A standard plug will not fit into a 220/240-volt outlet.

Service Disconnects

Electrical equipment is often connected to the electrical system with a plug or service disconnect as a safety measure. All equipment must have a readily available means of disconnection from the electrical system in case the unit needs servicing.

Common service disconnects:

- Furnace—"light switch" on the side of the unit

- Central air conditioner—switch or pull-out in a box next to the exterior unit

- Dishwasher—"light switch" above the kitchen counter.

Know where the service disconnects are located and how to use them.

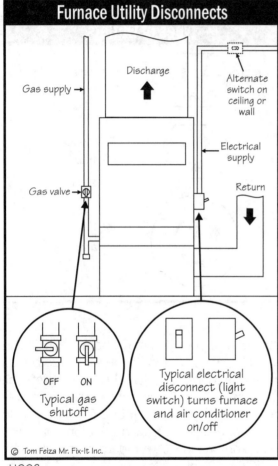

Furnace Utility Disconnects

Gas supply →
Discharge
Alternate switch on ceiling or wall
Electrical supply
Gas valve →
Return
Gas valve →

OFF ON
Typical gas shutoff

Typical electrical disconnect (light switch) turns furnace and air conditioner on/off

© Tom Feiza Mr. Fix-It Inc.

H008

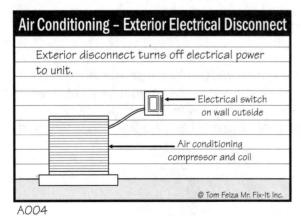

Air Conditioning – Exterior Electrical Disconnect

Exterior disconnect turns off electrical power to unit.

Electrical switch on wall outside

Air conditioning compressor and coil

© Tom Feiza Mr. Fix-It Inc.

A004

Dishwasher - Water & Electrical Supply

From Under Sink

Electrical disconnect above counter

Dishwasher

Valve

Hot water pipe

Water Hammer arrester

© Tom Feiza Mr. Fix-It Inc.

From Basement or Crawl

Electrical disconnect

Water Hammer arrester

Dishwasher

Hot → water pipe

Valve

Flexible pipe

P061

Electrical Polarity

Polarity is an important concept. For safety's sake, you need to understand the basics.

Electricity circulates through wires just like water moves through a hose. In the case of a lamp, for instance, electricity pushes through the "hot" wire, lights the bulb, and returns through the neutral wire. Got it?

Plugs on modern lamps and other devices have one wide blade and one narrow blade so that they can be plugged into an outlet in the correct position only—unlike plugs on old lamps, which could be reversed. Electrical devices with three-prong plugs have a ground wire; these, too, can only be plugged into an outlet in one position.

You may find a modern electrical tool with a plug that has two narrow blades that can be inserted in either direction. These are special "double insulated" tools with plastic housings that isolate the electrical components from contact with your skin.

What happens if you power a device with "reversed polarity"—that is, with the plug reversed? Stereo equipment may buzz; electrical and computer equipment may be damaged. Lights and lamps pose a serious hazard. When turning off the switch, you would be turning off the neutral (return) wire, not the live (hot) wire. This means that even when the lamp is off, the ring around the base of the bulb is still live, and if you touch the ring you can get a serious shock.

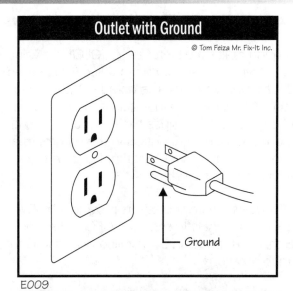

Outlet with Ground

© Tom Feiza Mr. Fix-It Inc.

Ground

E009

Polarity - Correct	**Polarity - Reversed**

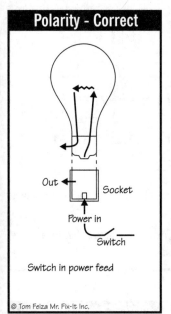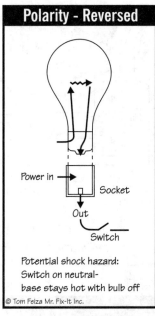

Out
Socket
Power in
Switch

Switch in power feed

Power in
Socket
Out
Switch

Potential shock hazard: Switch on neutral-base stays hot with bulb off

© Tom Feiza Mr. Fix-It Inc.   © Tom Feiza Mr. Fix-It Inc.

E008

What does all this mean to you? Never change a plug or outlet unless you understand polarity and know exactly what you are doing.

Electrical Grounding

Electrical devices with metal housings—stoves, dryers, tools—often have a grounded plug. A grounded plug has a third, round connector. Grounded plugs provide an extra level of safety by grounding the metal housing of the device. Never remove the grounding device from a grounded plug. Never use adapters that convert a grounding plug to a standard two-prong plug. If your electrical device has a grounded plug, it should only be used with a grounded outlet. If there's no grounded outlet where you need it, have one installed.

Outlet – Old Style

Polarized, non-grounded

Narrow: hot

Wide: neutral

© Tom Feiza Mr. Fix-It Inc.

E007

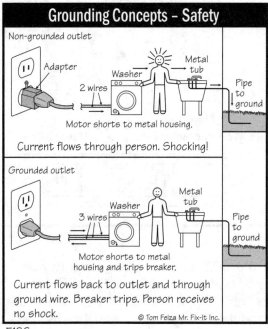

Grounding Concepts – Safety

Non-grounded outlet

Adapter
Washer
Metal tub
Pipe to ground
2 wires

Motor shorts to metal housing.

Current flows through person. Shocking!

Grounded outlet

Washer
Metal tub
Pipe to ground
3 wires

Motor shorts to metal housing and trips breaker.

Current flows back to outlet and through ground wire. Breaker trips. Person receives no shock.

© Tom Feiza Mr. Fix-It Inc.

E126

Ground Fault Circuit Interrupters

A ground fault circuit interrupter (GFCI) is a valuable safety device that should be installed in bathrooms, kitchens, sink locations, the garage, and exterior outlets. GFCIs have been required in new construction and remodeling since the mid-'70s. If you are remodeling, add GFCI outlets in the bathroom and any other damp or wet location. Have an electrician perform this work.

GFCI outlets or circuit breakers provide a high level of safety for very little cost. The GFCI outlet costs less than $10 and can be installed in a few minutes in most locations.

A tiny imbalance in the power and neutral lines will trip the GFCI. The imbalance indicates potential current leakage that could deliver a shock.

Don't confuse a GFCI with the fuse or circuit breaker in the basement. The fuse or breaker protects the wire from overloads, overheating and burning. A fuse will allow 15 or 20 amps to flow through the circuit before it trips. This is more than enough power to electrocute you.

pressing the reset button on the face of the outlet. Reset a GFCI breaker (at the main panel) by moving the switch from the center "tripped position" to fully "off" and then to the "on" position.

Unfortunately, most outlets are not tested. I provide home inspection services, and I find that 5% to 10% of existing GFCI outlets are not working properly.

GFCI Protects Outlets Downstream

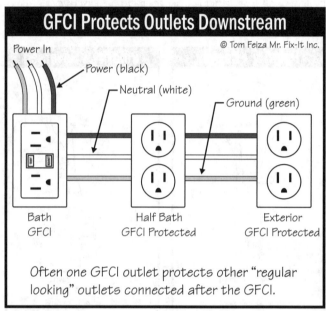

© Tom Feiza Mr. Fix-It Inc.

Often one GFCI outlet protects other "regular looking" outlets connected after the GFCI.

E022

Ground Fault Circuit Interrupter (GFCI)

© Tom Feiza Mr. Fix-It Inc.

GFCI outlet

Test and reset buttons

GFCI breaker-located in main panel

Look for test button

E016

Once the GFCI is installed, test it monthly with the test/reset button on the face of the breaker or outlet. Testing is simple and essential. Push the test button, and the GFCI will trip. Reset the GFCI outlet by

GFCI Breaker Reset

Ground fault circuit interrupter (GFCI) breaker found in main electrical panel

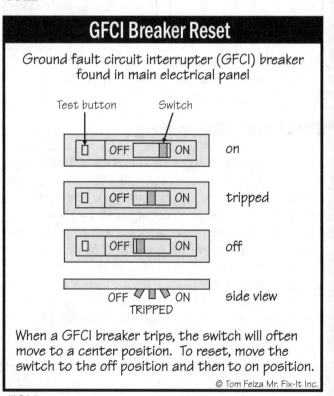

Test button   Switch

on

tripped

off

side view

When a GFCI breaker trips, the switch will often move to a center position. To reset, move the switch to the off position and then to on position.

© Tom Feiza Mr. Fix-It Inc.

E014

Safety of GFCI vs. Breaker

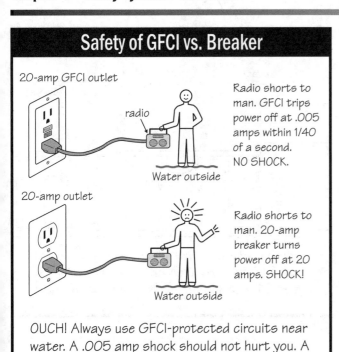

20-amp GFCI outlet

radio

Water outside

Radio shorts to man. GFCI trips power off at .005 amps within 1/40 of a second. NO SHOCK.

20-amp outlet

Water outside

Radio shorts to man. 20-amp breaker turns power off at 20 amps. SHOCK!

OUCH! Always use GFCI-protected circuits near water. A .005 amp shock should not hurt you. A 20-amp shock will hurt you – it could light you up like 24 100-watt bulbs before the 20-amp breaker trips.

© Tom Feiza Mr. Fix-It Inc.

E125

GFCI – Simple Test

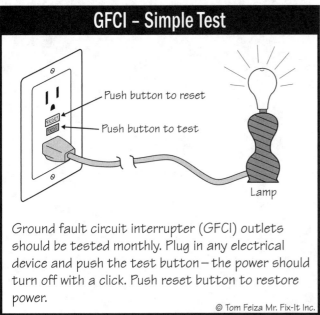

Push button to reset

Push button to test

Lamp

Ground fault circuit interrupter (GFCI) outlets should be tested monthly. Plug in any electrical device and push the test button – the power should turn off with a click. Push reset button to restore power.

© Tom Feiza Mr. Fix-It Inc.

E119

GFCI Requirements – Residential

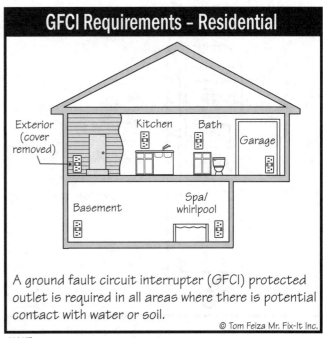

Exterior (cover removed)   Kitchen   Bath   Garage

Basement   Spa/ whirlpool

A ground fault circuit interrupter (GFCI) protected outlet is required in all areas where there is potential contact with water or soil.

© Tom Feiza Mr. Fix-It Inc.

E117

Arc Fault Circuit Interrupters (AFCI)

An Arc Fault Circuit Interrupter (AFCI) is an electrical safety device that started to appear in residential construction codes and some homes about 1999. It is designed to prevent fires by detecting an arc (spark) and then disconnecting the power before a fire starts.

An arc or spark may occur between two wires without tripping a standard circuit breaker because the current flow may not be high enough. Yet while the spark may not trip the breaker, it can ignite building materials. The AFCI contains sophisticated electronic circuitry that detects arc faults.

When required by code or installed by a conscientious electrical contractor, the AFCI usually protects circuits in bedrooms. A dangerous arc fault is likely to occur with damaged or frayed electrical cords. The AFCI is installed in the main circuit panel or as a special outlet and has a reset button on its face. Typically, the device protects several outlets.

Unlike a Ground Fault Circuit Interrupter (GFCI), the AFCI is designed to prevent fires. The GFCI is designed to prevent electrical shock. If your home has an AFCI, you should test it periodically with the test button. Most manufacturers suggest testing once per month. When the AFCI is tripped, there should be no power at the outlet or the circuit.

Arc Fault Circuit Interrupter – AFCI

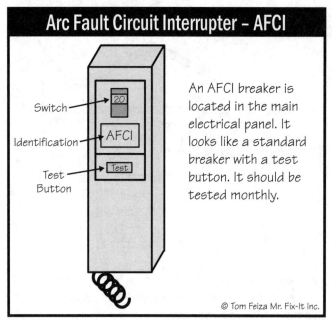

Switch

Identification

Test
Button

An AFCI breaker is located in the main electrical panel. It looks like a standard breaker with a test button. It should be tested monthly.

© Tom Feiza Mr. Fix-It Inc.

E020

Electrical Wiring in Modern Kitchen

Disposal switch   GFCI-protected outlets at countertop   Disconnect for dishwasher

Dishwasher

Modern kitchens have a minimum of two 20-amp small appliance circuits and GFCI protection for outlets. The dishwasher must have a disconnect.

© Tom Feiza Mr. Fix-It Inc.

E107

Disconnect – Safety Cord Option

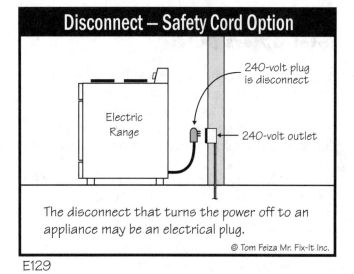

240-volt plug is disconnect

Electric Range

240-volt outlet

The disconnect that turns the power off to an appliance may be an electrical plug.

© Tom Feiza Mr. Fix-It Inc.

E129

Chapter 5 – Utility Systems – Plumbing, Water Supply

Water Service—Municipal

Most homes in urban areas receive water from municipal water systems. The original water source may be a lake, a river, or large, deep wells and storage facilities. Municipalities are required to test water for safety and purity. Often they filter the water and treat it with chemicals. If you have questions about the quality of your water supply, contact your local water utility.

In a cold climate municipal system, water is distributed through piping mains beneath the streets. It enters your home under the basement slab or at the first floor slab. In cold climates, piping is buried below the frost line.

Inside the house, there is usually a shutoff valve, a meter, and then a second shutoff valve. You can use either of these valves to turn off the water, but the second valve is used more often. Sometimes the valve on the street side of the meter can only be operated with a wrench.

In many cases there is no basement, and the water meter may also be installed in a shallow box near the street. Often the main water shutoff is located on the side of the home near the street, and the meter and additional valves will be located in shallow boxes near the curb. Any of these valves will turn off all water to the home.

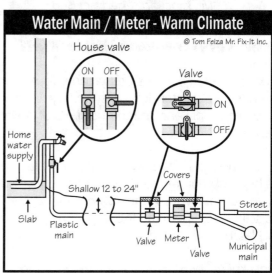

P063

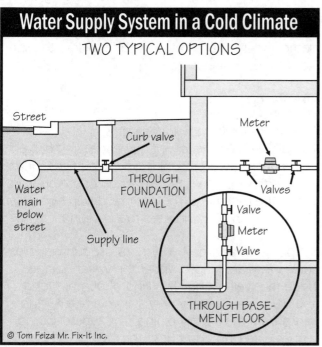

P005

In a warm climate, we don't need to worry about frozen ground and frozen pipes, so water mains can be installed just below the surface of the soil.

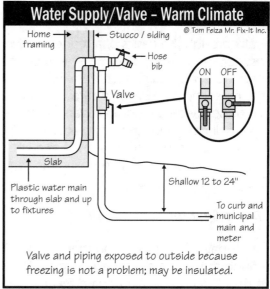

P064

Water is distributed through the house by steel, plastic or copper piping. Check your system, identify valves, and look for any potential problems. Locate the main that feeds the water heater, and check for a shutoff valve before the water heater in case you need to turn off all hot water in your home.

Must Know / Must Do
Municipal Water Supply

- Make sure that all adults in your home know how to turn off the main water shutoff valve.

- If the valve is old, rusted or leaking, have it serviced by a plumber so it will function when needed.

Water Service—Your Own Well

Well, well, well...OK, that's pretty corny; but if your home has a sick water delivery system, you can lose your water supply and spend hundreds of dollars on repairs.

Most damage to private wells comes from lack of basic homeowner knowledge. As one service company representative told me, "Waterlogged pressure tanks sell more replacement pumps than any marketing I could possible do."

Do you know the symptoms of a waterlogged tank? Can you correct simple well problems? Do you know how to turn off your well water system?

Let's walk through the basics of a residential well water system and discuss how you can recognize common problems and correct them. We will discuss the most common systems in residential use. If you are presently on a municipal water system, fine—you still may enjoy the information or save it for your brother up north. You should also know that most municipal water systems are just larger versions of residential systems.

The Basic System

Most wells have a 6" steel casing that is drilled into the ground to reach a clean water supply. The well casing may extend several hundred feet to reach a clean and adequate water supply. Water rises to a static level of equilibrium inside the steel casing and surrounds smaller internal piping. This internal piping is connected to a pump that lifts the water from the well and delivers it under pressure to your home plumbing system.

The top of the well casing is covered with a cap and should be 12" above the surrounding soil to prevent contamination from surface water and other sources. The cap should be securely fastened to prohibit tampering. Recently, problems with insects have prompted many people to replace older caps with modern vermin-proof caps.

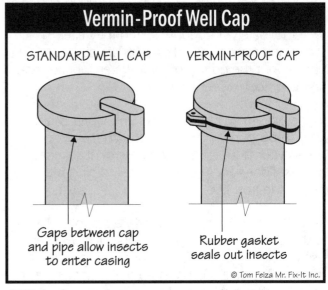

Vermin-Proof Well Cap

STANDARD WELL CAP

VERMIN-PROOF CAP

Gaps between cap and pipe allow insects to enter casing

Rubber gasket seals out insects

© Tom Feiza Mr. Fix-It Inc.

P030

From the well casing, piping extends underground into your home, entering the basement near a pressure tank. The piping may be steel, copper, or plastic and is installed at least 6 feet below the surface to prevent freezing.

The Pump

For shallow wells and older systems, a jet-type centrifugal pump lifts water out of the well and delivers it to your home's piping. This type of pump is surface mounted in a pit near the well head or the pressure tank in the basement. The pump is driven by an electrical motor and is connected to the piping.

Deeper wells and newer systems use submersible pumps that are placed under the water's surface inside the well casing. This kind of pump is long and slender—normally only 4" in diameter—and hangs from the supply piping. This type of pump pushes water up and out of the well.

When you "pull" a pump, you physically remove the cap of the well casing and pull the submersible pump out of the hole by the supply pipe.

Well - Two Pipe Deep Well

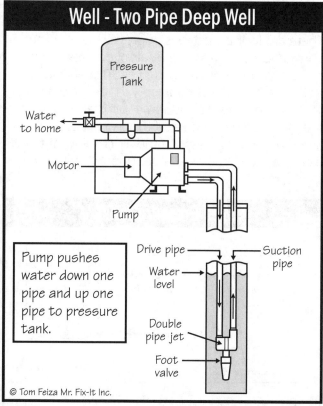

Pump pushes water down one pipe and up one pipe to pressure tank.

P058

Shallow Well System

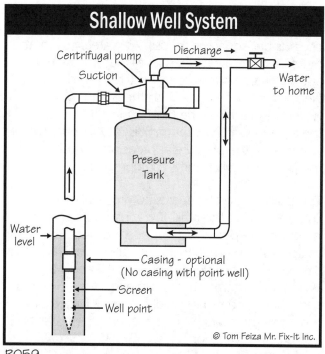

P059

Well Pump (Submersible) and Pressure Tank

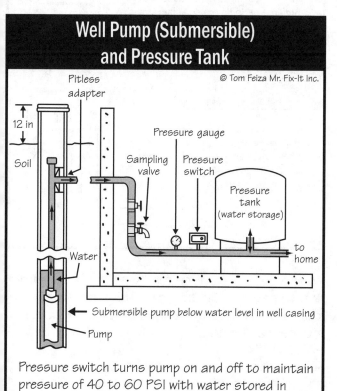

Pressure switch turns pump on and off to maintain pressure of 40 to 60 PSI with water stored in pressure tank. Water flows in and out of tank against air cushion.

P055

Well Pump - Submersible

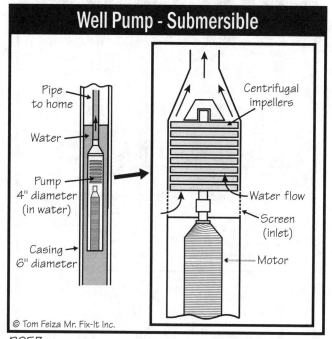

P053

Working Under Pressure

A pressure tank, normally located in the basement, stores water and prevents the pump from turning on and off every time you use water. There is a compressed air cushion above the water in the tank; it expands and compresses with changes in pressure. As you use water in your home, the air cushion in the tank expands to maintain pressure and force water into your piping.

The cushion of air generally varies in pressure within a normal operating range of about 40 to 60 pounds per square inch (psi). As water is used, the pressure decreases; when it reaches 40 psi, an automatic pressure sensing switch turns on the electricity to the pump. With the pump running, water is forced into the tank, raising the pressure of the air and water. As the tank is fully recharged with water, the pressure approaches 60 psi, and the pressure switch turns the pump off.

This pumping cycle repeats automatically as you use water from the tank. If you use a small amount of water, the pump will not need to start. You may notice a slight variation in pressure in your home as the system cycles slowly between 40 and 60 psi. When the system operates properly, the slow pressure changes are barely noticeable. A larger tank will draw more water per cycle, and there will be less pressure variation.

Tank Types Make a Difference

There are four basic types of pressure tanks. The conventional or galvanized "air over water" tank, generally found on systems over 30 years old, holds water in direct contact with the air cushion. This tank loses its air cushion as air is absorbed in the water, so you will need to service it several times per year to maintain the air cushion. You will recognize this type as a large, upright, galvanized steel tank.

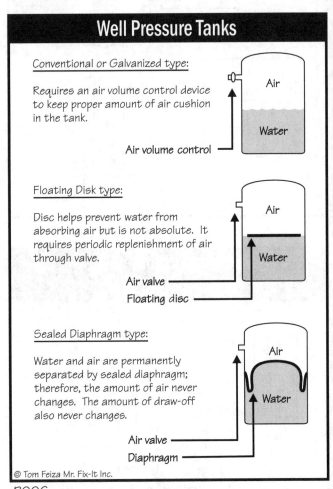

Well Pressure Tanks

Conventional or Galvanized type:

Requires an air volume control device to keep proper amount of air cushion in the tank.

Air volume control

Floating Disk type:

Disc helps prevent water from absorbing air but is not absolute. It requires periodic replenishment of air through valve.

Air valve
Floating disc

Sealed Diaphragm type:

Water and air are permanently separated by sealed diaphragm; therefore, the amount of air never changes. The amount of draw-off also never changes.

Air valve
Diaphragm

© Tom Feiza Mr. Fix-It Inc.

P006

An improved galvanized tank separates the air from the water with a floating disc. This tank will not lose air to the water as quickly, but it still requires routine maintenance.

Some systems are designed with a pump that adds a small amount of air to the system each time to pump starts. This system has a special air release tank, and every time the pump starts you will hear a little "gurgle" or "burp" if you are standing next to the tank. The "burp" results as air enters the tank.

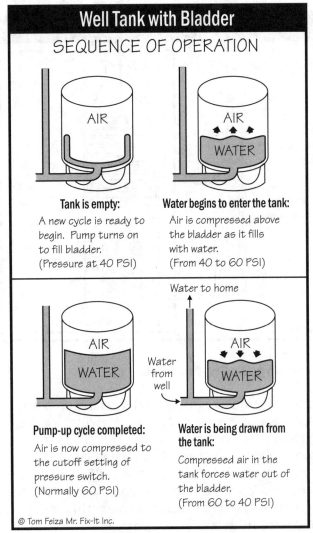

Well Tank with Bladder

SEQUENCE OF OPERATION

AIR

Tank is empty:
A new cycle is ready to begin. Pump turns on to fill bladder.
(Pressure at 40 PSI)

AIR
WATER

Water begins to enter the tank:
Air is compressed above the bladder as it fills with water.
(From 40 to 60 PSI)

AIR
WATER

Pump-up cycle completed:
Air is now compressed to the cutoff setting of pressure switch.
(Normally 60 PSI)

Water to home

AIR
WATER

Water from well

Water is being drawn from the tank:
Compressed air in the tank forces water out of the bladder.
(From 60 to 40 PSI)

© Tom Feiza Mr. Fix-It Inc.

P080

Well Tank with Air Volume Control

Air volume control

Float

Air release →

Level moves as water is used

Water to home

Water from well pump

The well pump adds a small amount of air when it starts. If there is excessive air in the tank, the float drops and releases air.

© Tom Feiza Mr. Fix-It Inc.

P057

This special air release or air volume control tank never needs additional air because the pump constantly maintains the air supply. If the system has too much air, a float in the tank drops with the water level and allows air to be released from the side of the tank. You will see a small plastic fitting on the side of the tank, and you may notice some water staining below the fitting. When air is released from the tank, some water is often released as well.

A tank with an air volume control is often installed when the well water has contaminates and odor problems. Because the tank eliminates the rubber bladder to hold water, it tends to reduce these problems.

Modern tanks are a big improvement over the older tanks. They are smaller and usually are made of painted steel. Inside the tank, the elements are separated by a sealed diaphragm or bladder which holds either the air or the water. Since there is no direct air/water contact, this tank system maintains the air cushion indefinitely.

Steps to Well Wellness

The best route to a trouble-free well is to become familiar with the system's important parts and know how it is supposed to look and sound when running properly. Take the time to identify the components of your system and to watch it operate. Read

any instructions and information available for your system. Look for the pressure tank, pressure switch, and gauges. Find the circuit breaker or switch that turns off the power to the pump.

Turn on a faucet and watch the pressure gauge to see the system's pressure vary. As it approaches 40 psi, you will hear a click when the pressure switch turns the pump on. With a submersible pump, you may hear a hum while the pump runs. When the pump is on, water flow into the tank will gradually increase the pressure to about 60 psi; then the pump will click off. It should take a minute or two for the pressure to increase from 40 to 60 psi.

If your system operates as described, now you know how a properly operating system responds when water is used.

The Helpful Turn-Off

It's important to know how to turn off the system completely. To stop the water flow to your home, you must turn off both the house service valve and the electrical supply to the pump. At least two people in your household should know how to do this.

Trace your home's piping back toward the pressure tank. The large valve in the line between the tank and the house piping is your house service valve.

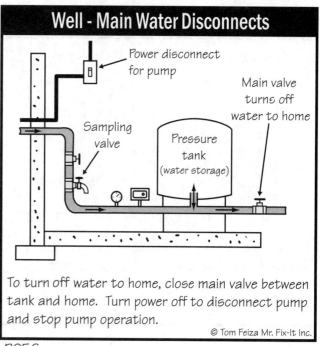

Well - Main Water Disconnects

Power disconnect for pump

Main valve turns off water to home

Sampling valve

Pressure tank (water storage)

To turn off water to home, close main valve between tank and home. Turn power off to disconnect pump and stop pump operation.

© Tom Feiza Mr. Fix-It Inc.

P056

If you turn off only the power to the pump, all the water under pressure in the tank will still flow into the piping system. If you turn off only the valve, the pump and electrical system can still malfunction.

Spotting a Waterlogged Tank

The most common and damaging problem in this system is a waterlogged pressure tank. A tank is waterlogged (full of water) when there is no air cushion in the tank. Without an air cushion, there is no air pressure to push water out of the tank into the home's piping. The pressure will vary quickly whenever a small amount of water is used.

This quick change in pressure causes the pump to start and stop almost every time you use water. As soon at the pump starts, the pressure will go up very quickly. For instance, if you are running a yard sprinkler, the pump will constantly turn on and off, and you will notice the pressure change at the spray of the sprinkler. If the pump is allowed to continue turning on and off (short cycling), eventually it will be ruined.

You can identify a waterlogged tank by quick changes in pressure and the way the pump switches on almost every time water is used. You must correct this situation to prevent damage to the pump.

Well Pressure Tank Problems

Normal Operation — Waterlogged

With adequate air in tank, air is compressed and expands with the draw of several gallons of water. Without air, pump cycles on and off with very little water draw.

© Tom Feiza Mr. Fix-It Inc.

P054

Correcting a Waterlogged Tank

If you need to correct a waterlogged tank but don't fully understand your well system's operation, call a service company. Watch their repair person service the tank. Ask lots of questions, and take notes so you can do it yourself next time.

The bladder-type tank should not lose its air cushion unless there is a bladder failure or a valve stem leak. If there is an air leak, you will need to recharge this bladder-type tank.

When an air-over-water tank requires replacement of the air cushion, follow these steps:

1. Turn off the electrical power to the pump.

2. Turn off the house service valve.

3. Open the drain valve at the bottom of the tank and drain off all the water under pressure. Normally, a hose is connected to this valve, and water is routed to a drain.

4. Using an air compressor or bicycle pump, add compressed air to the tank through its tire-stem-type fill valve.

5. Continue adding air until all the water is out of the tank and air flows from the drain valve.

6. Close the drain valve.

7. Pressurize the tank to about 5 psi below the normal operating range of the system. (In our example of a pump with a range of 40 to 60 psi, this would mean a pressure of 35 psi.)

8. Turn the electrical power to the pump back on and watch the pressure increase to the normal range as the pump fills the tank with water.

9. Open the drain valve again to drain away any debris that may have loosened inside the pipes and tank when they were under low pressure. Close the valve.

10. Slowly open the house service valve.

If your tank frequently becomes waterlogged, an air leak in the tank is probably the culprit. To check for this, make sure the tank has a full charge of air;

then sponge a strong solution of soapy water on the tank and its parts. Check the air fill valve, fittings, and weld joints. Bubbles will indicate an air leak. Fittings and valves can be replaced or sealed to eliminate leaks. However, if the tank welds are leaking, you may wish to replace the unit with a modern bladder-type tank.

Other Problems

Many other problems can occur with well systems. Jet pumps can lose their prime. Pressure switches can fail. Fuses can blow. Pipes can freeze. Excessive air can be pumped into the system. As with any home system, the list of potential problems goes on and on, and most of the more serious problems should be solved by a professional.

However, a properly maintained system will work smoothly and provide years of trouble-free service. Ironically, that may eventually lead to trouble, for we take the system for granted and forget to watch for symptoms of problems. We may fail to perform simple maintenance or notice quick changes in pressure.

What, Me Worry?

Even so...don't worry, be happy. Modern pumps and systems are almost trouble-free. Do your homework and understand your system. Consult a professional if you have any concerns or problems you don't understand. Watch for that water-logged tank—it can cost you a new pump. Consider replacing an old tank with a modern bladder-type tank if you don't like routinely replacing the air cushion.

Watch for any changes in the water; changes in water clarity, color, and odor can all indicate problems. You should also have your water tested for bacteria at least semi-annually. Some wells require routine chlorination.

For detailed informational brochures on wells, water, and water treatment, contact your local municipal health department or plumbing inspector or your state's department of natural resources. You can also obtain operational information from the companies that manufactured your well pump, tank, and pressure switch. Well service companies are another good source of information.

Must Know / Must Do
Your Own Well

- Make sure that all adults in your home know how to turn off the main water valve and the electrical power to the well pump.

- If water pressure varies as you draw a small amount of water, this indicates a pressure tank problem: the pump is "short cycling." Add air to the pressure tank, or call for service.

- Have your water tested routinely—perhaps once per year.

Water Heaters

A water heater is simply that—a device to heat water. A water heater consists of a storage tank with a gas, electric or oil heat source. If your home has an oil-fired hydronic boiler, there may be a coil in the boiler that heats water.

Water heaters work year after year with very little maintenance, so it is easy to ignore them. Yet routine maintenance checks should be performed on electric, gas and oil water heaters.

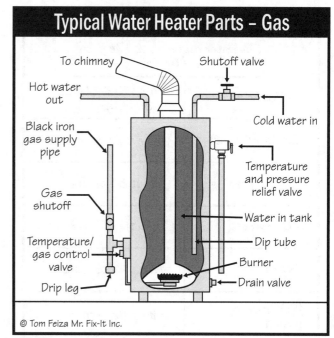

Typical Water Heater Parts – Gas

To chimney — Shutoff valve — Hot water out — Cold water in — Black iron gas supply pipe — Temperature and pressure relief valve — Gas shutoff — Water in tank — Dip tube — Temperature/gas control valve — Burner — Drip leg — Drain valve

© Tom Feiza Mr. Fix-It Inc.

P082

The water heater has a temperature dial. Keep it at a low or middle setting, and check your water temperature at the faucet. It should be about 120 degrees to prevent scalding.

The temperature dial controls a thermostat in the water tank. When the water cools, the burner or electrical heating element is switched on. When the water reaches the specified temperature, the heating unit shuts off. The water heater's tank stores hot water, giving you a reservoir to draw from.

Federal requirements mandate that new gas water heaters must be flammable vapor ignition resistant (FVIR). Some homes have tankless or instantaneous water heaters without a storage tank.

Routinely check your water heater for leaks. A leak is a sign of an impending failure, and you should replace the unit as soon as possible.

Typical Water Heater Parts – Electric

Electrical feed

Shutoff valve

Hot water out

Cold water in

Heating element inside tank

Temperature and pressure relief valve

Access panels for thermostat and heating elements

Dip tube

Drain valve

© Tom Feiza Mr. Fix-It Inc.

P081

FVIR Gas Water Heater

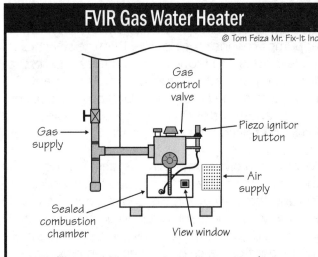

© Tom Feiza Mr. Fix-It Inc.

Gas control valve

Gas supply

Piezo ignitor button

Air supply

Sealed combustion chamber

View window

FVIR (flammable vapor ignition resistant) water heater has a sealed combustion chamber, spark (piezo) ignitor, and air supply. It prevents combustion of flammable vapors near the water heater.

W022

Water Scalding Chart

Set water heater to 120 degrees or less for safety!

TEMPERATURE	TIME TO PRODUCE SERIOUS BURN
120 degrees (hot)	More than 5 minutes
130 degrees	About 30 seconds
140 degrees	Less than 5 seconds
150 degrees	About 1 1/2 seconds
160 degrees (very hot)	About 1/2 second

© Tom Feiza Mr. Fix-It Inc.

W008

Temperature and Pressure Valve

(T & P) RELIEF VALVE

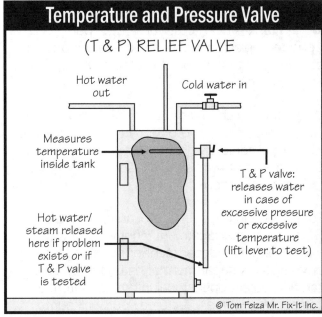

Hot water out

Cold water in

Measures temperature inside tank

T & P valve: releases water in case of excessive pressure or excessive temperature (lift lever to test)

Hot water/ steam released here if problem exists or if T & P valve is tested

© Tom Feiza Mr. Fix-It Inc.

W001

Also, routinely check the temperature and pressure (T and P) relief valve. This valve, which has a small lever, will be located on the top or side of the heater tank; the relief pipe should extend from the valve to within 6" of the floor. If water leaks from the relief valve, the valve should be replaced, because a leak may plug the valve with scale and debris. A plugged valve may fail to open if the tank overheats—a dangerous situation.

Manufacturers of T and P valves recommend testing the valve periodically by lifting the lever and allowing water to flow from the valve. They recommend this as a safety measure so you will know whether the valve will work if needed. But there's a risk that the valve won't close properly and will keep leaking, and then it will need to be replaced. When you do test the relief valve, do it when you can buy a replacement or get quick service from a plumber.

Manufacturers also recommend that you periodically drain water from the valve at the base of the water heater. This is a good procedure to follow if there is sediment in your water supply—but, again, few people follow this procedure, because their water systems have little sediment. If you do drain the tank, use a hose to direct water to a drain. Be careful—the water will be hot. If you haven't used the drain valve in several years, it probably won't close

properly because of sediment buildup. If the valve leaks, you must replace it or cap it with a hose cap.

For a gas water heater, routinely inspect the metal flue pipe to the chimney. It should be free of rust, and it must be securely fastened to the water heater and the chimney. Also, have a contractor routinely inspect and clean the burner. A burner covered with rust indicates that the unit is not drafting well; the internal flue pipe is rusty, and the unit could be producing carbon monoxide. Every time you have your gas furnace tested and tuned, ask the service technician to test the gas water heater and check the flue gas for carbon monoxide.

For an oil-fired water heater, follow maintenance procedures (including yearly service by a professional) recommended in the section on the oil burner furnace. For more info on gas and propane-fired heaters, see the end of this chapter.

Tankless Water Heater

- Combustion gas to outside
- Stainless steel vent to outside (some rated for PVC vent)
- Temperature sensor
- Hot water out
- Heats water in tubes
- Electronic control
- Cold water in
- 120V power
- Flame (variable)
- Flow sensor
- Gas in
- Gas valve
- Burner fan

The burner operates when water is flowing. Includes controls to maintain the proper hot water temperature at variable water flow rates by changing the burner output. Provides continuous hot water at a designated flow rate.

© Tom Feiza Mr. Fix-It Inc.

WO21

Must Know / Must Do
Water Heater

- Know how to operate the hot water shutoff valve.

- Know how to turn off the gas, oil or electrical power.

- Inspect the flue of a gas water heater yearly.

- Routinely check the water heater for leaks.

- Have an oil-fired water heater serviced yearly.

- Make sure the temperature and pressure valve is not leaking.

- Check the water temperature at the faucet; set the water heater temperature to about 120 degrees F.

- Whenever you have your furnace serviced, ask the technician to check the water heater, too.

Water Heater - Oil Fired

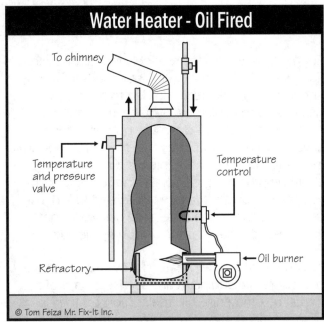

To chimney

Temperature and pressure valve

Temperature control

Oil burner

Refractory

© Tom Feiza Mr. Fix-It Inc.

W015

Water Heater in Garage

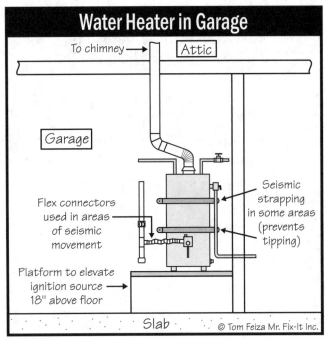

To chimney →

Attic

Garage

Flex connectors used in areas of seismic movement

Seismic strapping in some areas (prevents tipping)

Platform to elevate ignition source 18" above floor

Slab

© Tom Feiza Mr. Fix-It Inc.

W013

The following problems should be corrected by a professional: difficulties with the T and P valve; lack of hot water; failed electrical elements; and problems with the anode, dip tube, thermocouple, or pilot light.

Piping and Valves

Operating your home also requires a basic understanding of plumbing valves and piping. You may need to turn off the water in an emergency. You may need to shut off water to one sink or tub while it's being serviced.

Pipes route water from the main feed to individual fixtures. Piping can be galvanized steel, copper or plastic. Each type of piping has elbows, tees, couplings and reducers to connect lengths of pipe and route them through walls and framing. Take a look at your system. You will notice that it starts with 3/4" or 1" pipes and reduces to pipes of smaller diameters as fewer fixtures are served.

Valves control the flow of water and enable you to disconnect parts of the system. You will find a combination of valves. Take a good look at your plumbing system to identify valves, determine what they control, and learn how they operate. It is a great idea to place a small tag on each valve identifying what it controls. See Chapter 9 for tags.

Piping – Distribution

Let's trace the water flow from the municipal supply in the street or from your private well system. Water enters your home at the municipal main pipe or through the underground pipe connected to your private well system. You should locate the main valve and tag it for future use. Everyone in your home should know where this valve is located and how to operate it. We have provided tags in Chapter 9.

For homes with basements, the feed pipe enters through the basement floor or wall. The main feed will then have several valves at the meter in the basement or at the well storage tank. From there the water is fed to the water heater, and the system has two distinct feeds into the home—hot and cold water. If the water is hard and needs treatment, a piping system may also distribute softened water to the water heater and other fixtures. Typically, soft water is not provided to the kitchen sink and exterior hose connections.

In homes with crawl spaces, the main feed pipe enters through the floor or a side wall. The meter and main valves may be in the crawl space, in a closet, in the utility room, or outside. Distribution piping is usually routed through the crawl space and up the fixtures. If you are lucky, you will find a shutoff valve at each fixture or appliance.

In homes built on a concrete slab, modern construction usually places the piping in the slab. The pipes are laid out, and then concrete is poured around the piping. Some homes built on a slab will have pipes run in the attic instead, and repairs or retrofit piping may also be run in the walls or the attic.

Materials used for water distribution piping have changed over the years. In the early 1900s, lead piping was used. About 1910, this changed to galvanized steel, and around 1950 it changed to copper. The changes were made as better materials became available and companies looked for ways to reduce labor on installation.

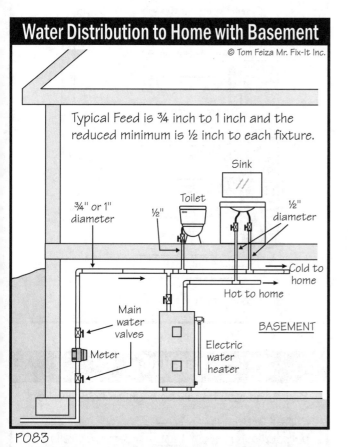

Water Distribution to Home with Basement

© Tom Feiza Mr. Fix-It Inc.

Typical Feed is ¾ inch to 1 inch and the reduced minimum is ½ inch to each fixture.

Sink

Toilet

¾" or 1" diameter

½"

½" diameter

Cold to home

Hot to home

BASEMENT

Main water valves

Meter

Electric water heater

P083

Water Distribution to Home with Crawl Space

© Tom Feiza Mr. Fix-It Inc.

Typical feed is ¾ inch to 1 inch, and the reduced minimum is ½ inch to each fixture.

Sink

Toilet

¾" or 1" diameter

½"

½" diameter

Cold to home

Hot to home

Meter

"Shorty" electric water heater

CRAWL

P084

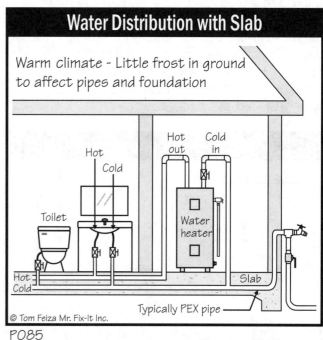

Water Distribution with Slab

Warm climate - Little frost in ground to affect pipes and foundation

Hot   Cold

Hot out   Cold in

Toilet

Water heater

Hot
Cold

Slab

Typically PEX pipe

© Tom Feiza Mr. Fix-It Inc.

P085

Metal Distribution Piping

Lead - 1900s
• Soft; gray color
• Preformed bends
• Decorative fasteners

Fasteners

Galvanized Steel - 1920s
• Silver coating over steel pipe
• Screwed fittings
• Pipe dope, sealer at joints

Threads

Pipe dope at fitting

Copper - 1950s
• Copper or brown color
• Soldered fittings
• Green corrosion for solder flux

Solder in Joint

Green corrosion common here

© Tom Feiza Mr. Fix-It Inc.

P086

59

Since about 1970, various plastic piping systems have been used. Some plastic piping systems have plastic-welded fittings and are installed much like metal pipe by starting with a large feed and reducing the pipe size toward the end of the run.

PEX is a unique piping system. It is installed with a large main feed pipe to a header (manifold). Small tubes feed each fixture. The piping is flexible and can be bent around some corners without fittings. Tight corners require fittings. Often, copper pipe is used for connections through walls and at fixtures. Fittings are compression type, installed by special tools.

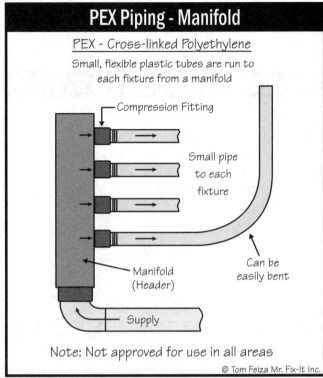

PEX Piping - Manifold

PEX - Cross-linked Polyethylene

Small, flexible plastic tubes are run to each fixture from a manifold

Compression Fitting

Small pipe to each fixture

Manifold (Header)

Can be easily bent

Supply

Note: Not approved for use in all areas

© Tom Feiza Mr. Fix-It Inc.

P088

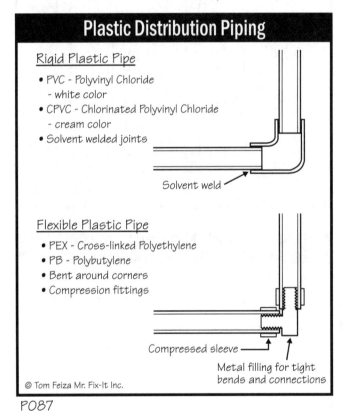

Plastic Distribution Piping

Rigid Plastic Pipe
- PVC - Polyvinyl Chloride
  - white color
- CPVC - Chlorinated Polyvinyl Chloride
  - cream color
- Solvent welded joints

Solvent weld

Flexible Plastic Pipe
- PEX - Cross-linked Polyethylene
- PB - Polybutylene
- Bent around corners
- Compression fittings

Compressed sleeve

Metal filling for tight bends and connections

© Tom Feiza Mr. Fix-It Inc.

P087

Ball Valve

Ball valves are used where full flow is required. This valve is unique in that it turns fully on and fully off with a 90-degree turn of a short lever. When the lever is parallel to the pipe, the water is on; when the lever is perpendicular, the water is off. Ball valves are often used at the main feed line and the water heater.

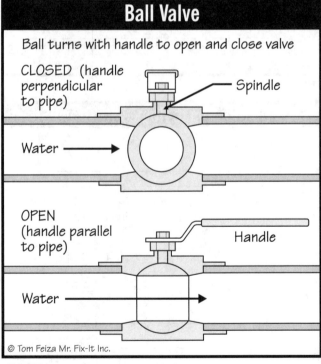

Ball Valve

Ball turns with handle to open and close valve

CLOSED (handle perpendicular to pipe)

Spindle

Water

OPEN (handle parallel to pipe)

Handle

Water

© Tom Feiza Mr. Fix-It Inc.

P007

Gate Valve

As you turn the handle, a "gate" inside the valve closes, controlling water flow. A gate valve is designed to be completely open or closed. It is often used at the main feed line.

Gate Valve

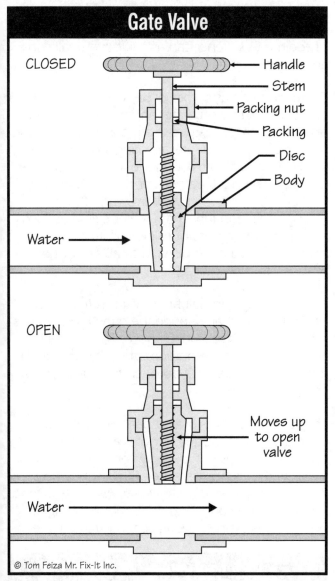

CLOSED

Handle
Stem
Packing nut
Packing
Disc
Body
Water

OPEN

Moves up to open valve

Water

© Tom Feiza Mr. Fix-It Inc.

P008

Globe Valve

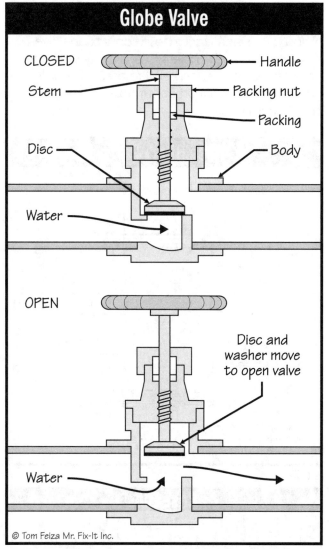

CLOSED

Handle
Stem
Packing nut
Packing
Disc
Body
Water

OPEN

Disc and washer move to open valve

Water

© Tom Feiza Mr. Fix-It Inc.

P009

Globe Valve

A globe valve uses a washer and a set. It can be throttled to control water volume, but generally it is not used in the main shutoff.

Saddle Valve

This is a small valve mounted on the side of a pipe like a saddle mounts on a horse. Saddle valves are frequently found on the water supply line for ice-makers and humidifiers. They provide only a low flow of water and are prone to leaks.

Small Saddle Valve

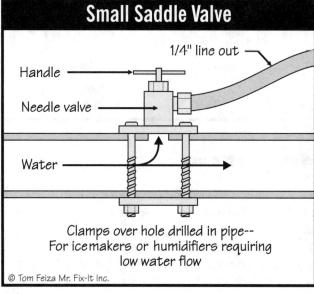

1/4" line out
Handle
Needle valve
Water

Clamps over hole drilled in pipe--
For icemakers or humidifiers requiring low water flow

© Tom Feiza Mr. Fix-It Inc.

P011

Hose Bib

A hose bib is an exterior hose connection valve. You may also find a hose bib at a utility sink. The hose bib has a threaded end to accept a garden hose. More information about hose bibs appears later in this chapter.

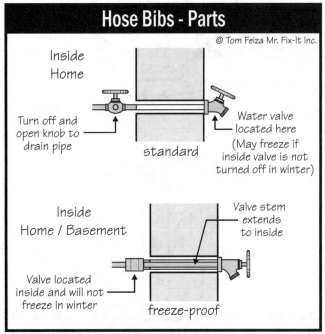

Hose Bibs - Parts

© Tom Feiza Mr. Fix-It Inc.

Inside Home

Turn off and open knob to drain pipe

Water valve located here (May freeze if inside valve is not turned off in winter)

standard

Inside Home / Basement

Valve stem extends to inside

Valve located inside and will not freeze in winter

freeze-proof

P077

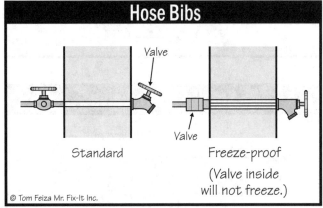

Hose Bibs

Valve

Standard

Valve

Freeze-proof

(Valve inside will not freeze.)

© Tom Feiza Mr. Fix-It Inc.

P010

Water Softener

If your home has hard water (minerals in the water), you'll probably want to use a water softener. Hard water can corrode piping and fixtures and cause a buildup of deposits. It leaves spots on dishes cleaned in the dishwasher, makes surfaces hard to clean, and interferes with detergents in the clothes washer and shampoos you use on your hair.

A water softener removes the offending minerals, calcium and magnesium and adds a small amount of sodium. A softener can also remove small concentrations of iron.

There are two basic types of salt brine water softeners. One has two separate tanks: a salt brine tank and a resin tank. Salt pellets are placed in the brine tank and soaked in water, creating salt brine. The salt brine is flushed through the resin on a routine basis, based on a time clock or usage meter. Salt ions attach to the resin. As hard water flows through the resin tank, hard water elements such as magnesium and calcium precipitate onto the resin surface. In the process, a small amount of salt is added to the water.

The second type of salt brine water softener has the resin tank located inside the brine tank. The system operates as described above. The only difference is that from the outside, the softener looks like it has only one tank. If you open the cover, you will see the second tank.

The softener is often located near the water main. Normally, it is connected to hot water and bathroom fixtures. It is not routinely connected to tap water in the kitchen because of the slight amount of sodium being added to the water. Also, the softener is not routinely connected to exterior hose piping because there is no need to soften exterior water.

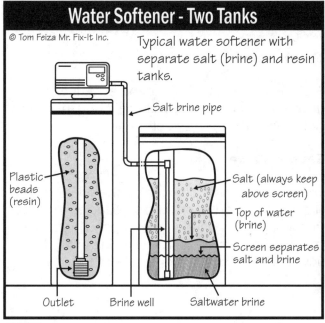

Water Softener - Two Tanks

© Tom Feiza Mr. Fix-It Inc.

Typical water softener with separate salt (brine) and resin tanks.

Salt brine pipe

Plastic beads (resin)

Salt (always keep above screen)

Top of water (brine)

Screen separates salt and brine

Outlet   Brine well   Saltwater brine

P089

Water Softener - Tank in Tank

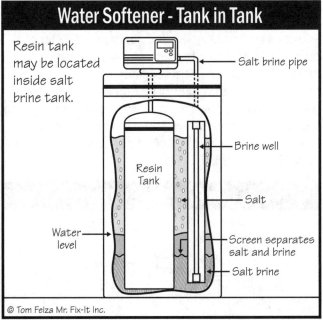

Resin tank may be located inside salt brine tank.

Salt brine pipe

Brine well

Resin Tank

Salt

Water level

Screen separates salt and brine

Salt brine

© Tom Feiza Mr. Fix-It Inc.

P090

Water Softener Installation - Typical

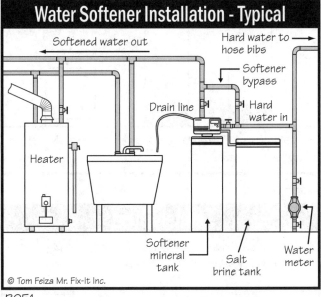

Softened water out

Hard water to hose bibs

Softener bypass

Drain line

Hard water in

Heater

Softener mineral tank

Salt brine tank

Water meter

© Tom Feiza Mr. Fix-It Inc.

P051

A professional should test water for hardness and estimate the amount of water usage, then set up the softener. Some of the better models of softener will base their cycle on the amount of water used. Others cycle on a timer device.

To maintain a water softener, you must keep a supply of salt in the salt brine tank. Use salt that has been processed into pellets, or whatever salt is recommended by the manufacturer. Do not use plain rock salt; it contains small amounts of impurities that will ruin the system over time.

Water treatment systems are almost always installed with a method to "bypass" the system for maintenance and repairs. The bypass involves three valves that are opened or closed to route the water through the system or to bypass the system.

Water Conditioner: Typical Bypass Valving

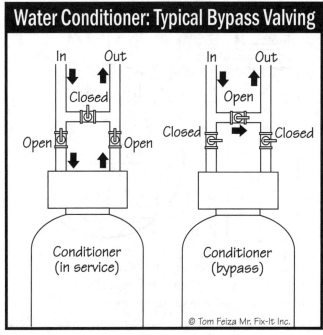

In   Out

Closed

Open   Open

Conditioner (in service)

In   Out

Open

Closed   Closed

Conditioner (bypass)

© Tom Feiza Mr. Fix-It Inc.

P029

Must Know / Must Do Water Softener

- Use the proper salt, and keep some salt in the brine tank at all times.

- Watch for leaks.

- If spots appear on dishes and the water doesn't feel "slippery," your softener is not working. Check the salt supply first.

- If the unit cycles on a timer, make sure it's set properly for the number of people in your home. Review the manufacturer's instructions.

Several types of water softeners have a bypass hidden behind the control panel on top of the softener. Sliding a control lever operates this type of bypass. The lever switches both the hard and soft lines and provides a passageway for water to bypass the softener. These valves are marked with the correct directions for operation, but to find them you must look behind the softener control panel.

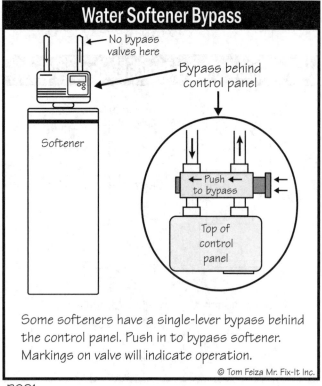

Water Softener Bypass

No bypass valves here

Bypass behind control panel

Softener

Push to bypass

Top of control panel

Some softeners have a single-lever bypass behind the control panel. Push in to bypass softener. Markings on valve will indicate operation.

© Tom Feiza Mr. Fix-It Inc.

P091

Other Water Treatment Options

If your home has water problems beyond basic hard water, consult a professional. Treatments for problem water include special iron filters, sediment filters, and reverse osmosis.

Iron Removal

Iron creates a difficult problem with many private water systems. Often a simple filter or softener will not remove large quantities of iron. Special treat systems are available; they are expensive but very effective. They use two treatment tanks, an air pump, and sometimes, additional chemical treatment. These systems should be installed and maintained by a professional.

Water Filter

Some water contains a small amount of sediment or particles that can be removed with a simple cartridge filter. Similar to the oil filter in your car, it passes water through a filtering element and removes particles. When the filter becomes plugged, the cartridge must be removed and replaced. Often, the housing is made of clear plastic so you can see the condition of the filter.

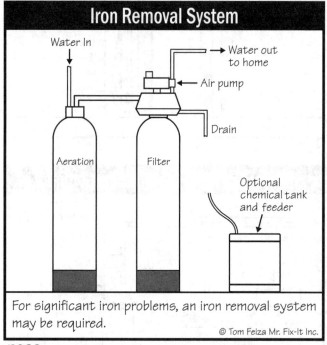

Iron Removal System

Water In

Water out to home

Air pump

Drain

Aeration

Filter

Optional chemical tank and feeder

For significant iron problems, an iron removal system may be required.

© Tom Feiza Mr. Fix-It Inc.

P092

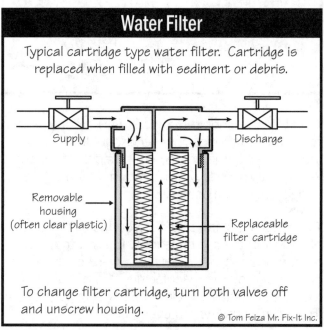

Water Filter

Typical cartridge type water filter. Cartridge is replaced when filled with sediment or debris.

Supply

Discharge

Removable housing (often clear plastic)

Replaceable filter cartridge

To change filter cartridge, turn both valves off and unscrew housing.

© Tom Feiza Mr. Fix-It Inc.

P094

Reverse Osmosis

A reverse osmosis water treatment system is a very fine and specialized filter that may be used to treat drinking water and perhaps the water used to create ice cubes in your refrigerator's icemaker. These specialized filters remove most of the particulate matter in water. Often they utilize a small storage tank because the water is processed at a relatively slow rate. Some systems use a chemical treatment, while others use electronic monitoring. This system needs to be provided and installed by a professional.

The system may be located in the basement, in the crawl space, or below the sink. Water may be routed to a small dispenser at the kitchen sink with a small plastic tube. A small tube and supply may also be provided to the icemaker in the refrigerator.

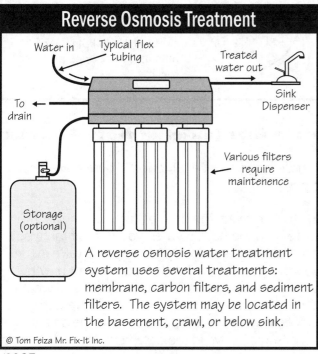

Reverse Osmosis Treatment

© Tom Feiza Mr. Fix-It Inc.

A reverse osmosis water treatment system uses several treatments: membrane, carbon filters, and sediment filters. The system may be located in the basement, crawl, or below sink.

P093

Garbage Disposal

A garbage disposal is a simple device that grinds food and washes it down the sewer system. I suggest that you use the disposal sparingly, placing larger quantities of food waste in the garbage or in a compost pile. Remember that any waste you put down the sewer system must be treated in a municipal sewage treatment facility or in your own private septic system.

Most experts suggest that you do not install a garbage disposal if you have your own septic or mound system. Introducing excess food waste can cause premature failure of the system. If you do use a garbage disposal, have the system pumped more often.

The key to using a disposal is to run the water before you add waste. Run a strong flow of cold water, turn on the unit, then slowly feed waste into it. Keep running water for several seconds after grinding stops to make sure all waste is flushed away. Never fill the unit and then turn it on—you will have a big, big mess of clogged pipes.

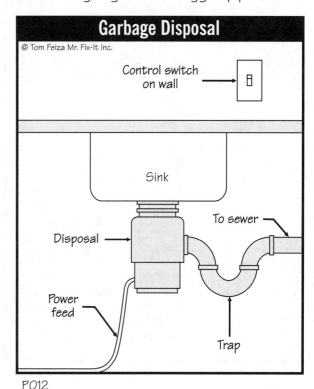

Garbage Disposal

© Tom Feiza Mr. Fix-It Inc.

P012

When a loud noise comes from the unit while operating, it usually means that a metal object like a spoon is caught in it. Turn the unit off and remove the object with tongs. Never put your hand in the disposal.

If you switch the disposal on and nothing happens (not even a hum), the thermal overload may have tripped. Under the sink, check the body of the unit for a small red or black button that may be marked "reset" or "overload." Turn off power to the disposal by flicking the "light switch" above the kitchen counter and then push in this button. Now try the unit again. If it just hums without running, it is stuck and needs to be cleared.

To clear the unit, turn off the power again. Look inside the unit for foreign objects, and if you see any, remove them with tongs. Next, look under the sink for a small six-sided wrench (usually stored in a plastic pouch near the disposal). Insert the bent end of this tool into a recessed hole at the center bottom of the disposal. Turn the wrench several revolutions in both directions until the shaft spins freely. Remove the wrench, turn the power back on, and try the unit again.

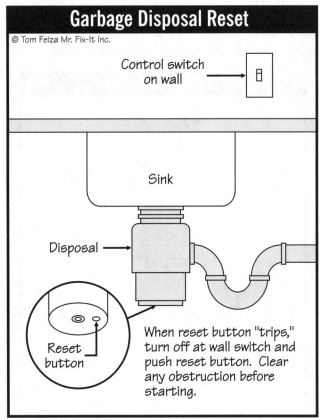

Garbage Disposal Reset

© Tom Feiza Mr. Fix-It Inc.

Control switch on wall →

Sink

Disposal →

Reset button

When reset button "trips," turn off at wall switch and push reset button. Clear any obstruction before starting.

PO13

Must Know / Must Do Garbage Disposal

- Always run a strong flow of cold water and start the disposal before you feed any waste into it.

- Never put your hand in the disposal.

- Know how to use the reset button and service wrench.

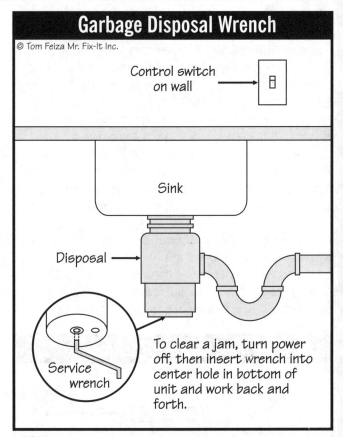

Garbage Disposal Wrench

© Tom Feiza Mr. Fix-It Inc.

Control switch on wall →

Sink

Disposal →

Service wrench

To clear a jam, turn power off, then insert wrench into center hole in bottom of unit and work back and forth.

PO14

Hose Bibs (Exterior Hose Faucets)

A hose bib is an exterior faucet. There are several types.

In a cold climate, the hose bib valve may extend up to 12" into the house. When you turn off this type of hose bib, you are actually turning off a valve inside your home…but (and this is important), it may not drain properly and could freeze during cold weather if there is a hose connected to it. To prevent this problem, some older installations provide an additional shutoff valve in the basement. Properly turning off water in the winter requires that you (1) turn off the inside valve, (2) open the outside valve, and (3) open the small drain knob (if there is one) on the inside valve to drain off the pipe.

A newer home may have a backflow preventer on the outside hose bib. This could trap water in the pipe and cause a freeze-up. To release water from the pipe, you must either push the little button in the center of the backflow preventer to release the pressure, or open the small knurled knob at the inside shutoff valve to drain water from the pipe.

Every hose bib should have a backflow preventer or an anti-siphon device to keep contaminated water from the hose out of your drinking water system. To find out if such a device is required in your area, check with your water utility, plumbing inspector, or health department.

Hose Bibs - Parts

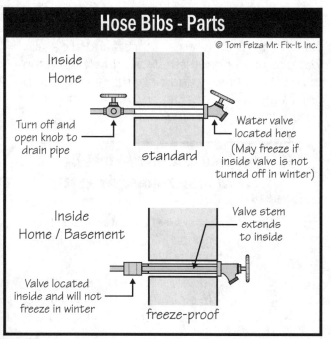

© Tom Feiza Mr. Fix-It Inc.

Inside Home

Turn off and open knob to drain pipe

standard

Water valve located here (May freeze if inside valve is not turned off in winter)

Inside Home / Basement

Valve stem extends to inside

Valve located inside and will not freeze in winter

freeze-proof

P077

Hose Bib – Backflow Prevention

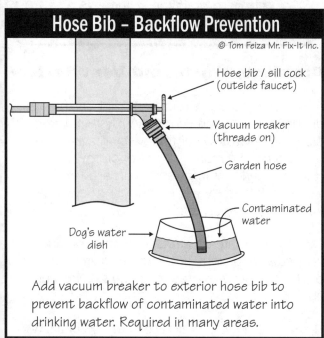

© Tom Feiza Mr. Fix-It Inc.

Hose bib / sill cock (outside faucet)

Vacuum breaker (threads on)

Garden hose

Contaminated water

Dog's water dish

Add vacuum breaker to exterior hose bib to prevent backflow of contaminated water into drinking water. Required in many areas.

P034

Laundry Tub Hose – Prevent Contamination

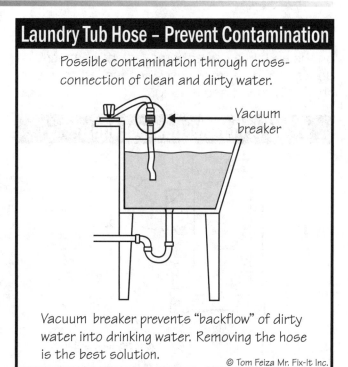

Possible contamination through cross-connection of clean and dirty water.

Vacuum breaker

Vacuum breaker prevents "backflow" of dirty water into drinking water. Removing the hose is the best solution.

© Tom Feiza Mr. Fix-It Inc.

P042

Must Know / Must Do Hose Bibs

- Keep all backflow devices in good working order.

- In colder climates, before winter begins, turn off the water supply to all exterior pipes and hose connections, and drain the pipes properly.

Water Hammer Arresters

Modern plumbing systems have water hammer arresters (anti-water-hammer devices) that prevent water pipes from pounding when water is quickly turned off. Basically, these are air chambers that can be compressed by moving water.

When halted quickly—for example, by an electrically-operated valve in a washing machine—water has lots of energy to dissipate. If the water can bounce against an air cushion, pipes won't pound. (For you electrical/electronic designers: this is equivalent to a capacitor in an electrical circuit.)

In older homes, anti-hammer devices are located near the main valve. In newer homes they are located near the washing machine, dishwasher, laundry tubs, and perhaps near the water main. They look like a short length of piping with a cap on the end. In a newer home, an anti-hammer device may be a small, specially designed chamber about 1" around and 4" long.

Modern Water Hammer Arrester

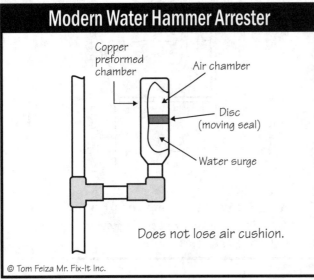

Copper preformed chamber

Air chamber

Disc (moving seal)

Water surge

Does not lose air cushion.

© Tom Feiza Mr. Fix-It Inc.

P032

Water Hammer Arresters

Old style – air chamber made with standard parts

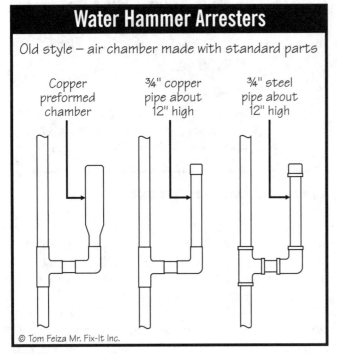

Copper preformed chamber

¾" copper pipe about 12" high

¾" steel pipe about 12" high

© Tom Feiza Mr. Fix-It Inc.

P015

If your pipes pound or bang when the water shuts off, add water hammer arresters or check any existing arresters. Old-style arresters may have filled with water and need to be drained. Before you try this, though, be sure the main valve is in good working order. If it leaks, is hard to turn, or has excessive corrosion, call a plumber. Also, be aware

that in older homes with steel piping, turning off the water may loosen sediment inside the pipes; you may see rust and debris in the water. And since this technique introduces air into the system, an air/water mix may shoot out of the faucets when you turn them on again.

To drain the system and restore air to the arresters, turn off the water main, shutting off all water to your home. Then open all faucets and allow all water to drain from them. Next, slowly open the main valve part way and close the faucets one by one as the water runs steadily. After all faucets are closed, fully open the main valve.

Must Know / Must Do
Water Hammer Arresters

- If pipes pound or bang when the water shuts off, check water hammer arresters.

- Consider draining the system to restore air in the chambers of water hammer arresters.

- If the main valve is hard to operate, don't drain the system; call a plumber instead.

Drainage, Waste and Vent System

After water is used in your home, it exits through a drainage, waste and vent (DWV) system. Large pipes allow wastewater to flow by gravity from your home to a municipal sewer or private septic system. A series of traps and vents allow wastewater to flow freely while preventing sewer gas from entering your home.

Older systems are constructed of cast iron and galvanized steel piping. Newer systems are made of plastic. Copper was used for some systems built about 1970.

The sketch shows common components of a DWV system, which uses pipes that are larger than those in the water-supply plumbing system. The pipes range from 1-1/2" to 4", with the larger pipes installed where the system exits your home. Horizontal pipes are angled to allow for proper waste flow.

The vent portion of the system starts with the vent pipe or stack routed through the roof. This open pipe allows air to enter the system so all pipes can drain properly. Think of the drainage system as a big straw. If you fill a straw with water, cover the top end with your finger and pick it up, water will not drain from the straw. When you release your finger and allow air to "vent" the straw, water drains quickly.

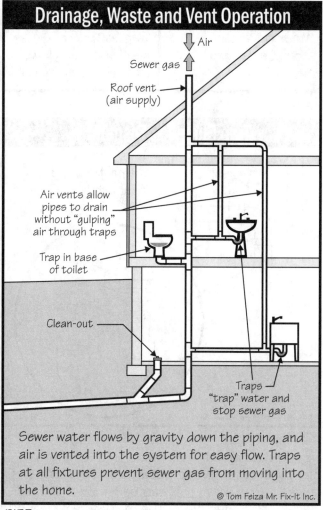

Drainage, Waste and Vent Operation

Sewer water flows by gravity down the piping, and air is vented into the system for easy flow. Traps at all fixtures prevent sewer gas from moving into the home.

© Tom Feiza Mr. Fix-It Inc.

P153

S Trap Not Allowed

In older systems or systems installed by an amateur, you may see a sink drained with an "S" trap. This type of trap has an S-shaped pipe below the sink, and instead of draining into the wall, it drains into the floor. Since there is no vent and no air supply, the trap will drain with a long slurp as air is drawn through it. The trap seal also may be lost.

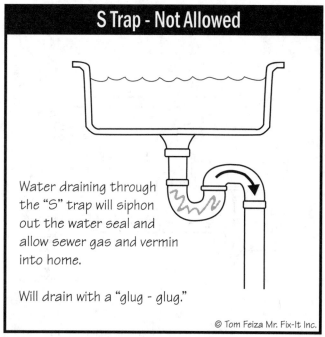

S Trap - Not Allowed

Water draining through the "S" trap will siphon out the water seal and allow sewer gas and vermin into home.

Will drain with a "glug - glug."

© Tom Feiza Mr. Fix-It Inc.

P037

Air Admittance Valve

In systems installed since about 2000, when plumbing codes changed, a new device called an air admittance valve may be added to the drain line. This valve allows air to enter the drainage system but does not allow sewer gas to escape. The device will be located in the horizontal run from a sink in place of a plumbed vent. It must be visible and accessible for maintenance. This valve may not be allowed on certain fixtures and may be prohibited in some communities.

Plumbing Vent of Island Sink

Island sinks present a special problem for running a typical vent pipe up a wall and into the attic, because there is no wall available. Island sinks have either a special vent arrangement with a vent loop under the sink or an air admittance valve if it is allowed.

All piping and fixtures must be vented. If problems occur with the venting system, drains will "glug-glug" and empty slowly.

Each fixture has a trap—a P-shaped device below a sink (or built into the base of a toilet) that remains full of water. "Trapping" water creates a seal that prevents sewer gas from entering through the drain. If a trap dries up, you will notice a sewage smell.

Air Admittance Valve

Air

Vent

Provides air
for drainage

Water traps
sewer gas

Air and water

Air

Air admittance
valve provides
air for drainage

Air and water

© Tom Feiza Mr. Fix-It Inc.

P035

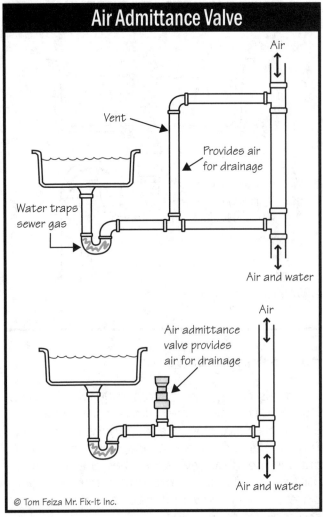

Plumbing Vent of Island Sink

© Tom Feiza Mr. Fix-It Inc.

Vent

Sink

Larger pipe

Cleanout

P036

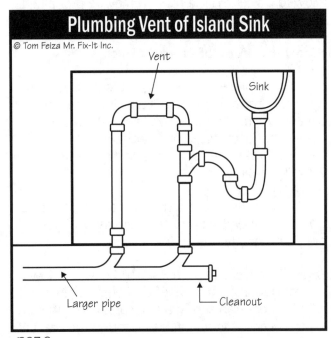

Floor Drain Trap — Sewer Smell

© Tom Feiza Mr. Fix-It Inc.

Sewer gas

Water

Water in trap
"traps" sewer gas.
No smell.

Sewer gas

Trap "water seal"
missing and gas flows
into home. Sewer smell.

P026

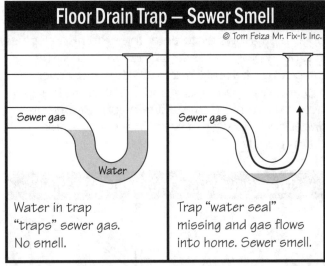

Trap Plugged - Dismantle

Loosen nuts

Dismantle trap and
clear debris.

Remove

Debris

Nut

Washer

Threads

Slides
off

© Tom Feiza Mr. Fix-It Inc.

P102

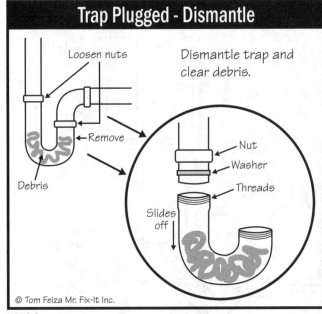

Traps are designed to be dismantled to remove
blockages or retrieve lost objects. Drain piping has
covers ("clean-outs") that can be removed to help
clean out clogged pipes. The main system cleanout
will be located in the basement floor or where the
main pipe exits your home.

If you have a septic system, this cleanout will be outside, about 4 feet below the soil. With slab construction, the cleanout will be in the slab or outside.

If the sewer drainage system is subject to backups from the municipal connection, the municipality may allow the installation of a sanitary sewer check valve. Typically this valve is located below the base-ment floor or wherever the main sewer line exits the structure. The valve is located in a box with a cover so the check valve can be maintained. Maintenance involves visual inspection of the operation, as well as clearing of any debris that would prevent the valve from closing.

Under normal conditions, the valve swings open to allow sewage to flow out of your home. When there is no flow, or if a backup occurs in the sewage system, the swing check valve drops closed, preventing sewage from backing up into your home.

Sanitary Sewer Cleanout

Cleanout cover is removed to allow a sewer cleaning machine into sewer line to street.

Vent

Trap in toilet

Clean-out

Street

Sewer lateral (pipe) – owner's responsibility

To sewer main

Sanitary sewer

© Tom Feiza Mr. Fix-It Inc.

P028

Must Know / Must Do
Drainage, Waste and Vent System

- If you notice a sewage smell, check for a dry trap.

- If a sink or other fixture backs up, there's a blockage in the trap.

- If your whole system backs up or wastewater backs up out of the lowest fixture, this indicates a problem with the main drainage line. Call a plumber.

- Any leaks from the waste system are potentially dangerous and should be repaired as soon as possible.

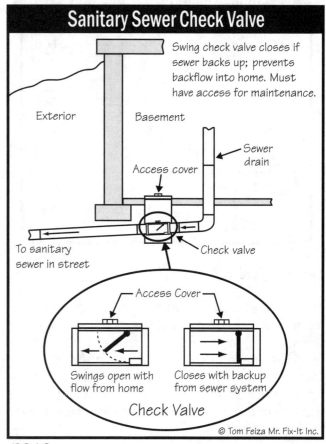

Sanitary Sewer Check Valve

Swing check valve closes if sewer backs up; prevents backflow into home. Must have access for maintenance.

Exterior   Basement

Sewer drain

Access cover

To sanitary sewer in street

Check valve

Access Cover

Swings open with flow from home

Closes with backup from sewer system

Check Valve

© Tom Feiza Mr. Fix-It Inc.

P040

Sewer and Septic Systems

After wastewater leaves your home, it must be treated and cleaned before it is released into the environment. In a municipal sewage system, wastewater is routed to a treatment facility. If you live in the country, your home will have its own private treatment system—a septic or mound system.

Sewer System

Municipal sewer systems collect sanitary waste (sewer water) through pipes below the street. Wastewater flows through a series of pipes that increase in size as they approach the treatment facility. Pipes can be 6 feet or more in diameter.

In many systems, all sewage flows by gravity until pumping stations "lift" (pump) it into the treatment facility. Once treated, the water is released to rivers and streams.

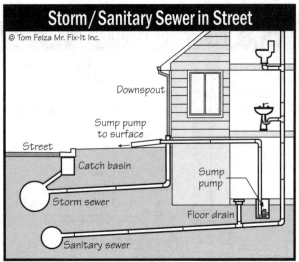

P017

Septic System

In rural areas without a municipal sewage treatment facility, residential sewage is treated in a septic system—a large underground tank and absorption field. Bacteria in the tank break down sewage solids. This treated sewage becomes sludge that settles at the bottom of the tank. Grease, fat and soap scum rise to the top of the tank, where they are trapped by baffles.

As wastewater enters the tank, processed water is released to a drain field or absorption field consisting of a series of perforated pipes that release the water into soil. The soil then filters the wastewater; soil microorganisms decompose many contaminants in the wastewater.

Although the septic system works automatically through the actions of bacteria, microorganisms, tank and piping, you must arrange for a professional to pump and inspect the tank.

Generally, a family of four should have the tank pumped and inspected every 2 years, but this varies with the type and size of the system and with local conditions. A professional septic service company can determine when your system should be pumped. Pumping the tank involves removing the sludge and scum before an excess builds up.

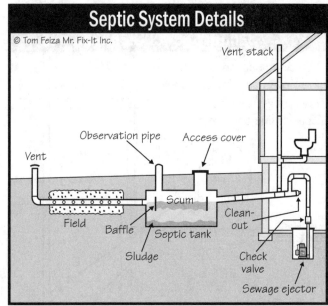

P121

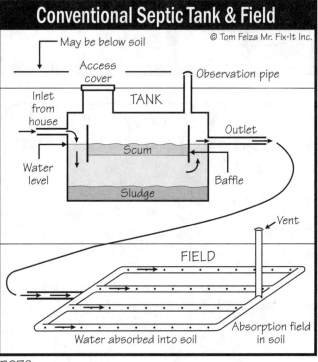

P078

Must Know / Must Do
Septic System

- Understand how your system works.

- Have the system pumped and serviced routinely.

- Do not put contaminants in the system.

- Learn ways to conserve water.

You also must limit the amount of water that enters the system. Use fixtures (toilets, showerheads) that limit water use. Repair all plumbing leaks promptly. Don't connect the sump pump discharge to the septic system—the sump handles clear rainwater that doesn't need treatment. Divert surface water away from the septic drainage field so it can work properly.

Never put grease, fat, coffee grounds, paper towels, food waste, sanitary napkins, or disposable diapers down the drains—they will clog the system. Also, do not put toxic substances like solvents, oils, paints, disinfectants, or pesticides down the drains.

Most experts agree that "sweeteners" or septic system "starters" are not useful.

For more information, consult local health officials, the local plumbing inspector, or your nearest department of natural resources.

Mound System

Mound systems are installed in rural areas where the soil can't accept water from a standard septic system. A mound system usually has a second holding tank/pump tank. After sewage is processed in the septic tank, water flows into the pump tank, which lifts the water to the top of the mound.

The mound is specially constructed of gravel and soil that's mounded above the surrounding surface. The mound functions the same as the absorption field in a conventional septic system, and the requirements for maintenance are the same as those described above for a septic system.

You should understand the operation of the pump/second holding tank. Also, there may be an alarm that goes off if the pump is not working. If the alarm sounds, contact professional help.

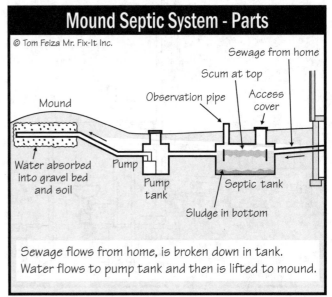

P079

Sewage Ejector

In most homes with basements and septic systems, sanitary system drainage will exit the basement 4 feet below the exterior soil depth, or about halfway up the basement wall. Sewage flows by gravity through the drainage pipe. But if there is a laundry tub, sink, bathroom, or floor drain in the basement, their wastewater must be pumped up to the main waste line. In this case, a sewage ejector or wastewater pump lifts the sewage water.

You can tell if your home has a sewage ejector by looking for a sealed crock with piping that leads to the septic system. Modern systems are sealed and vented. An older system may consist of an open crock if it just services a laundry tub or floor drain.

These pumps and crocks require little maintenance, but if the pump fails or water leaks from the crock, stop using water in the lower level, and call a plumber.

Sometimes a home that's on a municipal sewage system will have a sewage ejection pump. This depends on the height of the main sewer line in the street and the height of the connection to the home.

Sewage Ejector vs. Sump Pump

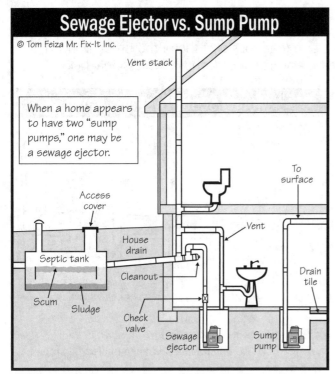

© Tom Feiza Mr. Fix-It Inc.

Vent stack

When a home appears to have two "sump pumps," one may be a sewage ejector.

Access cover

To surface

Septic tank

House drain

Vent

Cleanout

Scum   Sludge

Drain tile

Check valve

Sewage ejector

Sump pump

P120

Storm Sewer—Municipal or None?

Modern municipalities have two distinct sets of piping beneath roads and streets: sanitary sewers and storm sewers. The sanitary (municipal) sewer system routes all toilet, sink and drain water to a sewage treatment plant for processing, after which the clean water is released to rivers, lakes and streams.

Cities, and some subdivisions, also have a separate system—the storm sewer system—that handles rainwater. This system directly discharges untreated rainwater/runoff into rivers and streams. Your sump pump and rain gutters may be connected to this system through an underground pipe. The storm sewer line in your basement may look just like the sanitary sewer line except that it's not connected to toilets and sinks and doesn't have a vent on the roof.

If your sump pump is routed to the sanitary sewer system instead, you are sending clean rainwater to the sewage treatment plant. That overloads the plant and creates an unnecessary treatment expense. So don't connect your sump pump to the laundry tubs, because this water is routed to the sanitary sewer.

In rural areas, storm water may be routed into an open ditch beside the road. In densely populated areas, storm sewer piping below the street handles

rainstorm runoff from hard surfaces like roofs, driveways, and parking lots. Such runoff is too great to be absorbed by the limited area of exposed soil in the city. Whenever you see sewer grates in the street, you are looking at parts of an underground storm sewer system.

Municipal Storm/Sanitary Sewers

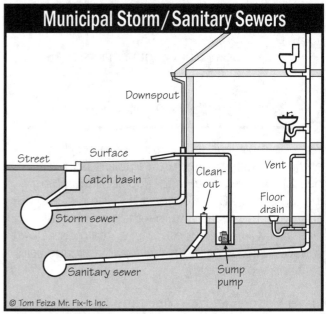

Downspout

Street   Surface

Catch basin

Clean-out

Vent

Storm sewer

Floor drain

Sanitary sewer

Sump pump

© Tom Feiza Mr. Fix-It Inc.

P122

Palmer Valve (Footing Drain)

In some metropolitan areas, homes built between the 1920s and the 1950s had a "palmer valve" that routed clear storm water into the sanitary sewer lines. This practice is no longer permitted in new home construction. We cannot afford to treat clear water in the sewer treatment plants. We also can't size sanitary sewer systems to accept large quantities of storm water during heavy rains.

If your house doesn't have a sump pump, it may have a palmer valve— and if so, you should maintain it. In the basement, remove the cover from the floor drain and shine a bright flashlight down into it. The palmer valve is a round brass disc at the side of the vertical pipe, just above the water in the trap.

Hook the lower edge of the palmer valve brass disc with a stiff wire or tool to make sure it moves freely—the brass disc should swing easily from the hinge at its top. If this disc is stuck closed (and most of them are), water that collects in the basement drain tile system cannot be drained away. You may end up with water rising in your basement.

To loosen a stuck palmer valve, spray it with lubricating oil a few times over several days, and bang it with a stick or tool. Try to hook the bottom and lift it up. You could also grab it with your hand if you are a brave soul. Or hire a plumber to free the valve.

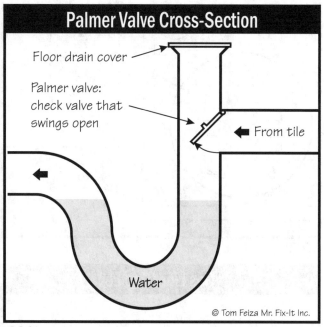

Palmer Valve Cross-Section

Floor drain cover

Palmer valve: check valve that swings open

From tile

Water

© Tom Feiza Mr. Fix-It Inc.

B001

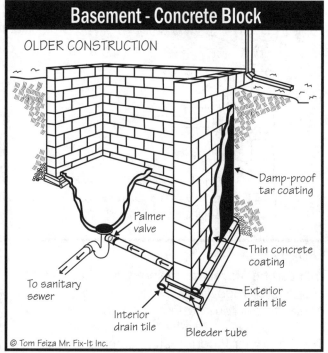

Basement - Concrete Block

OLDER CONSTRUCTION

Damp-proof tar coating

Palmer valve

Thin concrete coating

To sanitary sewer

Exterior drain tile

Interior drain tile

Bleeder tube

© Tom Feiza Mr. Fix-It Inc.

B002

Irrigation Systems

Landscape irrigation systems come in all designs and types. They are not common in northern climates, although they may be used for more expensive housing. In dry southern climates, drip systems often are buried to deliver moisture to soil below the plants.

In northern climates, water must be drained from an underground system to prevent winter freezing. A professional best performs this service. In addition, the system will need routine maintenance of sprinkler heads, automatic valves, and piping.

Most systems receive water from the home's drinking (potable) water system. In this case the irrigation system must be separated from the drinking water with a vacuum breaker or a backflow prevention device. Typically this device is located at least 12 inches above the soil in the feed pipe to the system. The backflow preventer stops any backflow that would contaminate the drinking water.

Where homes are on a metered municipal water system and a municipal sanitary sewer system, the irrigation system or even the exterior hose bib connections may be separately metered. This involves two water meters—one for the total amount of water used and one for the irrigation water. This allows the municipality to determine how much water is used for irrigation so the homeowner will not have to pay a sewer charge on it.

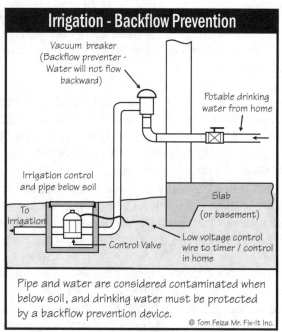

Irrigation - Backflow Prevention

Vacuum breaker (Backflow preventer - Water will not flow backward)

Potable drinking water from home

Irrigation control and pipe below soil

Slab

(or basement)

To irrigation

Control Valve

Low voltage control wire to timer / control in home

Pipe and water are considered contaminated when below soil, and drinking water must be protected by a backflow prevention device.

© Tom Feiza Mr. Fix-It Inc.

P098

75

Irrigation Meters - Shutoff and Drain

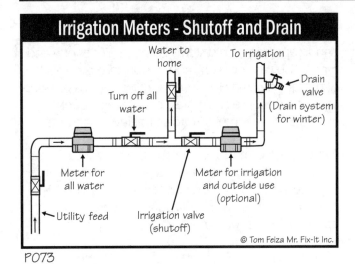

P073

Natural Gas and Propane

Natural gas and propane, commonly used in central heating systems, may also fuel the home's water heater. Know the basics of the distribution system in your home and how to turn off the system in an emergency.

Natural Gas

Natural gas is provided by a public utility in many areas. Underground piping distributes the gas, and a small line brings it to the house through a metering/control system outside or in the basement. Gas enters your home at very low pressure. There is a main shutoff valve near the meter, and the system has a relief valve and vent piping for safety.

Inside your home, natural gas may be distributed by "black iron" steel-screwed pipes. It can also be distributed by brass or copper pipes, depending on local requirements.

Natural gas piping should be well-supported and protected from damage. There should be a shutoff valve at each appliance connection to the piping. Most fixed gas appliances like the furnace or water heater will be directly connected to the gas piping without a flexible connector. Most connections will include a "drip leg," a small vertical pipe below the appliance connection that catches any contamination before it reaches the gas control valves.

All flexible connectors should be the modern type that extend directly from the gas piping and shutoff valve to the appliance. Normally, flexible connectors are used only with appliances like stoves or dryers

Exterior Gas Meter and Lockable Valve

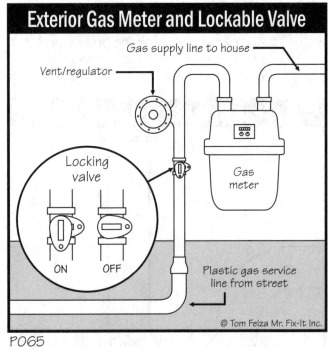

P065

Gas Line, Drip Leg

© Tom Feiza Mr. Fix-It Inc.

Drip leg collects debris and moisture from gas line to protect connected appliance.

P043

that can be moved for maintenance, but areas prone to earthquakes may allow or require flexible connectors at furnaces and water heaters.

The Consumer Product Safety Commission advises that older flexible gas connectors made of uncoated brass can leak. Your connectors should be made of plastic-coated brass or stainless steel. The CPSC advises that any uncoated brass connector should be immediately replaced by a professional. You will recognize uncoated brass by its coppery color, even

Water Heater Gas Connections

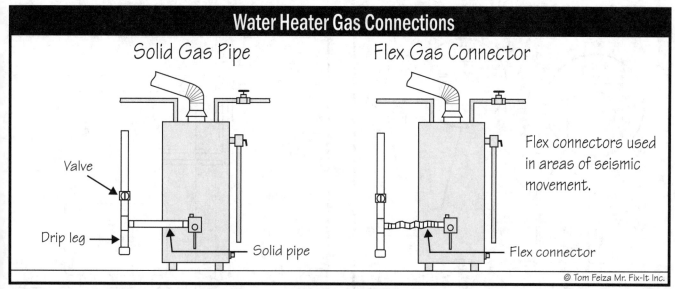

Solid Gas Pipe

Valve

Drip leg →

Solid pipe

Flex Gas Connector

Flex connectors used in areas of seismic movement.

Flex connector

© Tom Feiza Mr. Fix-It Inc.

P047

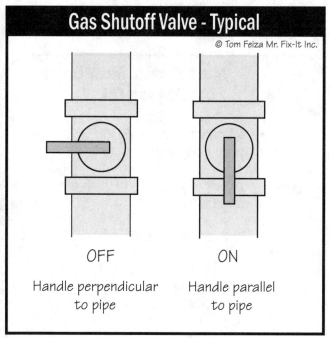

Gas Shutoff Valve - Typical

© Tom Feiza Mr. Fix-It Inc.

OFF

Handle perpendicular to pipe

ON

Handle parallel to pipe

P076

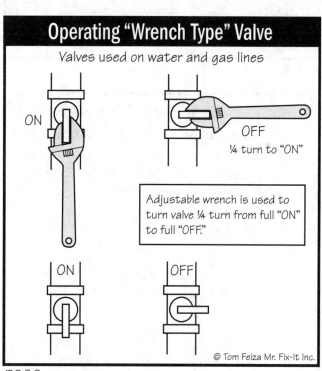

Operating "Wrench Type" Valve

Valves used on water and gas lines

ON

OFF
¼ turn to "ON"

Adjustable wrench is used to turn valve ¼ turn from full "ON" to full "OFF."

ON

OFF

P066

© Tom Feiza Mr. Fix-It Inc.

if it's old. Older connectors made of flexible aluminum or aluminum piping also should be replaced.

If a gas appliance is removed from the system, have a professional turn off the gas valve, cap the line beyond the valve, and check for leaks.

Gas valves turn off with a quarter-turn. When the valve handle is parallel to the piping, the valve is on. When the handle is perpendicular to the piping, the valve is off. Many valves must be turned with an adjustable wrench or pliers.

Propane

Propane is a gas that's similar to natural gas, except that propane is provided in a storage tank on your property. Distribution piping is similar to that for natural gas except that there is no meter; you pay for the gas when it's placed in the tank.

The main shutoff often is at the top of the tank. It may be a valve that requires several turns to shut off the gas. Review the valve and the rest of the system with your supplier. Follow all precautions noted above for natural gas.

Propane Gas Shutoff Valves

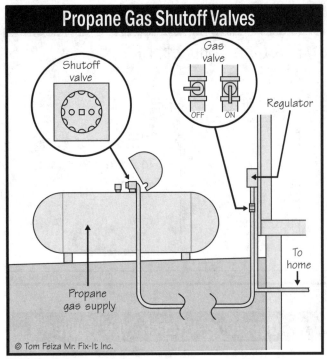

Shutoff valve

Gas valve

OFF   ON

Regulator

To home

Propane gas supply

© Tom Feiza Mr. Fix-It Inc.

P075

Typical Fuel Oil Tank in Basement

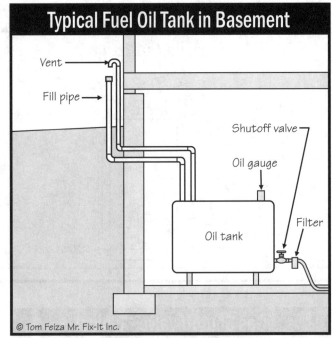

Vent

Fill pipe

Shutoff valve

Oil gauge

Oil tank

Filter

© Tom Feiza Mr. Fix-It Inc.

P003

Must Know / Must Do
Natural Gas and Propane

- Identify the main shutoff valve and know how it operates.

- Identify the shutoff for every gas appliance.

- Inspect all flexible gas connectors per CPSC standards (noted above).

- If you smell gas, leave the house. Don't light a match, and don't turn on a light. Use a neighbor's phone to call the gas supplier.

Must Know / Must Do
Heating Oil

- Identify the shutoff valve and know how to operate it.

- Never allow the system to run out of oil.

- The system should not smell or leak. Fix all leaks promptly.

- For underground tanks: contact municipal or state agency for registration and maintenance requirements.

It's wise to sign up with a supplier who automatically fills the tank as needed. Often, the supplier can also service your heating equipment.

Heating Oil

Oil can be used in a heating system and may also be used to heat water. An oil system consists of a storage tank, valve, filter, and distribution piping. A fill and vent line will extend to the exterior of the house.

The oil storage tank often is located in the basement, but it may also be underground in your yard. If your tank is underground, contact the oil supplier or your municipality or state to check maintenance requirements and code regulations. Usually, underground storage tanks are tightly regulated because of the potential for a spill that could contaminate the environment.

Arrange to have a supplier automatically fill the tank and maintain the oil burner. Never, never, never let the system run out of oil—this can lead to a very expensive service call.

Chapter 6 – General Home Systems

Foundation Basics

A foundation provides a stable, rigid base to support a home. The foundation supports the frame and structure and protects it from moisture and contact with the soil. The foundation must rest on firm soil and be protected from water entry or excessive dampness.

Full Depth Basement, Crawl Spaces

Foundation types vary with local weather conditions and accepted local practices. In northern climates, the foundation must be deep enough to extend below the frost line. This can be 4 feet or more, so full basements are common. (Frost causes soil to expand, and the foundation must be below the frost line so it won't move with this expansion.) In warmer climates that have little or no frost, the foundation may be a crawl space or concrete slab poured "on grade" or directly on the soil. In a coastal region, the foundation may be piers or posts that raise the house above potential high water levels. In some areas, foundations are made of pressure-treated wood.

The majority of homes in northern climates are built on foundations that form a crawl space or full basement. The basement rests on a footing that supports the home's weight. Foundation walls are constructed of brick, concrete block, poured concrete, clay tile, stone, or similar materials. The basement floor usually consists of poured concrete. Crawl spaces often have a dirt floor.

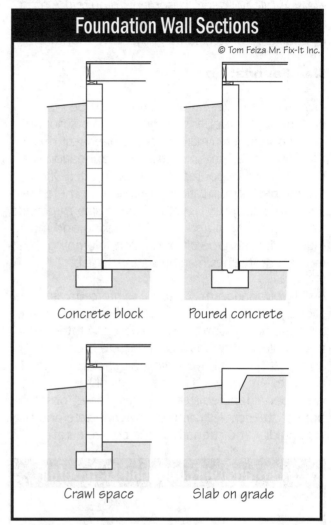

Foundation Wall Sections

© Tom Feiza Mr. Fix-It Inc.

Concrete block   Poured concrete

Crawl space   Slab on grade

S004

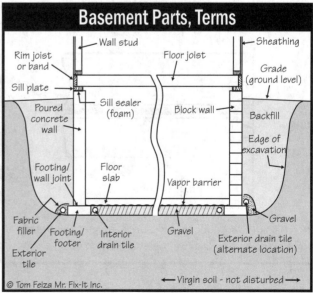

Basement Parts, Terms

© Tom Feiza Mr. Fix-It Inc.

B107

Must Know / Must Do Foundations

- Understand the type of foundation that supports your home.

- Protect your foundation from water damage. Never allow water to pond around the foundation.

- Protect your foundation and the rest of your home from insects.

Full-depth basements are the most complicated type of foundation because of potential water problems and the pressure of soil outside the basement walls. While full-depth basements require the most maintenance, crawl spaces and slab foundations must also be protected from excessive moisture.

Slab Foundations

In warmer climates, a foundation must be placed on firm soil for proper support, but frost is not an issue. In warmer climates, houses often rest on a "slab on grade," meaning that the foundation is a slab of concrete poured directly on grade. Often these types of foundations are thicker at the edge, and reinforcing steel is set inside the slab to provide structural strength and to resist cracking and movement. With this type of foundation, plumbing, heating and utility lines may be set in the slab.

A slab foundation may also be reinforced with steel cables pulled tightly inside tubes that are set in the concrete slab. During construction, the tubes and steel cables are set in place; concrete is poured, and it sets. Special hydraulic jacks stretch the cables, and they are fastened at the edges of the concrete with special tapered steel wedges. These "post tensioned" steel cables compress the concrete and provide rigidity and strength to the concrete slab.

Local conditions must be considered in maintaining a foundation. Slab foundations must be protected from changes in water in the soil supporting the slab to prevent heaving and cracking. Excessive moisture can make the soil swell, and lack of moisture can make the soil shrink.

Pier, Post, Pile, Caisson Foundations

In areas where soil conditions will not support a basement spread footing or a slab on grade, a post and beam foundation is an option. Generally, pier, post and caisson refer to a vertical post set into the soil down to a firm bearing soil or rock. These types of foundations are well suited for soft soils, soils that expand, and coastal or hillside construction. Usually, the post is constructed of poured reinforced concrete, and it supports a beam that forms the base of the home.

The hole may be drilled for the caisson, and then a steel-reinforced concrete post is poured. A pile is driven into the ground until it reaches suitable soil or rock that provides proper support. This type of construction requires a site evaluation and engineering design.

I will focus on the construction and maintenance of full-depth foundations. The necessary maintenance of crawl spaces is similar. For slabs on grade, follow the recommendations for protecting the foundation from water.

Post Tension Foundation Slab Detail

© Tom Feiza Mr. Fix-It Inc.

Slab
Steel cable
Fastener

Sleeve
Steel cable
Cable stretched inside sleeve

Tapered collars trap cable

Slab section

After poured concrete is cured, steel cables are stretched and locked in place with collars.

S035

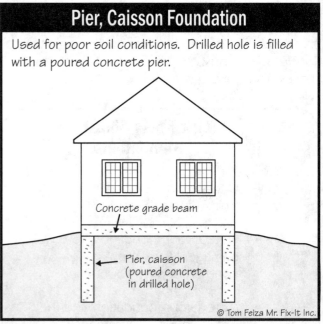

Pier, Caisson Foundation

Used for poor soil conditions. Drilled hole is filled with a poured concrete pier.

Concrete grade beam

Pier, caisson (poured concrete in drilled hole)

© Tom Feiza Mr. Fix-It Inc.

S037

Post Tension Cables in Slab

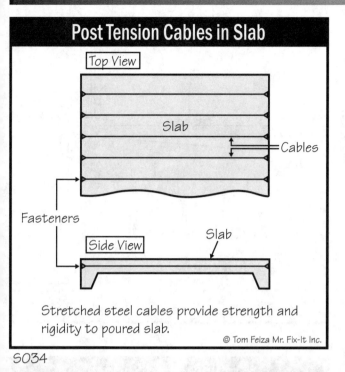

Stretched steel cables provide strength and rigidity to poured slab.

© Tom Feiza Mr. Fix-It Inc.

S034

Pile Foundation

Used for poor soil conditions. Pile is supported by friction to soil or rock.

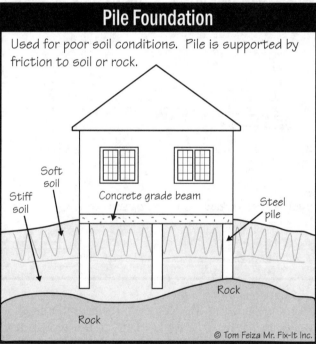

© Tom Feiza Mr. Fix-It Inc.

S036

Protecting Your Basement Foundation

Basements foundations require simple, routine maintenance to prevent damage that requires costly repairs. Since most damage to basements occurs slowly, over many years, if you ignore routine maintenance you may not notice a problem until there is a water leak or a major crack and wall movement. So take some time to inspect your basement and its

Basement – Concrete Block

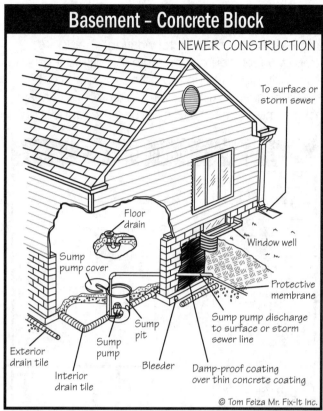

NEWER CONSTRUCTION

© Tom Feiza Mr. Fix-It Inc.

B005

environment. A little common sense and simple maintenance will prevent potentially serious problems and extend the trouble-free performance of your basement.

Over the years, your home's original water diversion systems require maintenance and repair. They simply can't be ignored. Let's walk through the basics of maintaining your hole in the ground.

Grading to Protect the Foundation

Proper grading around the house is your best protection against seepage into the basement that may cause expensive damage. When a home is built, workers dig the excavation several feet larger than the basement walls to allow for construction clearances.

Most of the hole around your basement is filled with soil from the site. This may contain gravel, rock, wood, paper, and unfortunately almost anything no longer useful for home construction. For the next 20 years, this soil and "stuff" settles around your basement walls. It settles quickly for the first few years and more slowly after that.

To divert surface water, the soil should pitch away from your home with a 1" pitch per linear foot for about 6 feet beyond the foundation. That is a 6" drop in 6 feet. You can measure this with a level and a straightedge held on top of the soil next to the foundation. At a minimum, the pitch should always have some slope for 6 feet beyond the foundation.

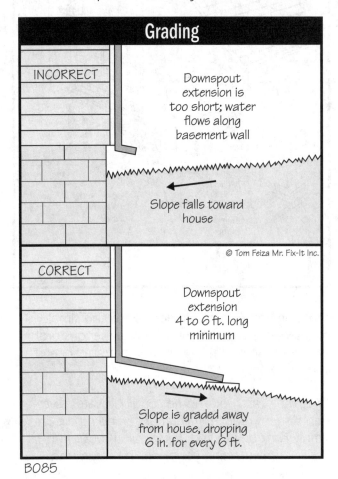

Grading

INCORRECT

Downspout extension is too short; water flows along basement wall

Slope falls toward house

© Tom Feiza Mr. Fix-It Inc.

CORRECT

Downspout extension 4 to 6 ft. long minimum

Slope is graded away from house, dropping 6 in. for every 6 ft.

B085

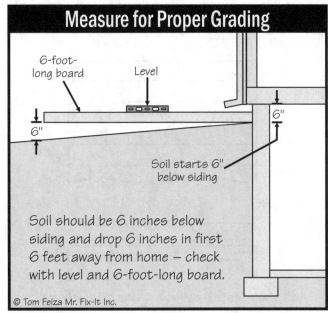

Measure for Proper Grading

6-foot-long board

Level

6"

6"

Soil starts 6" below siding

Soil should be 6 inches below siding and drop 6 inches in first 6 feet away from home — check with level and 6-foot-long board.

© Tom Feiza Mr. Fix-It Inc.

B011

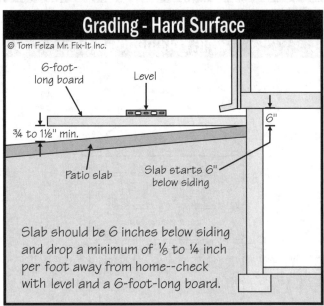

Grading - Hard Surface

© Tom Feiza Mr. Fix-It Inc.

6-foot-long board

Level

6"

¾ to 1½" min.

Patio slab

Slab starts 6" below siding

Slab should be 6 inches below siding and drop a minimum of ⅛ to ¼ inch per foot away from home--check with level and a 6-foot-long board.

B104

The soil should also be 6" below siding and wood trim to prevent water and insect damage. If wood siding touches the ground, water will wick up and rot the siding and framing.

To improve the grade, you have several options, depending on the landscape materials near your home.

Bushes near the foundation, planted above the original foundation hole, often settle. If there is bare soil under the bushes, just add more soil. However, adding more than a few inches of soil can damage bushes by eliminating air from the roots. Check with a professional landscaper on the potential damage to your type of bushes. You may need to raise the bushes and fill under them.

If the area around the foundation has a planting bed or bushes with a ground cover, the soil under the ground cover must pitch away from the foundation. Dig through the ground cover in several areas to check the grade of the soil. To improve this situation, remove the ground cover and fill with soil. Then replace the ground cover.

You may wish to use a fabric weed barrier or black plastic over the soil. The weed barrier will stop weeds while allowing air and water movement— good for plants but not ideal for the basement.

Black plastic does the best job of deflecting water and protecting your basement, but it can be hard on plants. If you use black plastic, cut large holes for plants to improve access to moisture and air.

Don't forget to grade areas under decks. You can use black plastic over the properly graded soil to deflect water and stop weeds. A thin cover of gravel or stone will hold down the plastic and make the area more attractive.

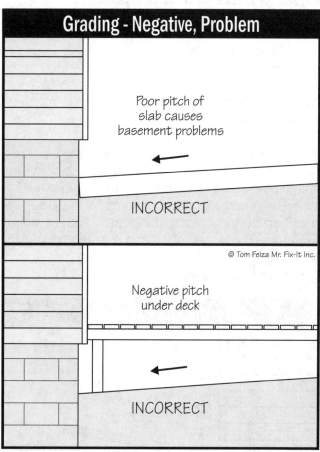

Slope and Grading, Ground Cover

INCORRECT

Water flows through the stone or bark chip ground covering and then toward the house

plastic

Slope falls toward house under ground cover

© Tom Feiza Mr. Fix-It Inc.

CORRECT

Water flows through the stone or bark chip ground covering and then away from the house

plastic

Slope is graded away from house (6 in. for every 6 ft.) under ground cover

B084

Grading - Negative, Problem

Poor pitch of slab causes basement problems

INCORRECT

© Tom Feiza Mr. Fix-It Inc.

Negative pitch under deck

INCORRECT

B008

If there is sod next to the foundation, cut it with a sod cutter and fold it away from the foundation. Add soil, then lay the sod back in place. You could add soil directly over the sod, but that would require re-seeding, and the area will settle as the buried sod decomposes. Cover the sod only if it is in very poor condition or if you need a dramatic change in grade. For flower beds and bare soil, just add topsoil fill.

When grading, don't use a light moss-type soil; it will settle too much and hold moisture. In areas where you will not be planting, you can use clay. In planting beds use a blended or brown planting soil, or garden soil. This heavier mixture will not wash away into the yard.

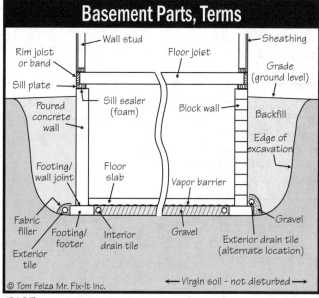

Basement Parts, Terms

Wall stud — Sheathing
Rim joist or band — Floor joist — Grade (ground level)
Sill plate —
Poured concrete wall — Sill sealer (foam) — Block wall — Backfill
Edge of excavation
Footing/ wall joint — Floor slab — Vapor barrier
Fabric filler — Footing/ footer — Interior drain tile — Gravel — Gravel — Exterior drain tile (alternate location)
Exterior tile
© Tom Feiza Mr. Fix-It Inc. ← Virgin soil - not disturbed →

B107

All hard surfaces such as walks and driveways should also be pitched away from your foundation. The good news is that only a slight grade, as little as 1/4" per foot, is adequate for hard surfaces.

Check Gutters and Downspouts

Gutters collect tremendous quantities of water from the roof and must deliver that water away from the foundation. Keep your downspouts extended at least 6 to 8 feet away from the foundation to a spot where the natural grade of the soil continues moving the water away.

If your area has underground storm sewers, make sure all downspouts are properly connected to the visible pipe fittings and that water flows into the storm sewer pipe during rainstorms. If this pipe backs up during a storm, it indicates that the storm sewer line is plugged or broken. Test the line by running a hose into the gutter. You can have this line cleaned by a sewer cleaner.

If dampness and seepage appear on basement walls near an underground storm sewer connection, a broken storm sewer line may be the cause. You can run water into the gutter during a dry spell; if moisture seeps into the basement, it indicates that the underground line is damaged. A sewer cleaner can evaluate and repair the line.

Keep gutters clean to prevent plugging and overflowing of downspouts and storm sewer lines.

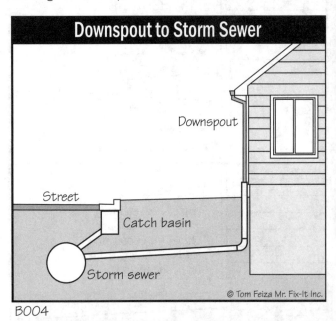

Downspout to Storm Sewer

Downspout

Street

Catch basin

Storm sewer

© Tom Feiza Mr. Fix-It Inc.

B004

Downspout Extension

INCORRECT

Extension pitched back toward house

Elbow too low; water leaks here

Slope falls toward house

© Tom Feiza Mr. Fix-It Inc.

CORRECT

Downspout extension (4- to 6-foot-long minimum)

Elbow raised

Slope is graded away from house, dropping 6 in. for every 6 ft.

© Tom Feiza Mr. Fix-It Inc.

B086

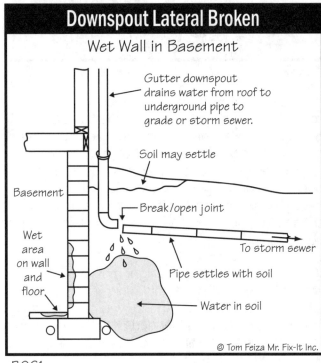

Downspout Lateral Broken

Wet Wall in Basement

Gutter downspout drains water from roof to underground pipe to grade or storm sewer.

Soil may settle

Basement

Break/open joint

Wet area on wall and floor

To storm sewer

Pipe settles with soil

Water in soil

© Tom Feiza Mr. Fix-It Inc.

B061

Window Wells

Window wells hold soil away from foundation windows as the grade is raised. The window well should fit tightly against the foundation wall to prevent leaks. The grade around the well should pitch away so water isn't directed into the well. If a window well fills with water, check the fit of the well and the grade around it.

Keep window wells clean and free of all plant material. Fill the bottom of the well with gravel to allow for good drainage and to stop any plant growth.

If the grade and fit around the window well are in good condition but the well still fills with water, dig out the bottom of the well about 18" and fill with washed stone. The stone will ensure proper drainage to the tile system. If you have a problem window well, dig down several feet inside it with a post hole digger; then fill the hole with washed stone. This channel helps drain the window well to the basement tile. However, you should only dig this channel if you know the drain tile system is working. If it isn't, you will create a tube of frozen water that can push against the basement wall.

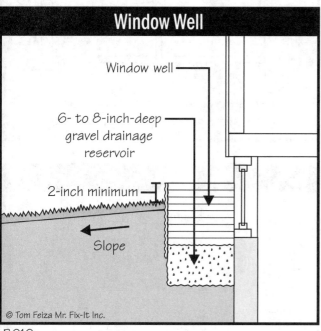

Window Well

Window well

6- to 8-inch-deep gravel drainage reservoir

2-inch minimum

Slope

© Tom Feiza Mr. Fix-It Inc.

B010

Foundations—The Bottom Line

If you follow these simple inspection and maintenance tips, your basement will perform for many years without failure. All foundations have some

problem symptoms, but if you maintain your foundation, minor problems will not become major crises. If you notice severe drainage problems, wall cracks or wall movement, contact a professional home inspector or basement consultant to evaluate your specific situation.

If a major problem is identified, don't feel threatened, and don't jump at the first evaluation or repair proposal. It often takes years for a basement or foundation problem to develop, and the situation will not require immediate repair. Take time to solicit several evaluations and repair proposals. Check each contractor's references, and make sure the contractor belongs to a professional builders' or remodelers' organization.

Termite Protection

In warmer climates, the wood structure of a home must be protected from termites and other pests. This often requires special construction techniques and constant diligence to check for potential problems. Often a pest control contractor should be hired on a routine basis.

Homeowners must eliminate soil contact with the wood structure of the home. Potential entry points for pests include contact points of trees and shrubs as well as firewood stacked against a home. In areas where termites are a problem, special precautions like a termite shield can separate the wood structure from the soil to prevent insect movement.

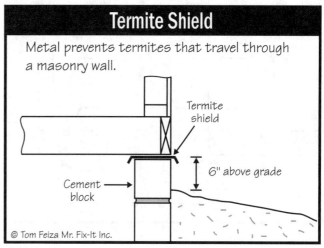

Termite Shield

Metal prevents termites that travel through a masonry wall.

Termite shield

6" above grade

Cement block

© Tom Feiza Mr. Fix-It Inc.

S032

Structure, Frame and Siding

The structural frame of your home rests on the foundation or basement and holds up the floors, interior walls, and roof. Most homes in the U.S. are framed with wood, but a few are built with a brick or block support structure. Once the frame and structure are properly designed and installed, little maintenance is needed except to protect the structure from water and insects.

Platform Framing

Most homes are built with platform framing. The framing starts with a "platform" of floor joists built over the foundation wall. The joists support the deck. There is usually a beam down the center of the foundation that supports the center of the joists. Posts rest on footings and the foundation wall support beam.

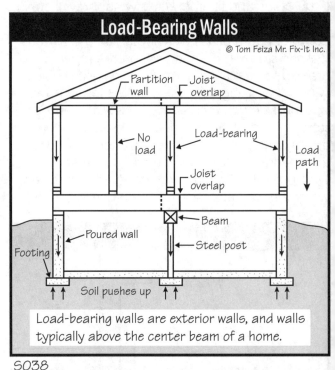

Balloon Frame / **Platform Frame**

© Tom Feiza Mr. Fix-It Inc.

- Sole plate
- 2nd floor joist
- Firestop
- Double top plate
- Ribbon
- Stud
- Stud
- Header
- 1st floor joist
- Sill
- Sill
- Foundation wall

S006

The wooden structure of the home is built to transfer weight loads to the foundation structure. Normally this includes load-bearing interior walls that run parallel to the supporting beam. The exteri-

or walls also carry loads. Some interior walls are partition walls and don't support the structure; they just divide or partition the space. Don't modify any walls without evaluating where the loads of the structure are supported.

Building up from the foundation structure, the floors are supported by floor joists covered with some type of subflooring material spanning the joists. Exterior walls are placed on the subflooring, and a second floor is added in a similar fashion. Exterior walls and the interior load-bearing walls support the roof structure and ceiling. Various materials have been used for floor joists and beams through the years.

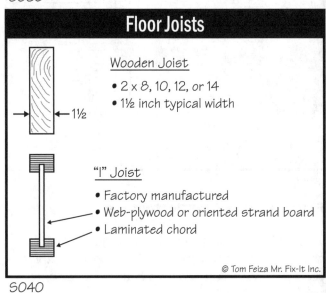

Load-Bearing Walls

© Tom Feiza Mr. Fix-It Inc.

- Partition wall
- Joist overlap
- No load
- Load-bearing
- Load path
- Joist overlap
- Beam
- Poured wall
- Steel post
- Footing
- Soil pushes up

Load-bearing walls are exterior walls, and walls typically above the center beam of a home.

S038

Floor Joists

© Tom Feiza Mr. Fix-It Inc.

Wooden Joist
- 2 x 8, 10, 12, or 14
- 1½ inch typical width
- 1½

"I" Joist
- Factory manufactured
- Web-plywood or oriented strand board
- Laminated chord

© Tom Feiza Mr. Fix-It Inc.

S040

Floor joists can be wood lumber or manufactured I-Joist systems. Wood joists have been constructed since wood or "stick" framing techniques started around 1880. Recently, I-Joist systems have been used because they enable longer spans and provide more dimensional stability than natural wood. Trusses can also be placed to provide floor support, allowing long spans and often eliminating the center beam or center support structure.

Subflooring covers the floor joist system and supports the floor loads. Materials used for subflooring have varied through the years. Until about 1960, solid 1" x 6" wood was used for subflooring. Around 1960, plywood became popular, and multiple layers of materials were often used. Now, specially designed, single-layer oriented strand board panels are used for subflooring.

Beams - Types

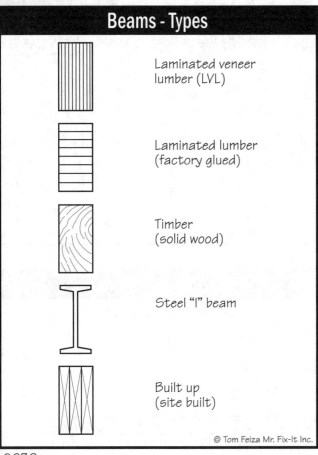

Laminated veneer lumber (LVL)

Laminated lumber (factory glued)

Timber (solid wood)

Steel "I" beam

Built up (site built)

© Tom Feiza Mr. Fix-It Inc.

S039

Subflooring - Typical Options

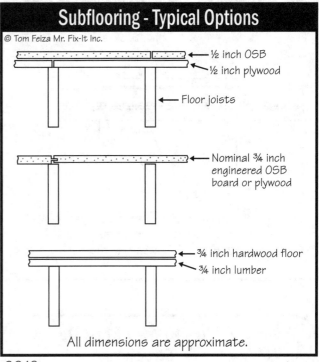

© Tom Feiza Mr. Fix-It Inc.

½ inch OSB

½ inch plywood

Floor joists

Nominal ¾ inch engineered OSB board or plywood

¾ inch hardwood floor

¾ inch lumber

All dimensions are approximate.

S042

Ceramic tile flooring presents a special challenge for wood frame construction. It requires additional support because any movement in the subfloor will create cracks in tile and grout and will loosen the tile. Years ago, subflooring was designed to hold a layer of poured concrete or grout to support the tile. Today, stronger subflooring and cement boards are used as a base for tile.

The rest of the structure arises above this first platform. It is supported with 2 by 4 or 2 by 6 exterior walls and interior support walls. For a two-story home, a second platform is built above the first floor walls, and then more walls are framed above this platform. Finally, a roof is framed above the wall framing.

The basic platform frame has many possible variations. An older home may have "balloon" framing in which exterior wall studs extend from the foundation to the roof without platforms. Some homes

Floor Truss Systems

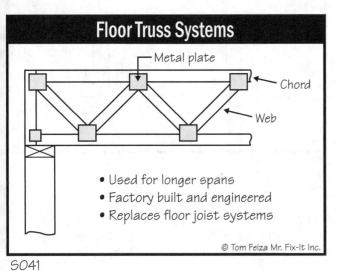

Metal plate

Chord

Web

- Used for longer spans
- Factory built and engineered
- Replaces floor joist systems

© Tom Feiza Mr. Fix-It Inc.

S041

are built with post and beam framing like that used for barns. Some homes have brick or block exterior walls that support the structure.

Since your home's framing is completed, all you need to know (if it's performing well) is that you shouldn't modify the structure of your home without contacting a professional.

Subfloor for "Mud-Set" Ceramic Tile

Tile
Mud-set tile
Grout
1" concrete (mud)
Building paper
1 x 3 blocking
¾" lumber

"Mud" or grout can be the base for ceramic tile. On wood framing, it is set over about 1 inch of concrete on lumber flush with the top of the joists.

© Tom Feiza Mr. Fix-It Inc.

S043

Must Know / Must Do Structure

- Understand the basic structure of your home.

- Never modify or remove structural framing without an expert's advice.

- Protect the structure from water and insects.

- Excessive cracking or movement indicate structural problems to be investigated.

Exterior Walls

The exterior walls are framed to support the structure, allow for window and door openings, and protect the structure from the elements. Most exterior walls are framed with 2 by 4 studs spaced 16" on center. The studs are braced in the corners and

doubled around window and door openings. Special "headers" are placed over openings to support the weight above the opening.

Exterior wall framing allows space for electrical, cable, telephone and heat distribution components. The framing also supports exterior siding or cladding and includes space for insulation.

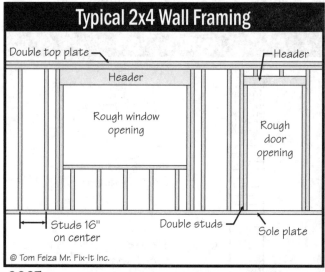

Typical 2x4 Wall Framing

Double top plate
Header
Header
Rough window opening
Rough door opening
Studs 16" on center
Double studs
Sole plate

© Tom Feiza Mr. Fix-It Inc.

S007

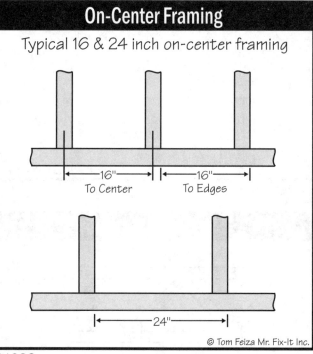

On-Center Framing

Typical 16 & 24 inch on-center framing

16" To Center
16" To Edges

24"

© Tom Feiza Mr. Fix-It Inc.

M029

Siding

Many options exist for siding homes: brick, stone, wood, aluminum, vinyl, cement, asbestos, logs, steel siding, wood products, stucco, and even steel panels. Identify the type of siding you have, and maintain the surface. This usually requires caulking and painting. Watch for excessive movement, water leaks and excessive paint damage.

Remember that homes built before 1978 may be painted with lead-based paints. Take special precautions if these finishes chip and flake or if you need to remove them. See the chapter on Environmental and Safety Concerns for more information on lead hazards.

Must Know / Must Do–Siding

- Maintain all painted surfaces.

- Maintain caulk and sealants.

- Be aware of potential lead hazards.

Brick

So you have an all-brick home, and it is beautiful, low-maintenance, cozy and warm. Brick homes are beautiful and valuable, but very few really have a brick structure; rather, they're brick veneer. Don't worry, you want a home that's brick veneer.

If your home was built before 1900, there is a chance that it actually has a brick structure. That means the exterior wall is solid brick, several layers thick, and the brick supports the home's framing and floors. Very few modern brick homes are built this way.

A typical modern brick home has a wood frame that supports the structure. The brick is applied as a veneer or siding over the outside. This method allows for better insulation of walls and a more user-friendly stucture that meets the needs of modern construction.

With brick veneer, you do need to watch for cracking and movement, as well as deterioration of mortar joints. Most brick veneer performs well for years with little maintenance.

One important element of maintenance involves the steel lintels over window and door openings. A lintel is a steel angle iron or beam that supports the masonry above the opening. Since window frames

and door frames are not designed to support masonry, the lintel spans the opening and transfers the load to the masonry on either side. The exposed steel of the lintel must be painted with exterior metal paint to prevent rust. If the lintel rusts, the metal expands, creating cracks in the mortar joints at the top corners of the openings. If excessive rust builds up, the lintel will fail and must be replaced.

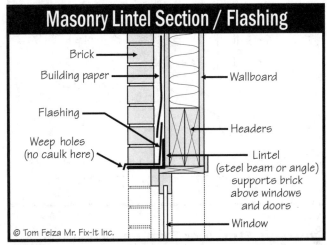

Masonry Lintel Section / Flashing

Brick — Building paper — Flashing — Weep holes (no caulk here) — Wallboard — Headers — Lintel (steel beam or angle) supports brick above windows and doors — Window

© Tom Feiza Mr. Fix-It Inc.

S027

Must Know / Must Do–Brick

- Maintain steel lintels.

- Watch for cracks or excessive movement.

- Maintain caulk and sealants at penetrations and windows/doors.

Look at any brick building and you'll probably see many rusted lintels causing mortar cracking and failure. You may also see that in some buildings, arches, cast concrete or large stones span the openings, eliminating the need for a metal lintel.

Stucco – Cement

Older homes and new homes in dry, warmer climates often have traditional cement stucco siding. Typically, this stucco consists of a three-part system applied over rigid sheathing material. Often a wire mesh is applied to the sheathing and over a building paper or drainage plane. The stucco is applied in three coats—base coat, scratch coat and a finish coat which often has a decorative surface.

Stucco – Traditional Cement Three-Coat

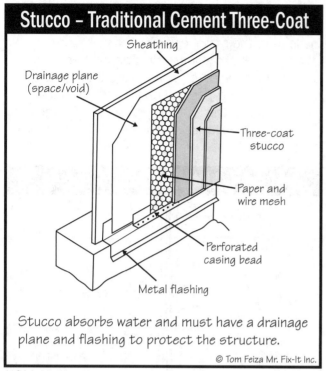

Sheathing

Drainage plane
(space/void)

Three-coat
stucco

Paper and
wire mesh

Perforated
casing bead

Metal flashing

Stucco absorbs water and must have a drainage
plane and flashing to protect the structure.

© Tom Feiza Mr. Fix-It Inc.

X014

EIFS – Synthetic Stucco

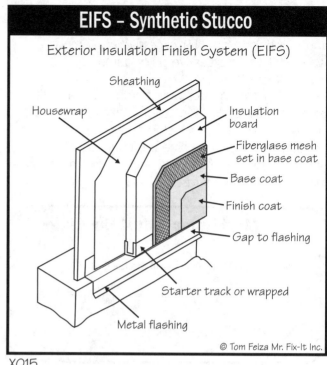

Exterior Insulation Finish System (EIFS)

Sheathing

Housewrap

Insulation
board

Fiberglass mesh
set in base coat

Base coat

Finish coat

Gap to flashing

Starter track or wrapped

Metal flashing

© Tom Feiza Mr. Fix-It Inc.

X015

Synthetic Stucco or Exterior Insulation Finish System – EIFS

Since about 1980, synthetic stucco material has been adapted to wood frame construction. This exterior insulation finish system, often referred to as EIFS, is a thin acrylic coating applied over rigid insulation board or cement board. Corners and joints are taped with a special mesh, and the finish is applied in two coats. The material looks like cement stucco or concrete. It can be painted and textured. In some cases, problems have occurred with moisture intrusion, and a specialized third-part inspector often evaluates this material. Properly installed, the material is effective and energy efficient.

Vinyl and Aluminum Siding

Many homes are covered with aluminum or vinyl siding that provides an economical and attractive surface. Since 1990, vinyl has because the more popular product because it maintains its color and does not dent. If your home has siding, you must maintain caulk where needed. Remember that fading aluminum siding can be easily cleaned or even cleaned and then painted with latex paint. Don't put the barbecue grill too close to the vinyl siding—the siding can melt.

Plywood, Wood Fiber, Wood Siding

All of these materials require routine maintenance of caulk and paint finishes. Watch for horizontal flashing at trim and windows. Often the flashing is not properly designed or installed, and rot can develop if you don't maintain caulk and paint.

Plywood or panel siding can present a unique problem with caulk at horizontal joints. These joints should have a "Z" or cap flashing, and there should be no caulk at the top of the metal flashing. This is left open to allow water to drain.

Cement Board

Cement board is a fiber and cement panel designed to replace wood siding, wood panels and trim. The siding is durable and needs minimal maintenance. The surface must be periodically painted, and caulk joints must be maintained. Currently this is the best alternative to cedar siding, and its texture and appearance imitate real cedar.

Masonry Veneer Flashing

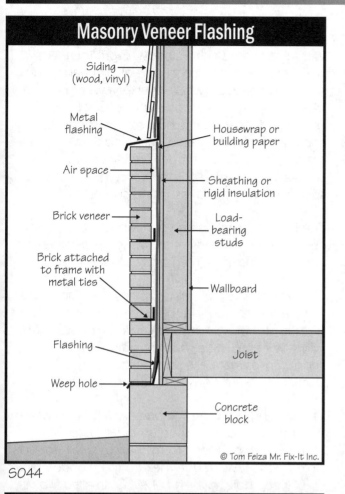

Siding (wood, vinyl)

Metal flashing

Air space

Brick veneer

Brick attached to frame with metal ties

Flashing

Weep hole

Housewrap or building paper

Sheathing or rigid insulation

Load-bearing studs

Wallboard

Joist

Concrete block

© Tom Feiza Mr. Fix-It Inc.

S044

Horizontal Panel Flashing and Problems

© Tom Feiza Mr. Fix-It Inc.

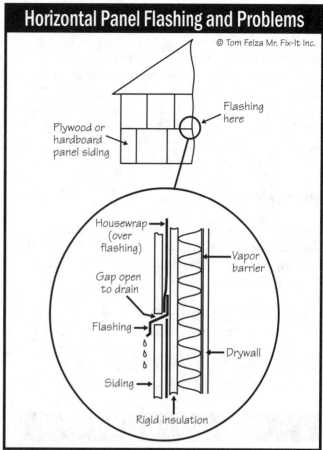

Plywood or hardboard panel siding

Flashing here

Housewrap (over flashing)

Gap open to drain

Flashing

Siding

Vapor barrier

Drywall

Rigid insulation

X008

Horizontal Trim Flashing and Problems

Horizontal Flashing

Siding

Building Paper or Housewrap

Paper over Flashing

Flashing

Drip

Trim

No Flashing

Caulk

Siding

Rot

Trim

Water enters

PROBLEM: Caulk always fails.
Water enters wall, causes rot.

© Tom Feiza Mr. Fix-It Inc.

X007

"Z" Flashing – Panel Siding

© Tom Feiza Mr. Fix-It Inc.

Sheathing

Wall framing

Housewrap over "Z" flashing

Building paper or housewrap

Gap and NO caulk here to drain water

Metal "Z" flashing or cap flashing

Water drips away

Building paper or housewrap

X006

Windows and Doors

It would take an entire book to cover all types of windows and doors and their maintenance. I will cover basic types and provide important mainte-nance tips. For specific information on maintaining and repairing the windows and doors in your home, contact the manufacturer.

Maintenance information and parts are readily available for windows and doors produced in the last 20 years. For older windows and doors, you will rarely find information and must rely on after-market products. Thousands of companies produced windows and doors through the years, and many are no longer in business.

Windows

Windows come in all shapes, sizes and types. Various types include double-hung, casement, sliders, hopper, fixed, garden, bow and bay. The list goes on and on.

Materials used for window frames include wood, steel, aluminum, vinyl, and combinations of these products. Higher-cost windows have wood framing on the inside for enhanced appearance and a metal coating on the outside for low maintenance.

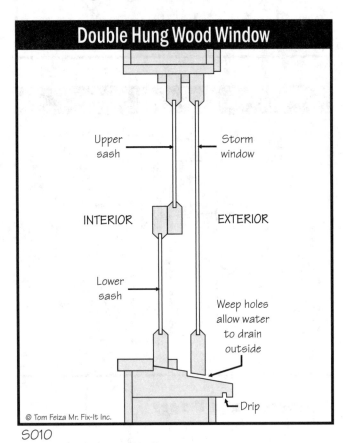

Double Hung Wood Window

Upper sash

Storm window

INTERIOR

EXTERIOR

Lower sash

Weep holes allow water to drain outside

Drip

© Tom Feiza Mr. Fix-It Inc.

S010

There are also many glass options. In older homes you will find the basic single-pane glass, usually with a separate storm window. From there we have insulated glass consisting of two panes with a sealed air space between layers. Newer insulated glass is improved with an invisible "low E" coating on one side that lowers heat transmission. Glass can also be tripled-glazed, meaning there are three sealed panes. Other modern advances include a special inert gas that fills the space between panes; special coatings; and insulating spacers.

The keys to maintaining your window are to (1) keep exterior portions of the window weathertight, and (2) maintain painted and varnished surfaces.

On the outside, maintain all painted surfaces and the glazing compound that seals the window glass to the sash. Make sure that caulk which seals the window frame to the brick or siding is tight and secure. Investigate excessive mildew or peeling paint—these are signs of moisture problems.

The spacing between the primary (interior) window and the storm window on an older system can cause problems. Most storms have a small slot or hole on the lower edge, next to the wooden sill. This "weep hole," which is 1/4" or smaller, allows condensation and water to drain ("weep") to the outside, preventing rot and mildew that could cause serious damage. However, well-intentioned homeowners sometimes caulk weep holes shut, hoping to save energy. Weep holes should always be left open.

Caution

Double-hung windows have a cord and a weight or spring that balances the weight of the window to keep it open. If the spring or cord breaks, the sash can crash shut, causing serious injury. If your window slams shut, repair the cord or spring, or secure the window to the frame with a metal clip and screw to prevent anyone from opening the window and getting injured.

Meticulously check and maintain the condition of painted wood-framed windows and doors. Pay special attention to south-facing surfaces because the sun accelerates deterioration of caulk, paint and glazing products. Check the corners and ends of wood framing; this is where wood rot starts, and it can cause serious problems.

If you are lucky enough to have casement windows—great. They seal tightly and work well. But when they stick, it is easy to damage the crank mechanism. If you are trying to open a sticky casement window, never force the crank. It will break. Remove the screen and then gently force the window open with your hand, not with the crank.

To open a sticky double-hung or slider window, try to jar the window closed by striking the frame with a closed fist. Be careful. Don't hit it so hard that you break the glass. If the window is painted shut, you must break away all the paint before you try to open it.

panel. Don't neglect the inside of the door panel, and don't neglect the edges.

Hardware—rollers, hinges and tracks—requires routine maintenance. Because the doors are open and closed so often, hardware and fasteners are always being jarred and bounced, which loosens bolts, screws and other fasteners and eventually affects the smooth operation of the door. Tighten all hardware on your garage door at least twice a year. Put the door in the closed position, make sure all hinges and rollers are aligned, and then tighten bolts and nuts. Inspect rollers to make sure that they line up with the tracks. Tracks should be parallel to the edges of the door. Replace any rollers that have damaged bearings. Lubricate rollers and hinges with a special garage door lubricant, silicone spray, or light oil.

Must Know / Must Do Windows

- Maintain paint, putty, caulk and glazing compounds.

- Check the "weep holes" of storm windows.

- Repair broken sash cords and springs to prevent injury.

- Peeling paint on older windows may be a lead hazard–See Chapter 2.

Garage Doors

Garage doors are made of hundreds of possible combinations of materials, rollers, tracks, operators, springs, locks, and other options. Your main responsibilities are to maintain finishes, tighten hardware, and test the safety of operation.

Many garage doors are made of wood and wood products that require routine painting. When you paint a garage door, paint all six sides of each

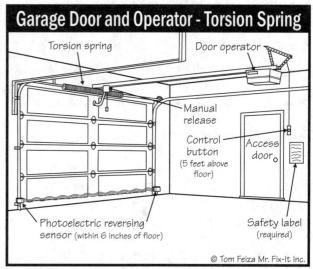

Garage Door and Operator - Torsion Spring

M012

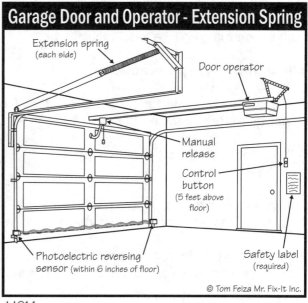

Garage Door and Operator - Extension Spring

M014

If the door has damaged springs, pulleys or cables, have them repaired by a professional. These springs store tremendous amounts of force, and they can cause serious injury if not handled properly. Professional service is also a good option if the door is not properly aligned to the tracks and the frame opening.

Must Know / Must Do
Garage Door

- Maintain painted finishes on the door.

- Tighten hardware twice a year.

- Hire a professional for repair of springs, cables and rollers.

- Check with the manufacturer of your door for specific maintenance information.

Garage Door Openers

Many of us take our garage door openers for granted: push the button, and we drive into our dry and lighted garage. These openers provide many years of trouble-free service, but they do require routine maintenance and safety tests. An improperly maintained garage door opener poses a safety hazard.

Contact the manufacturer of your opener for specific safety and maintenance requirements.

Follow these safety precautions:

- Do not stand or walk under a moving door. Do not try to rush under a door as it closes.

- Keep the remote control units away from children.

- Explain to children that garage doors are not toys and that the door can hurt them.

- Mount the pushbutton control at least 5 feet from the floor to keep it out of reach of children.

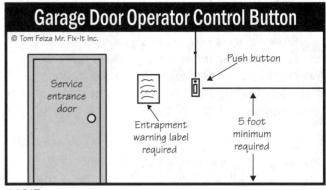

Garage Door Operator Control Button

© Tom Feiza Mr. Fix-It Inc.

Service entrance door

Push button

Entrapment warning label required

5 foot minimum required

M013

- When closing the door, observe it until it is fully closed.

- Check the safety reverse once monthly.

Every garage door should have a safety device that reverses the door if it meets resistance while closing. Very old units may not have a safety reverse; these should be replaced.

Must Know / Must Do
Garage Door Openers

- Follow all safety precautions.

- Perform monthly safety tests of the automatic reverse.

- Check the balance of the door once a year.

- Always consult a professional for repair of springs, pulleys and cables.

- Contact the manufacturer for specific safety and maintenance recommendations.

Openers manufactured after April 1, 1982, must have a safety reverse that activates after striking a 1"-high object. Openers manufactured before that time were required to reverse off a 2" object. If your door does not reverse with the 1" test, replace it.

Openers sold after 1993 also have a photocell. When anything blocks or crosses the photocell beam as the door is closing, the door reverses. If your garage door opener doesn't have this optical safety device, I suggest you replace it with one that does.

Here's the procedure for the monthly safety reverse test. (Check with the manufacturer of your operator for more specific details.)

1. With the door open, place a 1"-thick block under the center of the door. Use an actual 1"-thick object, not a nominal 1" piece of wood that is actually 3/4" thick. A 2 by 4 laid flat is often used for this test.

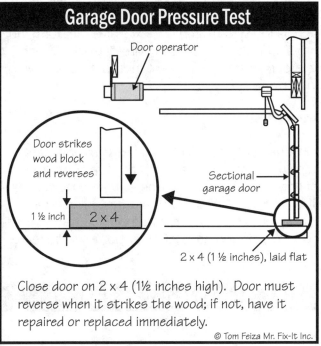

Garage Door Pressure Test

Close door on 2 x 4 (1½ inches high). Door must reverse when it strikes the wood; if not, have it repaired or replaced immediately.

© Tom Feiza Mr. Fix-It Inc.

M016

2. Activate the opener to close the door.

3. When the door hits the piece of wood, it should reverse and reopen.

4. Activate the opener again. This time, as the door closes, hold up the bottom of the door with your hand. The door should reverse with a few pounds of pressure.

5. If your door has a photocell safety control, perform the test again by breaking the beam as the door closes. The door should reverse itself. You can test the door with a 6 by 12 inch object placed progressively along the door opening. With the object in place, the door should stop and reverse to the full open position.

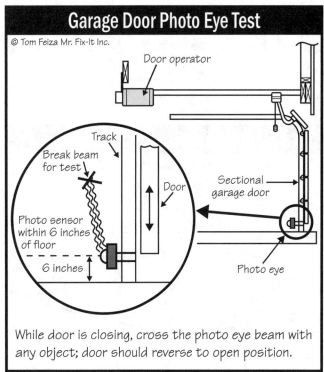

Garage Door Photo Eye Test

© Tom Feiza Mr. Fix-It Inc.

While door is closing, cross the photo eye beam with any object; door should reverse to open position.

M017

6. If the opener fails any of these tests, consult a qualified professional for adjustments and repair.

If the remote control fails to operate your garage door, first check for a weak or dead battery in the remote unit. A cold receiver unit with a weak battery could also cause this problem. If batteries are good, check the transmitter and receiver codes and the antenna on the receiver.

Your garage door opener is designed to open and close a balanced garage door. Strong springs provide lift that balances the weight of the door. If the operator unit sounds loud and works very hard to open or close the door, the door may be unbalanced or there may be a broken spring or damaged hardware.

Inspect the springs and hardware. If there is any damage, consult a professional.

You can also test the balance of the door if the springs appear to be in good condition. Start with the door closed. If you start with the door open, it can crash shut, causing damage and possible injury. With the door closed, disconnect the release mechanism—a cord or lever where the operator arm attaches to the operator frame. You should then be able to lift the door with little resistance;

the door should "balance" around the center of its motion. If the door is hard to lift and does not balance, consult a professional to adjust the spring mechanism. Don't attempt to adjust the springs yourself. They store a dangerous amount of energy and can easily injure you.

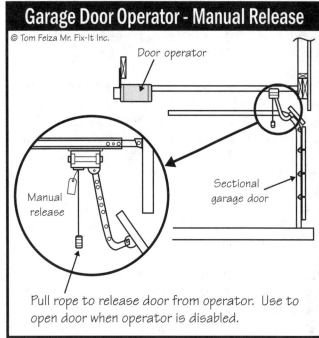

Garage Door Key Cable Release

(For detached garage with no access door.)

Remove lock from outside and pull cable on lock to manually release door from operator.

M018

Garage Door Operator - Manual Release

Pull rope to release door from operator. Use to open door when operator is disabled.

M015

If your garage has an automatic door operator but no service or entry door, how can you open the door when the power is out or the remote control

is dead? For this type of situation, there should be a key-operated garage door release on the outside of the overhead door. To open the door, remove the lock cylinder and pull the attached cable to release the door from the operator. Now you can lift the door manually.

Insulation and Ventilation

All homes are insulated in some fashion to protect against heat loss and gain. Older homes may have little insulation; newer homes have insulation that meets government standards for energy efficiency.

Ventilation systems remove excessive moisture and protect insulation from moisture damage. Vapor retarders or barriers prevent moisture from flowing into insulation.

Insulation

Most newer homes are insulated with fiberglass, cellulose fiber, rigid plastic foam, or a combination of these products. Older homes may have vermiculite, wood shavings, paper products, and other types of insulation. Often, homeowners add insulation to walls and attics of older homes to increase energy efficiency.

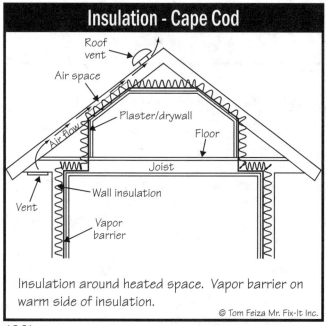

Insulation - Cape Cod

Insulation around heated space. Vapor barrier on warm side of insulation.

I001

A note of caution: vermiculite insulation has been found to contain asbestos in some cases. If your home has vermiculite insulation, it should not be disturbed and you should never breathe any related dust. Vermiculite looks like tan and gold gravel particles of about 1/4 to 3/4 inch. It is lightweight, like foam. If you think your home has vermiculite, have it tested by a professional.

Insulation is rated with an R-value, which simply indicates the resistance to heat flow. The higher the R-value, the higher the resistance. The key thing to remember is that when you double the R-value, you cut the heat loss in half; so the first several inches of insulation result in huge energy savings.

Most fiberglass is rated at about R-3 per inch of thickness. A 6"-thick section is fiberglass would be rated about R-19. The R-value for rigid foam ranges from 5 to 7 per inch. Cellulose and mineral wool provide about R-3 per inch.

Typical Wall Section (2x6 Framed)

6" R19 fiberglass insulation

½" drywall

½" exterior sheathing

Plastic vapor barrier

2" x 6" soleplate

Siding

Joist

Concrete block

© Tom Feiza Mr. Fix-It Inc.

S011

Insulation recommendations vary with climate conditions and state code requirements. In northern climates, attics are insulated to R-38 or more, and walls are insulated to R-19 or more. In southern zones, attics are insulated to about R-26 and walls to R-11.

Vapor Barriers

Vapor barriers or vapor retarders protect insulation and structural framing from moisture damage. Vapor barriers are usually made of polyethylene film. They can also be aluminum foil or kraft paper (brown paper coated with tar).

The vapor barrier, placed behind drywall, plaster or wood flooring and in front of insulation, prevents moisture from moving through the surface and penetrating the insulation. The barrier also prevents air movement through walls and floors; air movement carries tremendous amounts of water vapor.

If moisture were allowed to enter the insulation, it would condense on the cold wood framing of the exterior, causing water damage and potential rot.

In hot and humid climates, such as southern Florida, vapor barriers are not used because the relative humidity outdoors is greater than that in the home, and moisture tends to move into the house. If you have questions about requirements for vapor barriers in your area, consult the local building inspector.

Insulation vs. Heat Loss

Typical cost of heat loss through 1 square foot of exterior surface.

© Tom Feiza Mr. Fix-It Inc.

Material	R Value	Heat Cost / Sq. Ft.
Single Glass	R1	$2.40
Double Glass	R2	$1.20
4" of Wood	R4	$0.60
Basement w/ 1" Foam	R8	$0.30
Typical Wall	R20	$0.12
Attic Insulation	R40	$0.06

Double the R value and cut the heat loss (cost) in half. Actual cost will change on climate and heat source. The relationship is constant.

1004

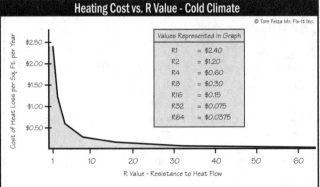

Heating Cost vs. R Value - Cold Climate

© Tom Feiza Mr. Fix-It Inc.

Values Represented in Graph	
R1	= $2.40
R2	= $1.20
R4	= $0.60
R8	= $0.30
R16	= $0.15
R32	= $0.075
R64	= $0.0375

This graph shows the relationship of R value to the cost of heat loss per square foot of exterior surface in a cold climate. The actual cost will vary; the relationship is constant.

1003

Attic Ventilation

No matter how well a home is constructed, moisture will reach the attic; it's impossible to completely seal this area. So ventilation is necessary to remove moisture and excessive heat from the attic. This is achieved through various combinations of roof vents, soffit vents, gable end vents, ridge vents, and ventilation fans.

Attic - Air Bypass

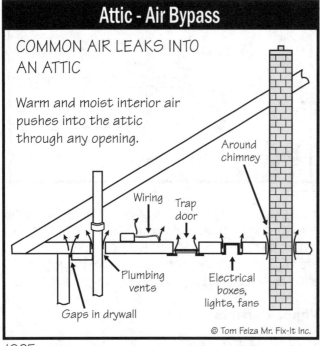

COMMON AIR LEAKS INTO AN ATTIC

Warm and moist interior air pushes into the attic through any opening.

Around chimney

Wiring

Trap door

Plumbing vents

Electrical boxes, lights, fans

Gaps in drywall

© Tom Feiza Mr. Fix-It Inc.

I005

Attic Ventilation

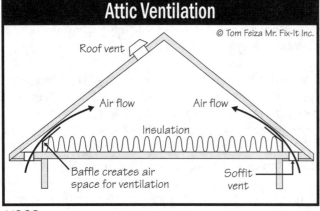

© Tom Feiza Mr. Fix-It Inc.

Roof vent

Air flow

Air flow

Insulation

Baffle creates air space for ventilation

Soffit vent

V002

For proper air flow, ventilation must be provided both high and low on the roof. Heat and wind help the vents move air through the attic. As an additional benefit, ventilation reduces the temperature inside the attic, lowering the cost of air conditioning and extending the life of an asphalt shingle roof.

Ventilation - Two Basic Types

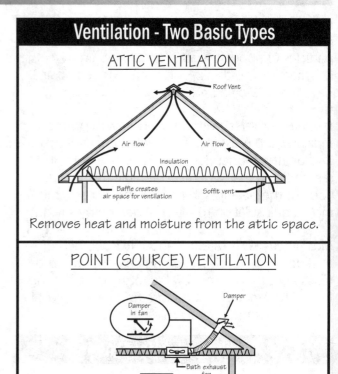

ATTIC VENTILATION

Roof Vent

Air flow

Air flow

Insulation

Baffle creates air space for ventilation

Soffit vent

Removes heat and moisture from the attic space.

POINT (SOURCE) VENTILATION

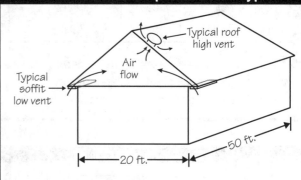

Damper in fan

Damper

Bath exhaust fan

Fan removes heat, contaminants, and moisture from point source to outside home.

© Tom Feiza Mr. Fix-It Inc.

V030

Attic Ventilation Requirements - Typical

Typical roof high vent

Air flow

Typical soffit low vent

50 ft.

20 ft.

Attic Area = 20 x 50 feet = 1000 sq. ft.

NFA

Min. Ventilation w/o Vapor Barrier = $\frac{1000}{150}$ = 6.6 sq. ft. = 960 sq. in.

Min. Ventilation w/ Vapor Barrier = $\frac{1000}{300}$ = 3.3 sq. ft. = 480 sq. in.

Typical attic ventilation requirements are based on the attic area divided by 300 to 150 depending on the type of construction. 50% of vent area must be high on the roof and 50% low on the roof. NFA is "Net Free Area" of the vent. The actual "free vent" area is reduced by screens and louvers on the vent.

© Tom Feiza Mr. Fix-It Inc.

V042

Bathroom and kitchen exhaust fans are needed to remove excessive moisture, but they must be routed to an exterior wall or through the roof. Make sure that the exhaust fans in your home aren't dumping moist air into the attic.

Must Know / Must Do
Attic Ventilation

- Check the attic periodically for signs of moisture condensation. Black or gray mildew stains indicate a need for increased ventilation.

- Make sure that the access door to the attic is insulated and weather-stripped to block air entry.

- Don't walk through the attic without taking special precautions. You could fall through the ceiling.

- Make sure that bathroom and kitchen exhaust fans aren't dumping moist air into the attic.

Vapor Barrier in Crawl Space

A crawl space or dirt floor in the basement can release significant amounts of moisture in your home. Even if the soil looks dry, moisture may evaporate from the surface. Cover any bare dirt with a thick (6-mil) poly vapor barrier. The barrier should provide a continuous cover with joints overlapped 12". Edges should lap up several inches on the foundation wall. Place stones or gravel atop the barrier to keep it in place.

Bathroom Ventilation

Ventilation for bathrooms has been required for many years. The minimum requirement is a window or an exhaust fan. Most of us would prefer, and our homes would like, a dedicated exhaust fan controlled by a switch in the bathroom. This allows us to effectively remove excessive moisture from showers and baths.

Confirm the discharge location of your fan. Make sure it discharges moisture through an exterior wall

or through the roof. These fans remove a tremendous amount of moisture, and you don't want that moisture in your attic.

Homes built prior to 1980 often have ventilation fans that exhaust into the attic space. These should be rerouted through the roof with a simple vent kit available at building supply centers.

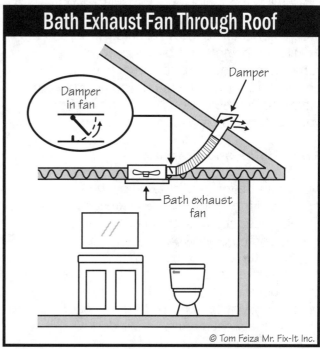

Bath Exhaust Fan Through Roof

Damper in fan

Damper

Bath exhaust fan

© Tom Feiza Mr. Fix-It Inc.

V006

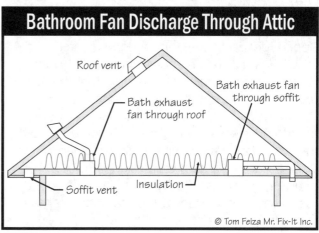

Bathroom Fan Discharge Through Attic

Roof vent

Bath exhaust fan through soffit

Bath exhaust fan through roof

Soffit vent

Insulation

© Tom Feiza Mr. Fix-It Inc.

V003

Often, bath exhaust fans can't keep up with the steam of a hot shower, and the bathroom remains full of moisture. This can cause excessive condensation, mildew, peeling paint, and damage to windows. A simple solution is to replace the ordinary fan switch with a timer switch—the type found on heat lamps. Use a timer that will operate for 1 or 2 hours, and run the fan for a timed period after you leave.

Roofs and Gutters

Roof framing and roofing materials contribute significantly to the look and style of your home. The roof also protects your home from the elements. While a roof is easy to ignore, its components do need routine maintenance.

Performing this maintenance requires access to the gutters and valleys and may involve walking on the roof. It's essential to follow all safety precautions for working at heights and climbing ladders. While some homeowners are comfortable with ladders and heights, others are not. If you are not completely comfortable with the idea of working on your roof, hire a professional.

Roof Styles and Framing

Many roof designs are dictated by the style of the home and the spans between exterior walls. Roofs are also designed to accommodate snow loads, winds, and other environmental factors.

All roofs have structural framing of joists or trusses that support a wood deck. The deck may be boards, plywood or oriented strand board. Roofing material is attached to the wood deck.

In general, the two basic styles are sloped and low-slope (or flat) roofs.

Sloped roofs are those with a slope greater than 4" in 12" or 4/12. This is equivalent to a 1/4 slope (just convert the fraction), meaning that the roof drops 1 foot for every 4 feet of horizontal run. To determine the slope of your roof, level a 4-foot board and measure the drop at the outer edge. If the pitch drops 4 feet within this 4-foot length, the slope is 4 in 4—and, by extension, 12 in 12. This is often expressed as a 12/12 roof. Styles of sloped roofs include gable, shed, hip, gambrel, mansard, and combinations of various types.

Low-slope or flat roofs have a slope that is less than 4 in 12. These require special waterproof or membrane materials because they do not shed water as well as roofs with a steeper slope. Most "flat" roofs do have a slight pitch to drain water to the edges or to roof drains.

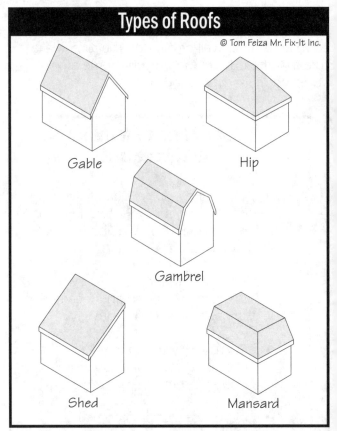

Types of Roofs

© Tom Feiza Mr. Fix-It Inc.

Gable

Hip

Gambrel

Shed

Mansard

R003

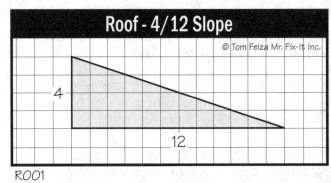

Roof - 4/12 Slope

© Tom Feiza Mr. Fix-It Inc.

4

12

R001

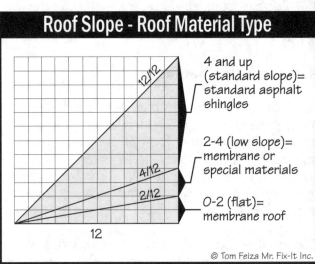

Roof Slope - Roof Material Type

12/12

4/12

2/12

12

4 and up (standard slope)= standard asphalt shingles

2-4 (low slope)= membrane or special materials

0-2 (flat)= membrane roof

© Tom Feiza Mr. Fix-It Inc.

R013

Other components of a roof include valley and sidewall flashings, edge flashings, and flashings at all roof penetrations. The roof will have a ventilation system and may have a gutter and drainage system.

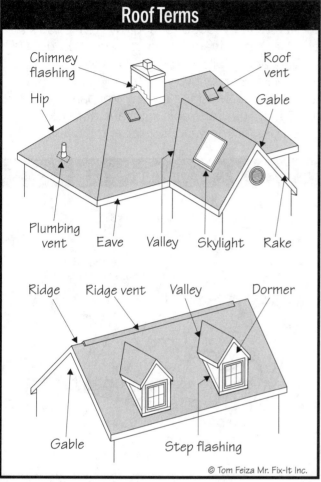

Roof Terms

Chimney flashing · Roof vent · Hip · Gable · Plumbing vent · Eave · Valley · Skylight · Rake

Ridge · Ridge vent · Valley · Dormer · Gable · Step flashing

© Tom Feiza Mr. Fix-It Inc.

R004

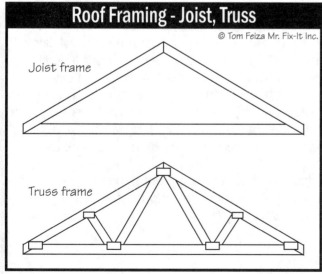

Roof Framing - Joist, Truss

© Tom Feiza Mr. Fix-It Inc.

Joist frame

Truss frame

S014

Roofing Materials

Asphalt shingles are the material most commonly used on conventional pitched roofs (1 in 4 and greater). An organic or fiberglass "mat" that forms the body of the shingle is covered with granules to protect the mat from the sun and add color and visual variety. A typical asphalt shingle will last from 15 to 40 years, depending on the original quality and local weather conditions. Asphalt shingles come in many shapes and sizes. Some are designed to imitate wood or tile.

Other materials used for pitched roofs include wood shakes, wood shingles, cement asbestos, tile, slate, metal, and cement tile. All of these are more expensive than asphalt shingles, but they offer unique design qualities and potentially longer life. Tile, slate and cement often last 50 years or more and are highly resistant to sun damage, wind and fire. However, heavier roof materials require special structural designs.

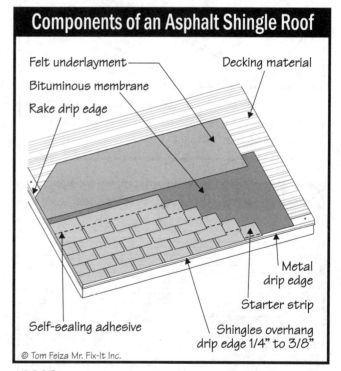

Components of an Asphalt Shingle Roof

Felt underlayment · Bituminous membrane · Rake drip edge · Decking material · Metal drip edge · Starter strip · Shingles overhang drip edge 1/4" to 3/8" · Self-sealing adhesive

© Tom Feiza Mr. Fix-It Inc.

R005

Wood Roofs

Years ago, most roofs had wood shingles. These flat, smooth shingles were applied without any tar paper beneath them. Today, most wood shingle roofs have been removed or covered with asphalt shingles.

Today when we see a wood roof, it is almost always a wood shake roof. Wood shakes are generally rougher and more irregular than wood shingles. Tar paper under the wood shakes provides a watertight covering. The wood shakes reject some water and protect the tar paper from the ultraviolet rays of the sun. Wood shake roofs need routine maintenance. The shakes must be kept clear of debris, and a periodic treatment may extend the life of the shakes.

Wood roof maintenance information is available at the Cedar Bureau: www.cedarbureau.org.

Tile Roofs

Tile roofs are found on older, expensive homes and on homes in the South or Southwest. Tile roofs are durable and resistant to sun damage. Because tile is slippery and fragile, you should never walk on a tile roof. Maintenance involves keeping gutters and valleys clear and watching for physical damage to the tile. Today some tile roofs are made from cement-based products in various styles and cross-sections.

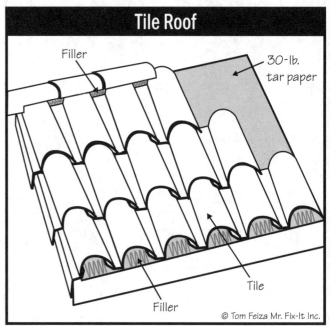

Tile Roof

Filler

30-lb. tar paper

Tile

Filler

© Tom Feiza Mr. Fix-It Inc.

R018

Low-slope or flat roofs require a special roofing material to seal against moisture. Since the slope is low, water does not easily run from the surface. Materials used include single-ply rubber, roll roofing, torch down (a modified bitumen), metal, and built-up roofing. Rubber roofing is quite common; technically, this material is ethylene propylene diene monomer, or EPDM. All of these materials require special installation and maintenance by experienced contractors.

A flat roof should have a slight slope to prevent ponding of water. Roof drains may be placed along the edges or in the center.

Wood Shakes

Roofing felt

Eaves protection

Wood shakes

Roofing felt makes the assembly watertight. The wood shakes shed most water and protect the roofing felt from sunlight.

© Tom Feiza Mr. Fix-It Inc.

R017

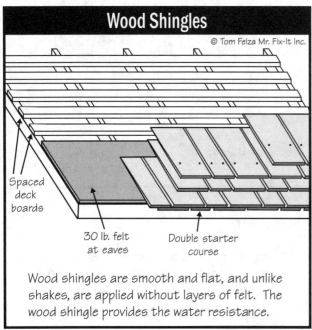

Wood Shingles

© Tom Feiza Mr. Fix-It Inc.

Spaced deck boards

30 lb. felt at eaves

Double starter course

Wood shingles are smooth and flat, and unlike shakes, are applied without layers of felt. The wood shingle provides the water resistance.

R020

Flat or Low-Slope Roof - Rubber, EPDM

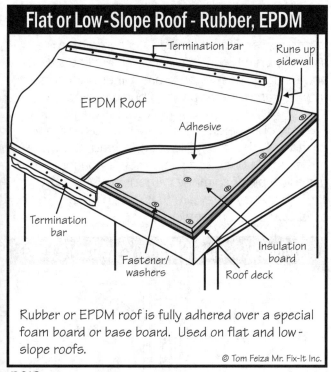

Termination bar
Runs up sidewall
EPDM Roof
Adhesive
Termination bar
Fastener/ washers
Roof deck
Insulation board

Rubber or EPDM roof is fully adhered over a special foam board or base board. Used on flat and low-slope roofs.

© Tom Feiza Mr. Fix-It Inc.

R019

Gutters and Downspouts

When it rains, your roof sheds a tremendous quantity of water that must be moved away from the foundation to protect the basement or crawl spaces. Gutters, downspouts and downspout extensions serve this function.

Gutters may drain to the surface of your yard. They may be channeled underground to drain into a lower area of your yard. In urban areas, where storm systems collect rainwater, gutters may drain underground into the storm sewer system. For more information on storm sewers, see the section about basements.

Roofing material manufacturers provide excellent free information in printed materials and on their websites.

Downspout Problem and Solutions

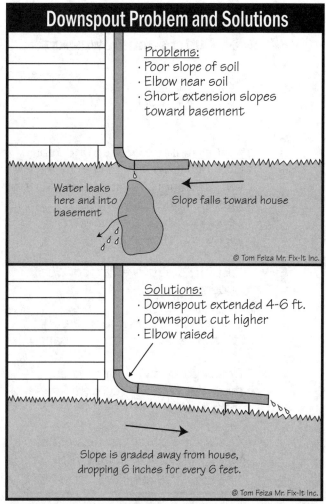

Problems:
· Poor slope of soil
· Elbow near soil
· Short extension slopes toward basement

Water leaks here and into basement

Slope falls toward house

© Tom Feiza Mr. Fix-It Inc.

Solutions:
· Downspout extended 4-6 ft.
· Downspout cut higher
· Elbow raised

Slope is graded away from house, dropping 6 inches for every 6 feet.

© Tom Feiza Mr. Fix-It Inc.

B126

Storm / Sanitary Sewer in Street

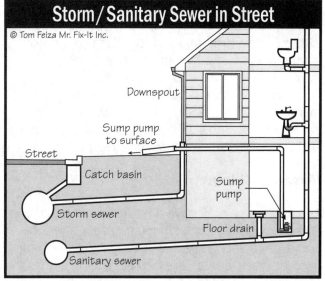

© Tom Feiza Mr. Fix-It Inc.

Downspout
Sump pump to surface
Street
Catch basin
Storm sewer
Sanitary sewer
Sump pump
Floor drain

P017

Must Know / Must Do
Roof, Gutters and Downspouts

- Inspect (or hire a professional to inspect) the roof and flashings twice a year.

- Gutters must be cleaned and kept clear of debris. Sometimes twice a year is enough. At other times this must be done once a week, depending on the prevalance of leaves and other materials.

- Keep the drains of a flat roof clear of debris.

- Make sure all downspouts are directed away from the foundation.

- Downspouts routed underground must be cleared or repaired if they "back up."

- Check the roof for wear every few years. Plan for eventual replacement based on professional advice.

Chimney, Flue and Vent

When you burn natural gas, oil, wood or any other fossil fuel, the toxic smoke and other products of combustion must be vented from your home through the chimney. Toxic gas rises up the chimney and flows outside because the gas is lighter than air. Various types of chimneys will accomplish this effect. You should understand chimney basics and know how to recognize problems.

Masonry Chimney

An older home may have a masonry or brick/stone chimney. This type of chimney can vent a wood-burning fireplace as well as an appliance like a furnace or water heater. The clay tile liner of a masonry chimney provides a smooth, uninterrupted surface that eases the flow of combustion gas. The liner harnesses combustion products and protects the brick of the chimney from heat and moisture.

You can view the tan or red tile liner by looking down into the chimney from the top or peering up the fireplace with a flashlight. It's common for a masonry chimney to have several flue liners. Gas and oil appliances often share a liner but cannot use the same flue as a wood-burning fireplace.

A home built before 1900 may have a masonry chimney with no clay tile liner; instead, the inside has exposed brick and some mortar coating. Never use this type of chimney without evaluation by a specialist. Also, be aware that this chimney can't be used to vent a gas appliance.

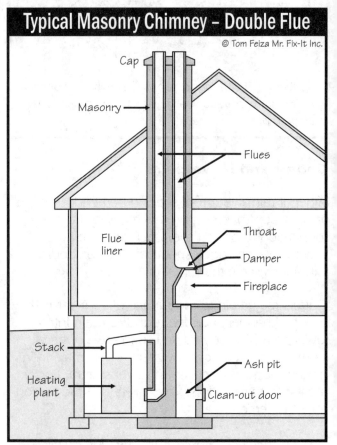

Typical Masonry Chimney – Double Flue

© Tom Feiza Mr. Fix-It Inc.

Cap

Masonry

Flues

Flue liner

Throat

Damper

Fireplace

Stack

Heating plant

Ash pit

Clean-out door

F002

Metal Chimney

A newer home may have a metal chimney, which may be a simple round chimney pipe with a metal liner. A metal chimney might be built into a masonry or wood chimney structure.

All Chimneys

Chimneys look simple, but they are actually complex devices, designed and installed with safety in mind. Chimney designs take into account the type of fuel burned, the heat of the fire, the size of the burner or fireplace, the height of the chimney, the horizontal distance to any appliance they vent, and other factors.

Typical Metal Chimney

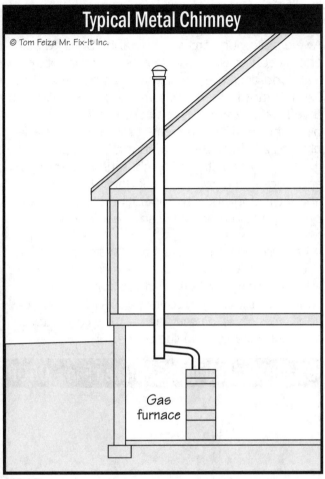

© Tom Feiza Mr. Fix-It Inc.

Gas furnace

F003

A flue pipe or smoke pipe connects gas- and oil-fired appliances to a chimney. This pipe, specifically sized for the appliance, must be pitched upward into the chimney. The gas appliance also has a special draft hood or draft diverter that allows air to enter the flue pipe, helping to create a proper draft up the chimney. At the chimney, the flue pipes are connected to the flue liner by special metal connectors or mortar.

Flue Pipe to Masonry Chimney

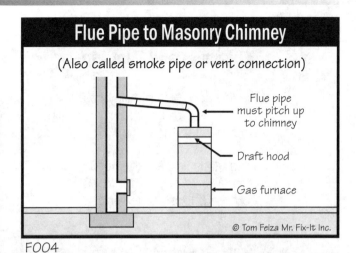

(Also called smoke pipe or vent connection)

Flue pipe must pitch up to chimney

Draft hood

Gas furnace

© Tom Feiza Mr. Fix-It Inc.

F004

Chimney Parts – Good Design

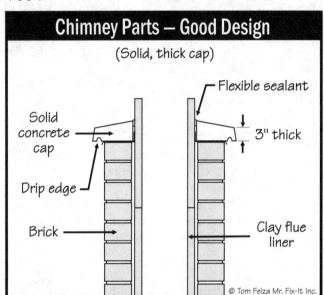

(Solid, thick cap)

Flexible sealant

3" thick

Solid concrete cap

Drip edge

Brick

Clay flue liner

© Tom Feiza Mr. Fix-It Inc.

Chimney Parts – Poor Design

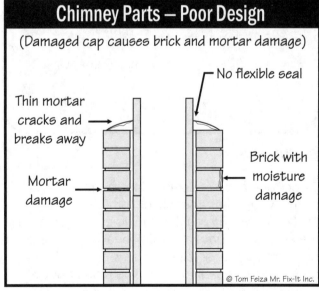

(Damaged cap causes brick and mortar damage)

No flexible seal

Thin mortar cracks and breaks away

Mortar damage

Brick with moisture damage

© Tom Feiza Mr. Fix-It Inc.

F008

Must Know / Must Do
Chimneys and Vent Pipes

- Never modify a chimney or flue pipe. Hire a professional for repairs and maintenance.

- Frequently inspect the vent pipe and draft hood. It should not be corroded, loose or leaking.

- Vent pipes are hot. Provide adequate clearance—at least 6" away from any combustible material. Don't use vent pipes as storage shelves or as racks to dry rags.

- Schedule professional inspection and cleaning for wood-burning stoves and fireplaces. The frequency of the need for maintenance depends on how often you build fires. Annual inspections are the norm.

- Routinely check the condition of the chimney top. A masonry chimney must have tile, brick mortar, flashings and the concrete cap in excellent condition to prevent serious moisture problems. A metal chimney must have a cap in good condition. Chimney damage can create safety problems.

- Install a carbon monoxide alarm.

- Add a rain cap to your chimney to keep out rain and animals.

Backdrafting

Proper operation of combustion appliances and chimneys requires a supply of combustion air and dilution air. A burning fire consumes oxygen from the air supply and draws additional air up the chimney. This additional (dilution) air is provided by the draft hood or opening in the flue pipe or above the burner in the housing of the appliance.

The air that's exhausted up the chimney must be replaced somehow. This may occur as air enters through small leaks in the structure of the house. If you've ever built a large fire in the fireplace and then opened the front door, you may have noticed that air rushes in to help replace air flowing up the chimney. This same exhaust process occurs with all combustion appliances.

As we build our homes tighter and tighter to aid energy conservation, we limit the number of air leaks and decrease the supply of combustible air. Exhaust fans in the bathroom and kitchen, clothes dryers, and downdraft cooktops also draw air out of the home. This can create problems with backdrafting and spillage of combustion products into the home. For instance, combustion gas from an appliance can be drawn back down the chimney, and if the appliance isn't operating properly, dangerous carbon monoxide can linger indoors.

What can you do to prevent this? Watch for signs of backdrafting. Check flue pipes for rust or water stains, and look for rust or burn marks at draft diverters. If you notice these signs, contact a specialist. Have gas appliances serviced yearly, and ask the contractor to check all chimneys and flue connectors.

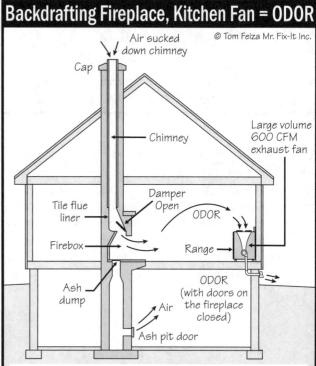

Backdrafting Fireplace, Kitchen Fan = ODOR

© Tom Feiza Mr. Fix-It Inc.

A large volume (600 CFM) range exhaust in a tight home can draw air down a chimney and cause a "stinky" odor in a home. A clothes dryer can also do this.

V031

Water Heater Signs of Backdrafting

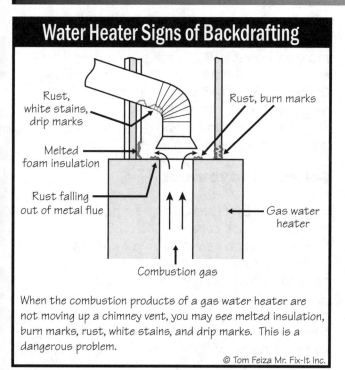

Rust, white stains, drip marks

Rust, burn marks

Melted foam insulation

Rust falling out of metal flue

Gas water heater

Combustion gas

When the combustion products of a gas water heater are not moving up a chimney vent, you may see melted insulation, burn marks, rust, white stains, and drip marks. This is a dangerous problem.

© Tom Feiza Mr. Fix-It Inc.

V033

Gas Water Heater with Signs of Backdrafting

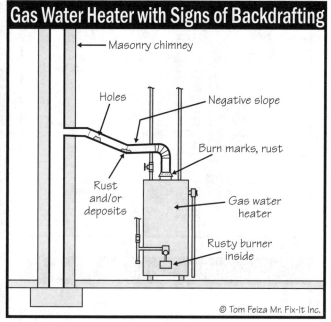

Masonry chimney

Holes

Negative slope

Burn marks, rust

Rust and/or deposits

Gas water heater

Rusty burner inside

© Tom Feiza Mr. Fix-It Inc.

W006

Also, install a carbon monoxide alarm. It's good insurance against a backdrafting problem that allows carbon monoxide into your home.

No Chimney for a Gas Appliance?

A modern gas furnace may have a sealed combustion system that doesn't require a chimney; the furnace is vented by plastic pipes to the exterior. Some gas water heaters also direct-vent through a side

wall with plastic pipe or a special metal vent. Newer gas fireplaces can vent directly through a side wall, and some have their own combustion air supply.

With today's tighter homes, always consider using fuel-burning appliances that have a built-in combustion supply that draws in air from outside.

High-Efficiency Warm Air Furnace

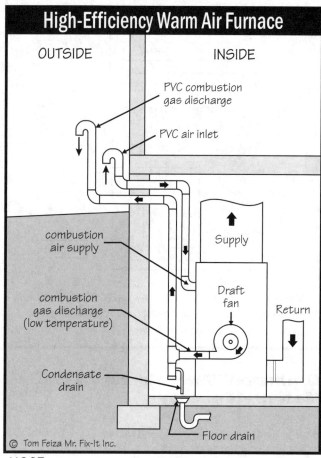

OUTSIDE

INSIDE

PVC combustion gas discharge

PVC air inlet

combustion air supply

Supply

combustion gas discharge (low temperature)

Draft fan

Return

Condensate drain

Floor drain

© Tom Feiza Mr. Fix-It Inc.

H003

Some states allow the installation of gas fireplaces without any vent or chimney, but many states forbid this type of installation because of the potential for safety problems. If you have any questions about the requirements in your area, check with the local building inspector.

Gas Fireplace Venting

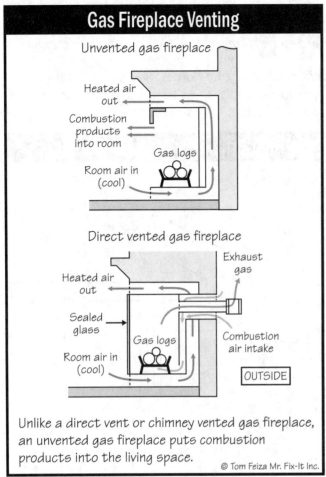

Unvented gas fireplace

Heated air out

Combustion products into room

Gas logs

Room air in (cool)

Direct vented gas fireplace

Exhaust gas

Heated air out

Sealed glass

Gas logs

Room air in (cool)

Combustion air intake

OUTSIDE

Unlike a direct vent or chimney vented gas fireplace, an unvented gas fireplace puts combustion products into the living space.

© Tom Feiza Mr. Fix-It Inc.

F036

Orphaned Water Heater in Masonry Chimney

Today many high-efficiency furnaces are installed to replace inefficient old furnaces. The new efficient furnace vents outdoors through a plastic pipe, and the old furnace connection to the masonry chimney is eliminated. Sounds great, right?

Well, it is great to use a high-efficiency furnace, but you can't just remove the exhaust flue from the masonry chimney if the chimney is shared with a gas water heater. The old furnace operated at only 50 to 65 percent efficiency. That means a lot of the energy from the gas flame went up the chimney, keeping the chimney nice and warm. When you remove this heat source, the chimney stays cold and the remaining (orphaned) water heater can't keep the chimney warm.

This results in condensation of the products of combustion in the chimney. Since water (steam) is a major component of the combustion gas, water condenses inside the chimney flue. This condensation will damage the chimney and can even leak into your home. You can solve the problem by adding a lightweight metal liner to the chimney. This thin, flexible metal liner runs from the water heater to the top of the chimney. The liner quickly warms from the combustion gas of the water heater, and condensation does not occur.

Seismic Movement

In certain parts of the country, earthquakes and tremors are a real concern. When a home shakes, piping can break, causing a major gas or water leak. In areas prone to seismic movement, water heaters often are strapped to the structure to prevent tipping, and flexible gas and water lines are attached to fixed appliances to accommodate movement. (Interestingly, flexible gas lines to fixed appliances are not allowed in some areas of the country.)

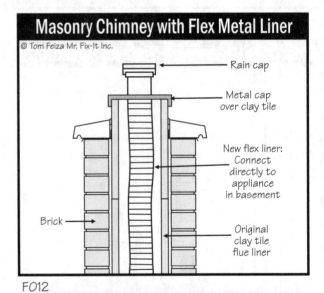

Masonry Chimney with Flex Metal Liner

© Tom Feiza Mr. Fix-It Inc.

Rain cap

Metal cap over clay tile

New flex liner: Connect directly to appliance in basement

Brick

Original clay tile flue liner

F012

Water Heater - Earthquake Areas

Flex connector

Gas line

Strapped to wall (prevents tipping)

Flex gas connector

Allows for some movement

© Tom Feiza Mr. Fix-It Inc.

W014

Chapter 7 – Fun Yet Serious Systems

Fireplaces and Wood Stoves

Before modern heating sources were available, fireplaces were a primary source of heating. Today a fireplace can't compete with a modern heating system. Fireplaces and wood stoves are great fun and provide a cozy, romantic amenity to our homes, but you do need to understand their basic components and how they operate.

Poor maintenance and improper operation can cause a fire inside your home. Fireplaces and wood stoves can produce dangerous products of combustion, such as carbon monoxide.

Basic Fireplace Types

There are three basic types of fireplaces: masonry, prefabricated metal and direct vent. Masonry fireplaces are designed to burn wood and can be adapted for a gas log set. Prefabricated metal fireplaces can be designed to burn wood, wood and gas, or just gas. Direct vent fireplaces are sealed high-efficiency units that only burn gas. We will look at each type and learn what's involved in safe operation.

A wood stove or fireplace insert should not be operated until a professional has checked it and determined that it conforms to local building codes and requirements. If you have any concerns or specific questions about your fireplace or wood stove, contact a local member of the Chimney Safety Institute of America (CSIA). Local fireplace and wood stove dealers can also provide assistance.

Masonry Fireplace

Masonry fireplaces have been the standard method of home heating for centuries. Since about 1900, when efficient central heating systems were developed, fireplaces have taken on the role of a desirable feature that adds value to our homes and provides a gathering place for family and friends.

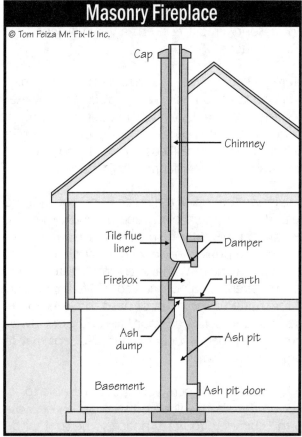

F005

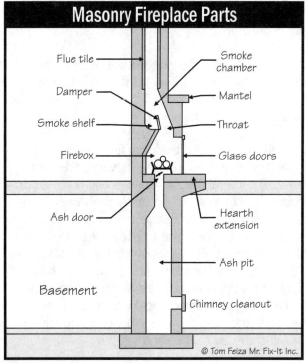

F006

109

A standard masonry fireplace is constructed of brick, firebrick, cement block and clay tile to contain the fire and products of combustion. The fireplace is custom built on-site by skilled masons. The design has changed little over the last 100 years, and masonry fireplaces aren't a very efficient source of heat.

Before you build a fire, you should understand the components of your masonry fireplace. Start by examining the firebox (the area where the fire is built). You will notice that the box is built of smooth brick or firebrick. If the wall of the firebox is metal, you have a metal framed or metal fabricated fireplace.

Look inside the top of the firebox and you will see a metal damper (metal plate) and a handle that operates the damper. Most dampers are made of cast iron and are pushed open with a handle or pulled open with a chain. With the chain-operated units you will often see a pull marked "O" for open and "S" for shut. Pull the chain or push the lever to open the damper. Keep your face and body away from the damper as it opens, because soot may fall from the opening.

With the damper open, you should be able to peer up the clay tile flue and see part of the way up the chimney. You may notice some soot- and tan-colored fluff or deposit. This is creosote. If you see a heavy buildup that is 1/16" to 1/4" thick, have your chimney and fireplace cleaned before you build a fire.

When you build a fire, the hot gases of combustion flow past the damper and up the chimney flue. The firebrick and firebox contain the heat of the fire and radiate some heat back into the room.

A variation on a solid masonry fireplace uses a metal firebox placed inside a masonry fireplace frame. The metal firebox replaces the firebox constructed of firebrick. These units often were constructed with an air passage around the metal box and air duct connections to the room. The lower duct opening draws air from the room at the base of the fireplace. The metal firebox warms the air, which then flows upward through a duct above the fireplace and enters the room through a grill. This gives the fireplace some heating capacity, warming the air of the room.

You might also find a wood-burning metal stove insert fitted inside a masonry fireplace. These custom-designed units provide heat to a room. Often, such a unit has a partially sealed combustion chamber. It requires a special flue and custom installation. This kind of unit needs yearly maintenance; flue gases exit at a lower temperature, and the unit is prone to a buildup of deposits in the stove and chimney flue.

Metal-Framed Prefabricated Fireplace

Many fireplaces built since about 1970 consist of a metal fireplace and flue built in a factory, which is then installed in a wood frame inside the home. These are called metal-framed, zero clearance, prefabricated, or factory-built fireplaces. They are designed and tested as a unit. Don't be confused by a solid brick or masonry front and mantle on such a fireplace; many metal fireplaces have a masonry front.

If yours is a factory-built fireplace, you will see a metal firebox with refractory panel liners, metal damper and a metal flue. The refractory panels will look like brick cast into a flat panel on three sides of the firebox. The side of the firebox may show the manufacturer's data and nameplate. Outside the house, there will not be a brick chimney; instead, you will see a wood-framed chimney chase and a metal-capped flue pipe. The flue or discharge pipe at the top of the chimney will be metal. The chase can also be covered with masonry materials, but this is not common.

A prefrabricated fireplace functions like a masonry fireplace but doesn't require the foundation and more expensive masonry construction. Glass doors are often included with the firebox, and the fireplace may have an outside air supply that provides combustion air for the fire. This reduces the need for inside air for combustion and makes the fireplace more efficient.

Many prefabricated fireplaces are equipped with a fan to circulate room air around the firebox so that the fire provides some heat in the room. The grills for air circulation are often placed directly above and below the glass doors.

Metal-Framed Prefabricated Fireplace

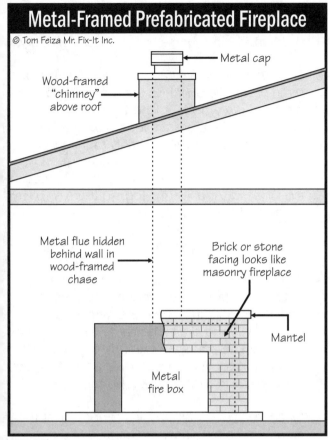

© Tom Feiza Mr. Fix-It Inc.

Metal cap

Wood-framed "chimney" above roof

Metal flue hidden behind wall in wood-framed chase

Brick or stone facing looks like masonry fireplace

Mantel

Metal fire box

F007

Direct Vent Fireplace

Around 1985, fireplaces were greatly improved as heating appliances when "direct vent" and "sealed combustion" fireplaces started to become popular. These are natural gas or propane burning fireplaces that vent combustion gases directly through a sidewall or up a special metal chimney. They use an outside air supply for combustion. The front glass is totally sealed.

This fireplace may have a pilot light or ignition device, just like a gas furnace. With a good set of gas logs, it provides an attractive flame and is an efficient source of heat. Some of these units are rated heating appliances, just like a warm air furnace, and can be connected to a thermostat for automatic control. The fireplace will have a fan to circulate heated air into the room. Many units are almost as efficient at heating the room as a good warm-air furnace.

Direct Vent Fireplace

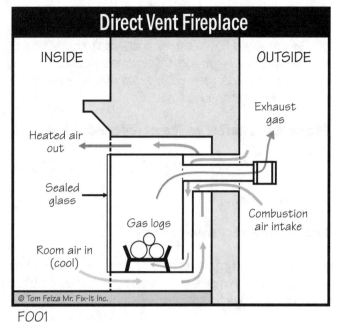

INSIDE

OUTSIDE

Exhaust gas

Heated air out

Sealed glass

Gas logs

Combustion air intake

Room air in (cool)

© Tom Feiza Mr. Fix-It Inc.

F001

Gas Fireplace Logs

A "gas" fireplace generally refers to a set of ceramic logs, a gas burner, and related equipment that allows the feel and look of a real fire while burning natural gas or propane. The advantages of a gas fireplace are that it requires no fuss and creates no mess. You can have an instant fire, and when you turn it off, you know the fire is out. There is no wood to haul in and no ash to clean up.

Gas fireplace logs are often adapted to a wood-burning masonry fireplace or to a metal-framed fireplace that is designed to burn wood.

Since each system is a little different, refer to the manufacturer's instructions for your unit. Some will have a pilot light or an automatic ignition device. Some use a wall switch or even a remote control.

With most manually operated gas fireplace logs, the first step is to open the damper in the flue above the logs. Then you place a match or flame in the log set. Use a long fireplace match or a lighter with a long handle. Carefully and slowly open the gas valve after there is a flame in the log set.

If you smell gas near the gas fireplace, do not attempt to light the unit. Turn off the gas valve located in the floor or in the firebox near the log set. Call for service. There should also be another safety valve in the basement or near the fireplace.

If you intend to burn real wood in a gas fireplace, consult a specialist first. Some metal-framed fireplaces are rated for gas only and won't burn wood. If your unit has a gas log set and gas piping, it would be very dangerous to burn real wood without converting the unit.

How to Build a Real Wood Fire

Masonry fireplaces and wood burning metal-framed fireplaces are safe and easy to use if you follow a few simple steps.

First, get everything ready:

1. Assemble a simple set of tools for maintaining the fire. At a minimum, you need some type of poker to move logs as needed when the fire is hot.

2. Always use a grate in the fireplace. The grate raises the wood off the base of the firebox to allow for air circulation, which aids complete combustion. Place the grate to the rear of the firebox.

3. Use dry or seasoned hardwood. This wood will burn hotter and prevent excessive smoke and soot from building up in the chimney flue. Dry or seasoned wood will have been cut and stored out of the weather for about 12 months. It will feel dry and will have cracks and splits in the end grain.

4. Never burn treated wood, Christmas trees, plastic, or trash in a fireplace. Never use a flammable liquid.

5. Remove ashes as they build up below the grate. There must be room for air circulation below the grate. If yours is a real masonry fireplace, you can put cold ashes down the ash pit door. Leave a base layer of about one inch of ash in the fireplace.

Now, to build the fire:

1. Open the damper. Take a look up the flue with a flashlight to make sure the damper is open. (Once you have mastered the operation of the damper, you can stop checking with the flashlight.)

2. If your home is very "tight," you may need to open a window to allow for combustion air to reach the fire. You will learn about this as you use the fireplace; if there is a poor draft, or if smoke builds inside your home, try opening a window.

3. Start loading the fireplace with small pieces of scrap wood (kindling) on the grate. Using small pieces of dry wood for kindling is the key. Woodworking scraps are ideal. These will light quickly, spreading the fire easily to the logs.

4. Add three or four small logs in the grate atop the kindling. Arrange the logs so there is space for air and fire circulation between them.

5. Place wadded newspaper below the grate.

6. You may need to help start the draft with a torch made from rolled newspaper. Light the paper and hold it up near the damper until there is a strong draft. The flame will warm the air in the flue and start a draft (a draw) up the chimney. After you have burned a few fires, you will know whether you can skip this step.

7. Once there is a draft up the chimney, light the crumpled paper below the grate.

8. Keep the screen closed while you are burning a fire.

9. Add and move the logs if needed. Don't build a huge fire.

10. Monitor the fire as it burns. Allow it to burn out before you leave the room. If your fireplace has glass doors, close them when you leave the fire.

11. Don't close the damper until the next day, and make sure the grate and remnants of logs are totally cold. A wood fire can smolder for a long time, and if you close the damper when the fire is still burning, you will trap smoke and dangerous products of combustion inside your home.

Fireplace Draft Problems

One problem with fireplaces in newer, more airtight homes is that they lack combustion air unless a window is open. This was not a problem with older homes, which had so many air leaks around windows, doors and framing that there was plenty of air for combustion.

Must Know / Must Do
Building a Fire

1. Keep the damper open overnight after burning a wood fire.

2. Routinely have the fireplace and flue cleaned by a professional.

3. Watch for soot and creosote buildup.

4. Consider glass doors; they're a great addition to your fireplace. They contain the fire and help prevent excessive room air from entering the fireplace.

5. Never light a gas fireplace if you smell gas. Treat this as a serious safety hazard.

6. If you see cracks, crumbling, or movement of the masonry surface inside the firebox or flue, have them checked by a professional.

7. A professional should check excessive rust on a metal-framed fireplace.

8. If you are not sure how to use your gas or wood-burning fireplace, get help from a professional.

This condition can be dangerous: as a fire is starting or burning out, it may lack draft, and it can back up dangerous carbon monoxide into your home.

A fire with a strong draft can cause gas-fired appliances such as a water heater or furnace to back-draft combustion fumes into your home. Any gas-burning appliance vented by gravity up a chimney could be affected. The draft of a fire can overcome the natural venting of these gas appliances.

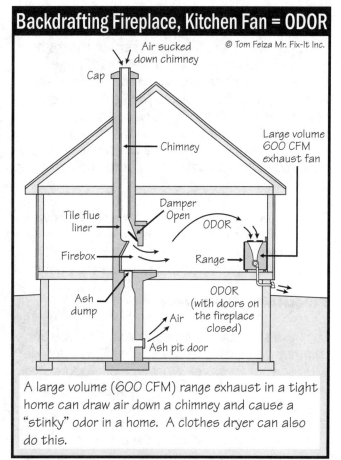

Backdrafting Fireplace, Kitchen Fan = ODOR

A large volume (600 CFM) range exhaust in a tight home can draw air down a chimney and cause a "stinky" odor in a home. A clothes dryer can also do this.

V031

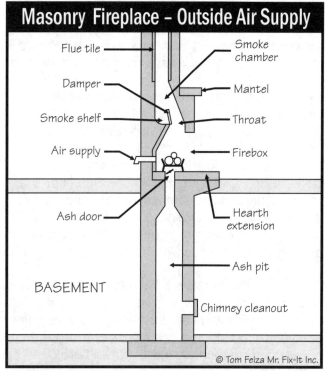

Masonry Fireplace – Outside Air Supply

F009

An air supply directed into the firebox would be a good solution. Consult a qualified brickmason, fireplace contractor or chimney sweep for the installation. This is definitely not a do-it-yourself project. The vent must penetrate an outside wall and the side or front of the fireplace. The vent may also need to be combined with fireplace doors.

Remember that when most natural fireplaces are operated in cold weather, most of the heat goes up the chimney.

There is one situation when a fireplace works well: if the home has excessive moisture levels in the winter, the fireplace will draw lots of air into your home for ventilation (provided that a window is open!)

Fireplace Cleaning

The ideal schedule for cleaning your fireplace and chimney depends on many factors. How often do you use your fireplace? What type of wood do you burn? Is the wood always dry hardwood? Is your home in a wooded area? Is there a cap on the chimney? Have you had problems in the past? Do you close the glass doors? Is there always a good draft? Is the chimney in the center of the home or on an outside wall?

If you live in a wooded area, you may wish to have the chimney checked every year just to make sure that no animals or their nests have blocked the flue.

You should inspect your fireplace, damper and flue every year. Operate the damper to see that it opens fully and latches open. The damper should also close tightly. Peer up the flue while shining a bright flashlight on it. You should not see any buildup of creosote or soot on the sides of the firebox or liner. The shelf behind the damper should not be full of debris. Proper inspection also includes looking at the top of the chimney, inspecting the cap, and peering down the flue with a bright light.

Creosote buildup creates a fire hazard. Creosote, a black or brown deposit, can be crusty and flaky, tar-like, or shiny and hardened. You might see different types of buildup on one fireplace. If creosote builds up in sufficient quantities, it can burn, destroying the chimney and even burning down your home.

Wet wood, restricted air for combustion, and cool chimney temperatures all increase the buildup of creosote, so no general rule of thumb can safely determine when a fireplace needs to be cleaned.

Have your fireplace cleaned, and ask the chimney sweep for recommendations on routine maintenance. He or she can determine how often your chimney needs cleaning, based on all the variables in your case. Select a sweep who belongs to the National Chimney Sweep Guild and is certified by the Chimney Safety Institute of America (CSIA). A chimney sweep must pass an examination to be certified. Remember that it's the worker, not the company, who should be certified. To find the names of certified members in your area, call the CSIA at (317) 837-5362 (www.csia.org).

"Rain" in the Fireplace

To avoid severe condensation problems that mimic rain in the fireplace, check the fit of the fireplace damper. If the damper leaks (or is left open) during the winter, warm moist air will flow up the chimney. This warm air will condense into water on the flue if the chimney is cold from lack of use; when temperatures are below freezing, the condensation will turn to ice on the flue. When you build a fire, this ice can fall like "rain."

"Rain" that falls onto your fire could also result from a leak in the flashing, a damaged cap, damaged brick and mortar, or a liner problem. If the problem persists, hire a certified chimney sweep to do an inspection.

Wood Stoves

Wood stoves, wood heaters, wood-burning fireplace inserts and related wood-burning devices have become popular over the years. Many are well-designed and safe to use. Some are homemade contraptions that are not safe. Some are excellent factory-built units installed by amateurs in an unsafe fashion.

If your home has any type of wood-burning device other than a professionally installed fireplace, have it checked by a professional before you use it. It may not be safe.

Wood-Burning Stove

NEEDS PROFESSIONAL INSTALLATION

To chimney

Special flue design

Fire-resistant surfaces

Clearance to prevent a fire

© Tom Feiza Mr. Fix-It Inc.

FO10

Whirlpool Bath

A whirlpool bath is a tub fitted with a circulating pump, jets, air induction, and possibly a heater. The tub can be small or large and is usually located in a bathroom. Most whirlpool tubs let you adjust the direction and amount of air in the jets for a more invigorating flow of water. Water is recirculated through the pump, the jets and a return opening.

The pump system usually is controlled by a switch on the side of the tub that uses pneumatic operation for safety. There may also be a timer and disconnect switch mounted on the wall away from the tub. The electrical system must be protected by a ground fault circuit interrupter (GFCI) outlet or breaker.

To use the tub, fill it with comfortably warm water to a level above the jets; then turn on the airflow to the jets, which should be pointed downward unless you want water spraying into your adjacent closet. You can adjust the jets to vary the amount and strength of the airflow. Adjust the temperature to your liking by adding more hot or cold water.

Whirlpool tubs should be flushed periodically, up to twice per month depending on usage. Debris can build up in the piping system if the unit is not used and flushed periodically.

The Kohler Co., a premier manufacturer of plumbing fixtures and whirlpool tubs, provides excellent information on whirlpool operation and mainte-

nance information at its website, www.kohler.com. According to Kohler, whirlpool flushing should be done as follows:

1. Adjust the jets fully clockwise so there is no air induction.

2. Fill the bath with warm water to a level 2" above the highest jets, or leave water in the bath after using.

3. Add 2 teaspoons of a low-foaming dishwasher detergent and 20 ounces of household bleach (5 to 6 percent sodium hypochlorite) to the water.

4. Run the whirlpool for 5 to 10 minutes. Then shut off the whirlpool and drain the water.

5. If desired, rinse bath surfaces with water.

6. Clean bath surfaces as needed with recommended cleaners.

Whirlpool Tub

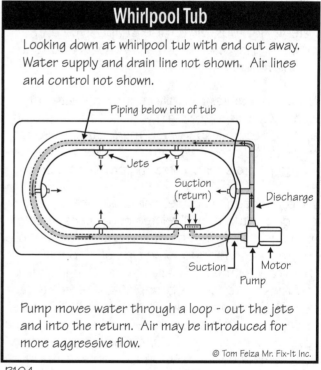

Looking down at whirlpool tub with end cut away. Water supply and drain line not shown. Air lines and control not shown.

Piping below rim of tub

Jets

Suction (return)

Discharge

Suction

Motor

Pump

Pump moves water through a loop - out the jets and into the return. Air may be introduced for more aggressive flow.

© Tom Feiza Mr. Fix-It Inc.

P104

Must Know / Must Do
Whirlpool Tubs

- Periodically flush and clean the unit.

- Test the GFCI routinely.

- Never use bubble bath or similar detergents.

- Never allow children to use the tub without supervision.

Hot Tub/Spa

A hot tub or a spa is a heated, water-filled tub that circulates water and often air through jets below the water line. Water is not drained from a hot tub as it is from a bathroom whirlpool tub.

The hot tub can be made of fiberglass, wood, acrylic or even poured concrete as part of a pool system. Hot tubs vary in size, shape, type and location. They have automatic controls and require routine maintenance.

A hot tub requires carefully controlled treatment with chemicals to maintain water quality. Ozone is also used to treat spa water. There are numerous methods for chemical treatment; some are manual and some are sophisticated, automated systems.

Self-contained (sometimes called portable) spas include the tub and all related equipment—heater pump, jets, filter, air system and automatic controls. They may also include some type of automatic chemical treatment. Usually the heater is electrical and the unit requires a large 240-volt electrical service with ground fault circuit interrupter (GFCI) protection. In most climates these tubs are fitted with a cover to conserve energy and water and maintain the chemical balance. Automatic controls maintain the temperature and operate pumps and heaters.

An in-ground spa installed with a pool usually has a separate pump, filter, heater, air system and chemical treatment. The equipment is often located outside but can be located in a pool room or basement. The heater for this type of spa is usually gas-fired—basically, it's a small gas boiler.

You may wish to hire a contractor for routine maintenance and chemical treatment. The chemicals and equipment must be carefully controlled to provide a safe system and to prevent equipment damage.

Hot Tub, Spa Equipment

Simple schematic - not to scale
Hot tub with separate equipment

Flex piping

Pump

Motor

Jets

Return

Filter

Gas supply

Gas heater

© Tom Feiza Mr. Fix-It Inc.

P105

Must Know / Must Do
Hot Tubs and Spas

- Maintain water quality through chemical treatment.

- Keep covered to control water and chemical loss.

- Periodically flush and clean the unit.

- Test the GFCI routinely.

- Never use bubble bath or similar detergents.

- Never allow children to use the hot tub without supervision.

- Watch for leaks.

- Listen for unusual equipment noises.

Swimming Pools

A swimming pool is a man-made tub of water designed for recreation, exercise, and staying cool on a hot summer day. Swimming pools come in all types, shapes and sizes. Some are above ground, some below. Most of them share common systems and components.

Most pools include a pump, filter, strainer, skimmer, drain, valves, and piping that connects all these components. In addition, a pool may have a heater, lights and an automatic treatment system. The treatment may be chemical, salt or oxygenation.

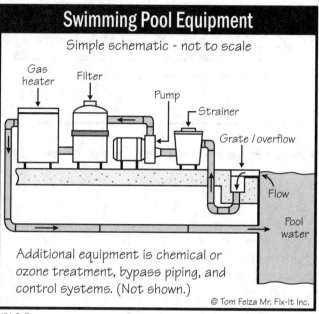

Swimming Pool Equipment

Simple schematic - not to scale

Gas heater
Filter
Pump
Strainer
Grate / overflow
Flow
Pool water

Additional equipment is chemical or ozone treatment, bypass piping, and control systems. (Not shown.)

© Tom Feiza Mr. Fix-It Inc.

P106

Pools are constructed of poured reinforced concrete, vinyl lined in ground or above ground, or a spray of cement and sand over a metal framework. Some pools are covered with ceramic tile, and some are surrounded with concrete or concrete and tile walking surfaces.

The basic operation of a pool starts with a skimmer and water return lines from the pool. Water from the pool runs through a screen to remove larger debris like leaves and swimming suits (just kidding). From the screen, water is routed through an electrically operated pump and into a filter. After the water is filtered it may be heated, treated, and then returned to the pool through an opening in the side of the pool.

Routine maintenance of the mechanical equipment requires cleaning the screen to remove debris. The filter is replaced, backwashed or cleaned, depending on the type of filter. To perform any maintenance, you must understand how your specific system operates, and you must use valves to turn off or bypass equipment as needed. Often, pool maintenance is best left to professionals. At the least, the homeowner should be trained by a professional and obtain specific operating and maintenance instructions.

Water treatment is required to limit bacteria and keep the water clean. Often, chlorine compounds are used as a disinfectant. It is important to keep the pH of the pool within a certain range so the chlorine remains useful.

Must Know / Must Do
Swimming Pool

- Hire a service contractor to routinely check equipment.

- Establish a maintenance routine based on your equipment.

- Treat the water to maintain chemical balance.

- Keep records on maintenance and water chemistry.

- Routinely check for leaks at piping and other systems.

- Regularly change or clean filters and screens.

- Never allow children to use the pool without adults present.

- Use an alarm to alert you to water movement when the pool is not in use.

- Secure the pool with a proper enclosure, and maintain the enclosure.

- Periodically test the GFCI and related safety equipment.

Your pool should be protected by a pool cover. The cover limits evaporation of water and loss of chemicals. It also helps protect the pool from leaves and debris.

Pool Safety

Children must always be supervised when using a swimming pool. It is a good idea to have more than one adult around when using a pool. A fence with locking and self-closing gates should protect the pool. All doors to living areas should be equipped with self-closing hardware and locks at least 54 inches above the floor. An electronic or automated safety monitoring system should be in place to detect water movement when the pool is not in use. A pool cover may also be used for additional safety.

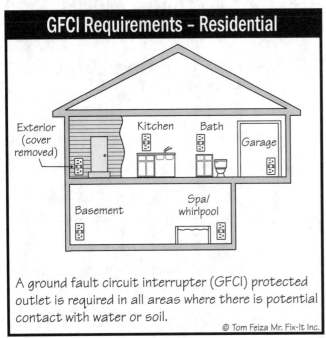

GFCI Requirements – Residential

A ground fault circuit interrupter (GFCI) protected outlet is required in all areas where there is potential contact with water or soil.

© Tom Feiza Mr. Fix-It Inc.

E117

All electrical outlets must be spaced away from the water and be protected by a ground fault circuit interrupter (GFCI). Overhead electrical conductors must be eliminated. All systems must be grounded and bonded. If you have any concerns about the electrical system, have it checked by a qualified electrician.

Pool owners should ensure that all safety requirements of the local municipality and state are followed. You may wish to have the local building inspector check the pool and its equipment for safety. It is a good idea to have a phone near the pool with local emergency assistance numbers next to it.

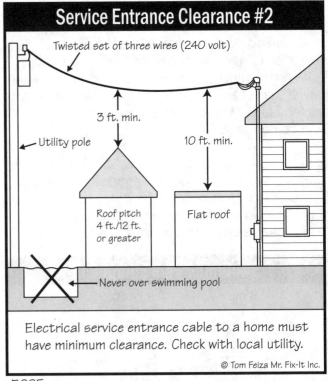

Service Entrance Clearance #2

Twisted set of three wires (240 volt)

3 ft. min.

Utility pole

10 ft. min.

Roof pitch 4 ft./12 ft. or greater

Flat roof

Never over swimming pool

Electrical service entrance cable to a home must have minimum clearance. Check with local utility.

© Tom Feiza Mr. Fix-It Inc.

E025

Waterfront Property and Seawalls

Property on lakes and streams must be protected from erosion of soil adjoining the water. This may require some type of retaining wall or rock. Surface water drainage also must be directed around or channeled through any retaining wall to prevent damage. Your local municipality or Department of Natural Resources can provide information on requirements and maintenance.

Property on major bodies of water with wave action may need special protection. Often an engineered and specially constructed seawall is used. Seawalls may consist of poured concrete, steel sheet pile, concrete block, rock or timber. The seawall or bulkhead protects banks by separating the earth or sand behind them from water movement. Provisions must be made to allow surface drainage around or through a seawall.

Generally, seawalls do not protect inland areas from water movement. Your state or municipality can provide local requirements and restrictions for a seawall barrier.

Chapter 8 – Service Requirements by the Calendar

Service Requirements by the Calendar

Home operation and maintenance is easy if we understand our home systems and stay organized. A home operates just like a car—with the right maintenance, you can avoid major problems and efficiently run your home for many years. The key is preventing problems or catching small problems before they become home disasters.

If you don't change the filter on the furnace on a routine basis, you can freeze up the coil, and you will come home to a very warm house. If you don't turn off the exterior hose connection in the winter, you can come home to a flood.

This chapter provides that little bit of organization that helps us all remember to perform important preventive maintenance tasks. It offers lists of maintenance tasks to be performed on a routine basis. Refer to specific chapters in the book for detailed information on the specific tasks. Follow manufacturers' instructions for all service.

Remember, not every maintenance item will be applicable to your home or its systems. You need to do the homework here—study and understand the systems in your home.

Exercise caution before attempting inspection, maintenance or repairs. Turn off the power and disconnect other utility services. Follow any owner's manual supplied by the equipment manufacturer. If you don't understand a problem or system, consult a professional.

Daily and Weekly

Be aware of any changes or strange sounds in your home. If the automatic garage door opener is groaning, the door and track may need lubrication, or perhaps a roller is broken. If you smell sewer gas in the basement, it may be due to a dried-out floor drain trap. If the central air conditioner is squeaking, this may indicate a bad bearing on the fan motor. If a gutter is overflowing, expect water in the basement or crawl space. Just watch for changes, and address issues as they arise.

Be watchful during drastic weather changes. Weather can have a huge effect on our homes. A big snowstorm may make it necessary to clear your furnace's intake and discharge vent pipes. During periods of heavy rain, it is wise to check gutters and downspouts and make sure that the sump pump is working properly. If the furnace runs constantly or more often than you expect, check for a problem.

Furnace Utility Disconnects

Gas supply →

Discharge

Alternate switch on ceiling or wall

Electrical supply

Return

Gas valve →

OFF   ON
Typical gas shutoff

Typical electrical disconnect (light switch) turns furnace and air conditioner on/off

© Tom Feiza Mr. Fix-It Inc.

H008

Monthly

When these systems are in use, perform the following checks monthly.

System	Check	Condition
❏ Fire and smoke alarms	Test alarm.	_____
❏ Fire extinguishers	Check pressure; service as needed.	_____
❏ Carbon monoxide alarm	Test alarm, and check reading.	_____
❏ Warm air heating system	Check and change or wash filter (unless it is a special type).	_____
❏ Furnace, high efficiency	Check condensate drain to make sure it is clear and draining.	_____
❏ Gas heat, water heater	Check flue pipe (smoke pipe) to chimney for rust or other damage.	_____
❏ Air conditioning	Check and change or wash filter (unless it is a special type); check condensate drain to make sure it is clear and draining.	_____
❏ Heat pump	Check and change or wash filter (unless it is a special type).	_____
❏ Steam heating system	Check water level. Service as needed.	_____
❏ Shower and tub drains	Clear out hair and other debris.	_____
❏ GFCI	Test GFCI (Ground Fault Circuit Interrupter) outlets and breakers.	_____
❏ Plumbing	Check for any leaks at fixtures, traps and piping.	_____
❏ Water softener	Check salt supply.	_____
❏ Clothes dryer	Clean lint from filter (after every use) and check duct for lint.	_____
❏ Garage door operator	Test auto-reverse safety feature.	_____

Spring

System	Check	Condition
❑ Air conditioning	Schedule professional service. Check that the unit is level and clean and has proper clearance. Adjust main duct dampers if needed.	_____
❑ Room air conditioner	Install or uncover unit. Check filter.	_____
❑ Humidifier	Turn off unit and water supply. Switch humidifier's duct damper from winter to summer setting as needed.	_____
❑ Duct dampers	Adjust dampers for a switch from heating to cooling if necessary.	_____
❑ High and low returns	Open high returns and close low returns for cooling season.	_____
❑ Whole house fan	Check belt; lubricate and clean.	_____
❑ Gutters, downspouts	Clean gutters, and make sure downspouts are attached and extended.	_____
❑ Roof	Inspect for damage. Trim trees if needed.	_____
❑ Roof vents	Inspect for damage or bird nests.	_____
❑ Chimney	Inspect for damage to cap, flashing and masonry.	_____
❑ Sump pump	Test sump pump to make sure it removes water from the crock.	_____
❑ Exterior, general	Check condition of paint, caulk and putty.	_____
❑ Exterior, grounds	Check that grading of soil and hard surfaces slopes away from the basement.	_____
❑ Attic	Check for signs of leaks, mildew, condensation.	_____
❑ Basement	Check for signs of leaks, cracks, movement, rot, mildew.	_____
❑ Crawl space	Check for adequate ventilation to remove excess moisture.	_____

(Continued, next page)

Spring (continued)

System	Check	Condition
❏ Dehumidifier	Clean; start operation in basement as needed.	_____
❏ Plumbing	Open outside hose connection shutoff.	_____
❏ Clothes dryer	Clean lint from duct and from unit per manufacturer's instructions.	_____
❏ Refrigerator	Clean coil, clean drain pan, and check drain.	_____
❏ Range hood	Clean filter, wash fan blades.	_____
❏ Bathroom exhaust fans	Clean grill and fan.	_____
❏ Bathroom tile	Check grout, caulk and tile for damage.	_____
❏ Water heater	Draw sediment from tank as needed.	_____
❏ Sprinklers, irrigation	Service and start system.	_____
❏ Decks	Clean and seal as needed.	_____
❏ Swimming pool	Arrange for service at start of season. Check filter, pump, chemicals, etc.	_____

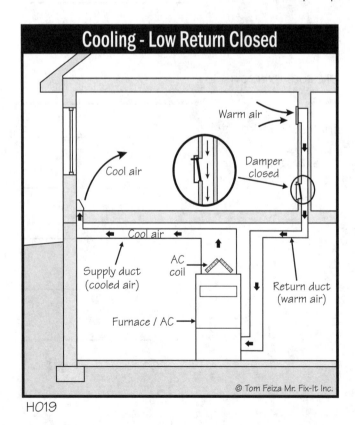

Cooling - Low Return Closed

Warm air

Cool air

Damper closed

Cool air

Supply duct (cooled air)

AC coil

Return duct (warm air)

Furnace / AC

© Tom Feiza Mr. Fix-It Inc.

H019

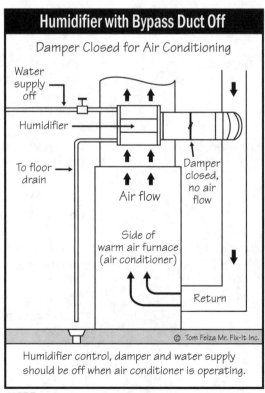

Humidifier with Bypass Duct Off

Damper Closed for Air Conditioning

Water supply off

Humidifier

To floor drain

Air flow

Damper closed, no air flow

Side of warm air furnace (air conditioner)

Return

© Tom Feiza Mr. Fix-It Inc.

Humidifier control, damper and water supply should be off when air conditioner is operating.

H033

Summer

System	Check	Condition
❏ Air conditioner	Keep bushes and plant material clear of unit. Maintain air conditioner's filter on furnace. Keep drain lines clear.	_____
❏ Gutters, downspouts	Clean gutters, and make sure downspouts are attached and extended.	_____
❏ Sump pump	Test sump pump to make sure it removes water from the crock.	_____
❏ Exterior	Complete any major paint, putty, wood repair and caulking projects.	_____
❏ Fireplace	Schedule professional cleaning and service as needed.	_____
❏ Wood stoves	Schedule professional cleaning and service.	_____
❏ Chimney and roof	Schedule professional service as needed.	_____
❏ Exterior metal	Check metal railings. Paint as needed.	_____

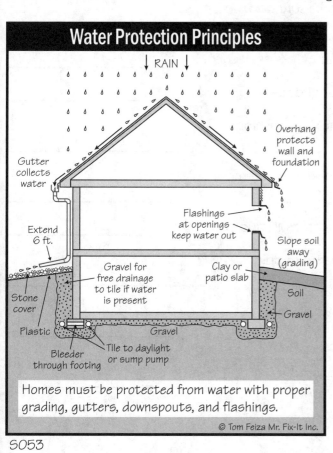

Water Protection Principles

Homes must be protected from water with proper grading, gutters, downspouts, and flashings.

© Tom Feiza Mr. Fix-It Inc.

S053

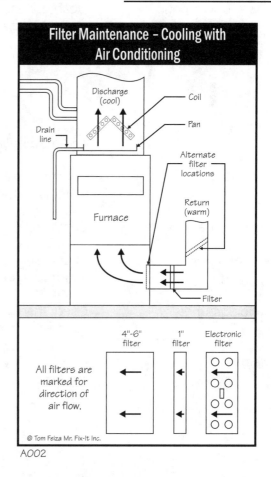

Filter Maintenance – Cooling with Air Conditioning

All filters are marked for direction of air flow.

© Tom Feiza Mr. Fix-It Inc.

A002

123

Fall

System	Check	Condition
❑ Air conditioning	Cover top of unit if desired at end of cooling season.	_____
❑ Heating	Schedule professional service; lubricate fan, motor, and pumps.	_____
❑ Oil heat	Arrange for maintenance and oil delivery.	_____
❑ Water heater	Service gas and oil water heaters. Draw sediment from tank as needed. Check for carbon monoxide.	_____
❑ Humidifier	Service, clean, and change water panel as needed. Switch duct damper as needed from summer to winter setting.	_____
❑ Duct dampers	Adjust dampers for the switch from cooling to heating if necessary.	_____
❑ High and low returns	Open low returns and close high returns for heating season.	_____
❑ Gutters, downspouts	Clean gutters, and make sure downspouts are attached and extended.	_____
❑ Roof	Inspect for damage; trim trees as needed.	_____
❑ Roof vents	Inspect for damage or bird nests.	_____
❑ Chimney	Inspect for damage to cap, flashing and masonry.	_____
❑ Sump pump	Test sump pump to make sure it removes water from the crock.	_____
❑ Exterior, general	Check condition of paint, caulk and putty.	_____
❑ Weatherstripping	Check and repair weatherstripping on windows and doors.	_____
❑ Exterior, grounds	Check that grading of soil and hard surfaces slopes away from basement.	_____
❑ Basement	Check for any signs of leaks, cracks, movement, rot, mildew.	_____

(Continued, next page)

Fall (continued)

System	Check	Condition
☐ Crawl space	Check for adequate ventilation to remove excess moisture.	_____
☐ Plumbing	Close outside hose connection shutoff.	_____
☐ Clothes dryer	Clean lint from duct and unit per manufacturer's instructions.	_____
☐ Bathroom tile	Check grout, caulk and tile for damage.	_____
☐ Garage door	Tighten all hardware, and lubricate moving parts.	_____
☐ Fireplace	Check flue, damper, firebox.	_____
☐ Sprinklers, irrigation	Drain and service system.	_____
☐ Room air conditioner	Remove unit, or install cover.	_____
☐ Swimming pool	Service and close.	_____
☐ Hoses	Remove from hose bibs; drain to prevent freezing.	_____

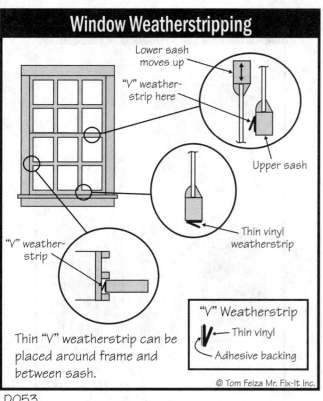

Window Weatherstripping

Lower sash moves up

"V" weather-strip here

Upper sash

Thin vinyl weatherstrip

"V" weather-strip

"V" Weatherstrip

Thin vinyl

Adhesive backing

Thin "V" weatherstrip can be placed around frame and between sash.

© Tom Feiza Mr. Fix-It Inc.

D053

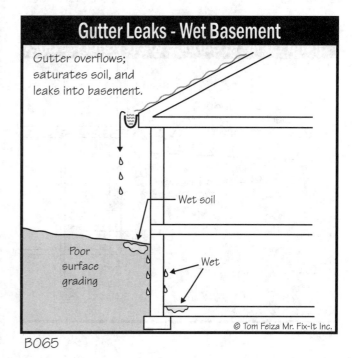

Gutter Leaks - Wet Basement

Gutter overflows; saturates soil, and leaks into basement.

Wet soil

Poor surface grading

Wet

© Tom Feiza Mr. Fix-It Inc.

B065

Winter

System	Check	Condition/Date
❏ Fire and smoke alarms	Change batteries, vacuum to remove dust, and test.	_____
❏ Carbon monoxide alarms	Change batteries, and test.	_____
❏ Roof and gutters	Monitor for ice dams, and record problems for future corrective work.	_____
❏ Sump pump	Test sump pump to make sure it removes water from the crock.	_____
❏ Furnace	Lubricate fan, motor, and pumps as required at mid-season.	_____
❏ Washing machine	Check supply hoses for damage. Clean screens in hose connections.	_____
❏ Doors and hardware	Lubricate hinges and moving parts.	_____
❏ Boiler	Lubricate pump twice each winter.	_____
❏ Steam boiler	Check water level.	_____
❏ Gutters	Keep downspouts extended.	_____

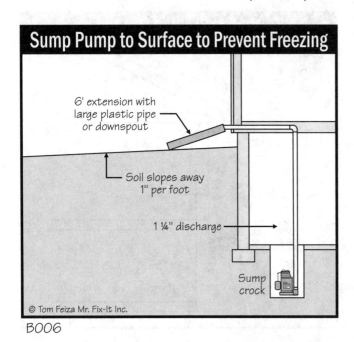

Sump Pump to Surface to Prevent Freezing

6' extension with large plastic pipe or downspout

Soil slopes away 1" per foot

1 ¼" discharge

Sump crock

© Tom Feiza Mr. Fix-It Inc.

B006

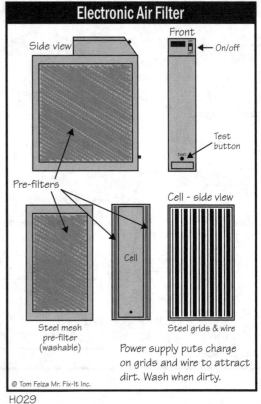

Electronic Air Filter

Side view

Front

On/off

Test button

Pre-filters

Cell - side view

Cell

Steel mesh pre-filter (washable)

Steel grids & wire

Power supply puts charge on grids and wire to attract dirt. Wash when dirty.

© Tom Feiza Mr. Fix-It Inc.

H029

Periodic Maintenance and Service as Needed

System	Check	Condition/Date
☐ Septic system	Schedule professional pumping and inspection at least every 2 years.	_____
☐ Water softener	Clean brine tank and screens or filters as needed.	_____
☐ Well system	Test water for bacteria and other contaminants. Check pressure tank operation.	_____
☐ Fire and smoke alarms	Replace alarms every 10 years.	_____
☐ Fireplace	Schedule cleaning and inspection as needed, depending on use.	_____
☐ Water filters	Replace as needed.	_____
☐ Water treatment units	Replace and service as needed.	_____
☐ Electric baseboard	Vacuum and clean based on usage.	_____
☐ Gas appliances	Check flexible gas connectors for stove, dryer, etc., yearly.	_____
☐ Range hood	Clean filter and fan.	_____
☐ Shutoffs	Periodically review all utility disconnects with your family.	_____
☐ Termites and other pests	Schedule professional inspections and service as needed.	_____
☐ Electrical	Eliminate extension cords. Check for damaged cords, plugs or outlets.	_____
☐ Water heater	Test temperature and pressure relief valve. Replace leaking valves.	_____
☐ Plumbing	Test main water shutoff. If it is hard to operate, call a plumber.	_____

Door Maintenance Tips

Patio Door Adjustment

© Tom Feiza Mr. Fix-It Inc.

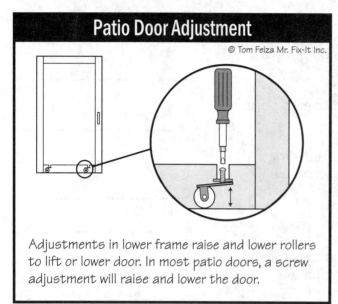

Adjustments in lower frame raise and lower rollers to lift or lower door. In most patio doors, a screw adjustment will raise and lower the door.

D037

Bypass / Sliding Door Adjustment #1

Various roller bracket adjustments:

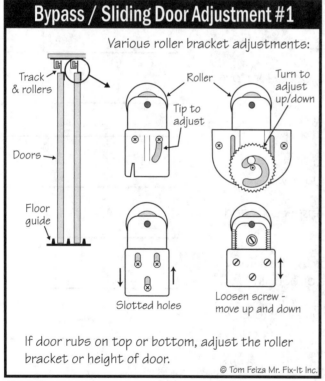

Track & rollers

Roller

Tip to adjust

Turn to adjust up/down

Doors

Floor guide

Slotted holes

Loosen screw - move up and down

If door rubs on top or bottom, adjust the roller bracket or height of door.

© Tom Feiza Mr. Fix-It Inc.

D030

Bypass / Sliding Door Adjustment #2

© Tom Feiza Mr. Fix-It Inc.

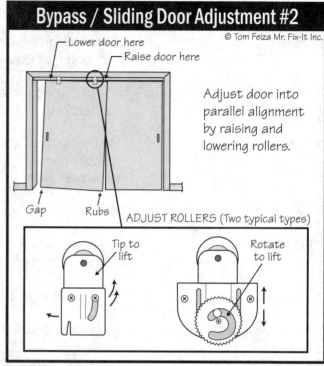

Lower door here

Raise door here

Adjust door into parallel alignment by raising and lowering rollers.

Gap

Rubs

ADJUST ROLLERS (Two typical types)

Tip to lift

Rotate to lift

D031

Bifold Door - Up/Down

Adjustment options:

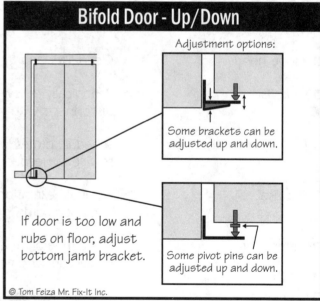

Some brackets can be adjusted up and down.

If door is too low and rubs on floor, adjust bottom jamb bracket.

Some pivot pins can be adjusted up and down.

© Tom Feiza Mr. Fix-It Inc.

D036

Chapter 9 – In Case of Emergency: Things Everyone in the Household Should Know

In Case of Emergency: Things Everyone in the Household Should Know

It's a great idea for every homeowner to set up an emergency plan and create a list of things everybody in the household should know. Your safety plan could involve maintaining a list of emergency shutoffs, compiling information sources, and gathering basic tools.

You may need to find an expert to help locate, repair or maintain some of these valves and switches. Locating and tagging them is a helpful exercise for homeowners. Use the tags provided in this journal. After tagging each item, take a tour with all family members explaining what these items do and how to operate the controls. In addition, develop a list of emergency numbers and an escape plan.

Here is a checklist to help you get started:

☐ **Main electrical disconnect**. This will be located at the main fuse box or breaker panel. Usually there is one main switch or fuse block, but older systems may have multiple disconnects.

☐ **Water main valve**. This valve turns off all the water to your home. If the valve looks old, worn or rusty, have a plumber check it for proper operation. If you use a municipal water supply, the valve will be located in the basement on the "street side" of your home near the water meter. If your house has its own well, the valve will be near the pressure tank. In this case, to disable the system you must turn off the main valve and the electrical switch for the well pump.

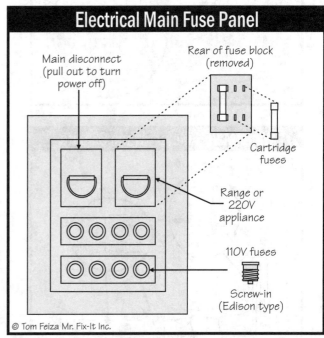

E003

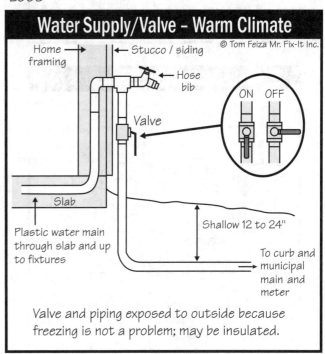

P064

Water Supply System in a Cold Climate

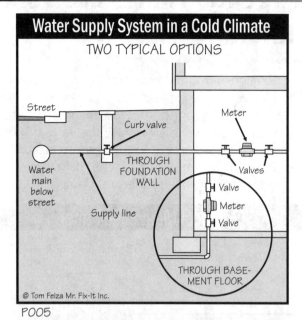

TWO TYPICAL OPTIONS

P005

Water Main / Meter - Warm Climate

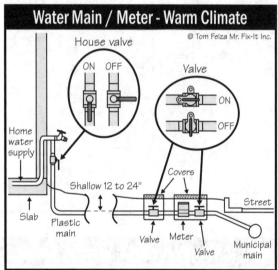

P063

Well - Main Water Disconnects

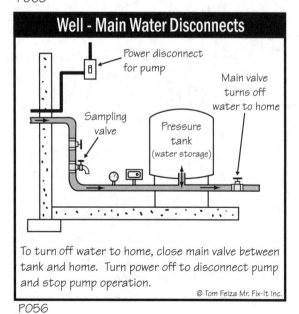

To turn off water to home, close main valve between tank and home. Turn power off to disconnect pump and stop pump operation.

© Tom Feiza Mr. Fix-It Inc.

P056

❒ **Water heater shutoff**. This valve is located on the cold-water inlet at the top of the water heater. It turns off the hot water supply to your home by closing the cold supply to the water heater.

❒ **Natural gas main**. This will be located near the meter, either outside or inside your home. Many of these valves require a wrench to operate; a quarter-turn moves the valve from on to off. When the handle is parallel to the pipe, the valve is open.

Water Heater Valves / Disconnects

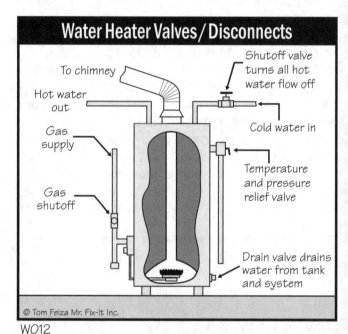

W012

Exterior Gas Meter and Shutoff

© Tom Feiza Mr. Fix-It Inc.

P002

☐ **Local gas valves**. These should be located at each gas appliance; they, too, close with a quarter-turn.

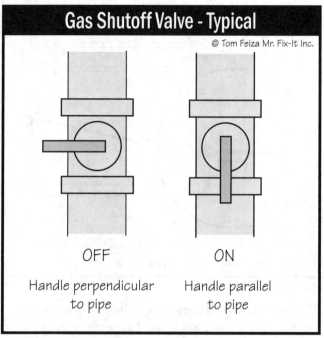

P076

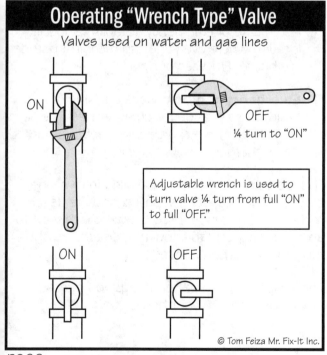

P066

☐ **Air conditioning disconnect**. This switch, near the exterior air conditioning unit, turns off the 240-volt electrical supply.

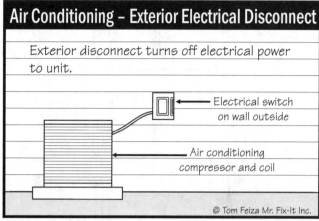

A004

☐ **Furnace and air conditioning main switch**. This is usually mounted on the furnace. In a modern system, it will look like a light switch. It turns off the central heating and cooling system.

☐ **Emergency release for garage door**. The automatic garage door opener has an emergency release so you can open the door when there is a power failure. Show everyone how it operates. Do this with the door down, because a poorly balanced door may crash to the ground. The release is located where the door attaches to the opener track. Pull the handle to release it—remember, do this with the door down—and then lift the door.

☐ **Emergency release for garage door—with a key** (when there is no service door to detached garage). In this situation, to release the garage door opener when the power is out, you must open a special lock and remove a cable. You'll find a circular lock near the top center of the garage door. Open this lock and pull the attached cable out through the opening. Doing this will release the opener from the garage door so you can open the door manually. Always remember that the door should be down before you test the release.

☐ **Emergency phone numbers**. Keep a list of how to reach the fire department, ambulance/rescue, police, Mom, Dad, relatives, workplace(s), and others appropriate to your household.

Furnace Utility Disconnects

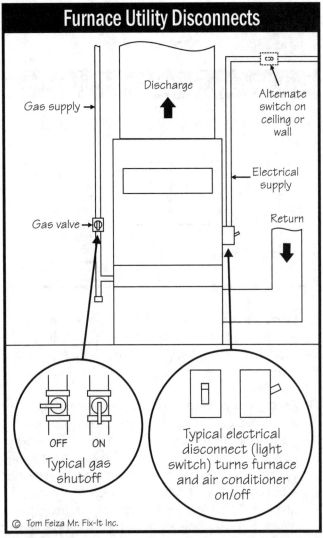

Gas supply →

Discharge ↑

Alternate switch on ceiling or wall

Electrical supply →

Gas valve →

Return ↓

OFF   ON

Typical gas shutoff

Typical electrical disconnect (light switch) turns furnace and air conditioner on/off

© Tom Feiza Mr. Fix-It Inc.

H008

Garage Door Operator - Manual Release

© Tom Feiza Mr. Fix-It Inc.

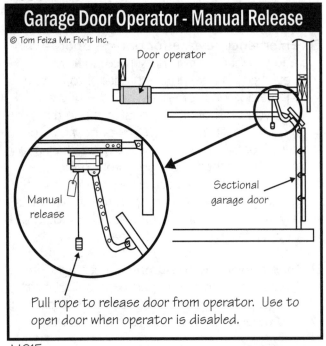

Door operator

Manual release

Sectional garage door

Pull rope to release door from operator. Use to open door when operator is disabled.

M015

Garage Door Key Cable Release

(For detached garage with no access door.)

Door operator

Cable to manual release

Cable

Open lock and pull cable

Lock & key

© Tom Feiza Mr. Fix-It Inc.

Remove lock from outside and pull cable on lock to manually release door from operator.

M018

☐ **Fire extinguishers**. Place fire extinguishers in your kitchen, garage, and basement. Make sure everyone knows how to use them.

☐ **Escape plan**. Have a plan for how to get out fast in case of emergency. Establish a specific location where everyone can meet just outside the house. Practice your plan.

☐ **Emergency toolbox**. Have a flashlight and basic tools set aside for emergencies. The flashlight should be rechargeable; keep it mounted on its charger.

This is a basic list. For more detailed information, contact your local utilities, police, and fire department. It is very important to know how to react to an emergency and to know that emergency shut-offs will work when needed.

This chapter provides a set of tags you may attach to various utilities in your home.

Water main valve, cold climate (Municipal water system)
Usually located on street side of home

Water Supply System in a Cold Climate

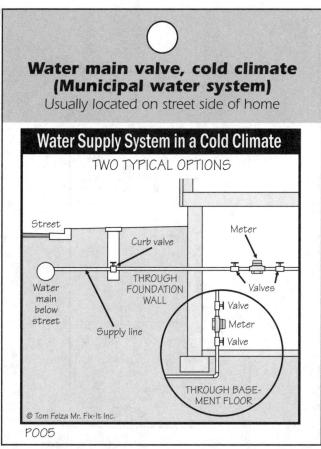

P005

Main valve for water (Well-water system)
Located near well pressure tank

Well - Main Water Disconnects

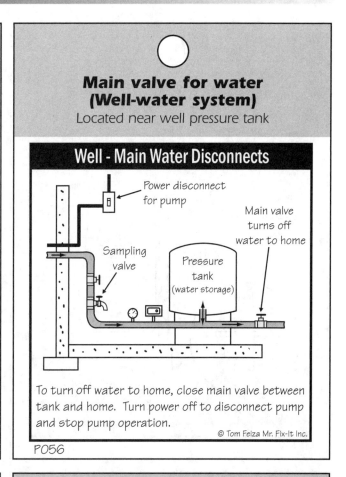

To turn off water to home, close main valve between tank and home. Turn power off to disconnect pump and stop pump operation.

© Tom Feiza Mr. Fix-It Inc.

P056

Main disconnect for power (Well-water system)
Located near well pressure tank

Well - Main Water Disconnects

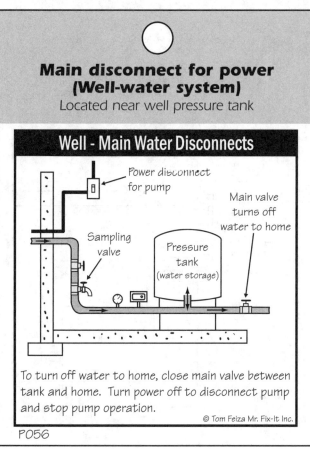

To turn off water to home, close main valve between tank and home. Turn power off to disconnect pump and stop pump operation.

© Tom Feiza Mr. Fix-It Inc.

P056

Water main valve, warm climate
Located outside on street side

Water Main / Meter - Warm Climate

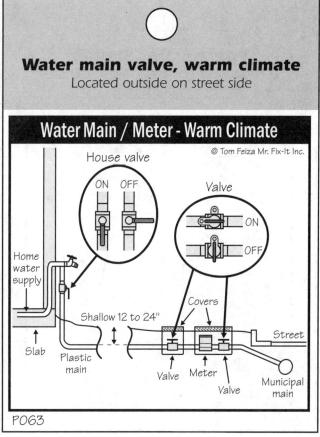

P063

Natural gas main valve
Located at gas meter

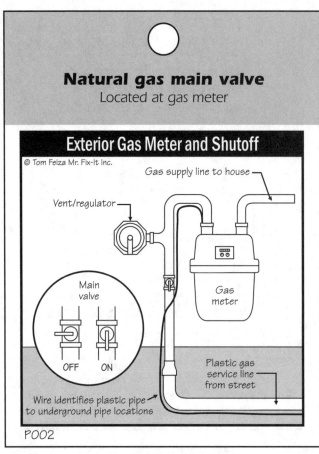

Exterior Gas Meter and Shutoff

© Tom Feiza Mr. Fix-It Inc.

Gas supply line to house

Vent/regulator

Main valve

OFF   ON

Gas meter

Plastic gas service line from street

Wire identifies plastic pipe to underground pipe locations

P002

Furnace / Air Conditioner main switch
Located on or near furnace

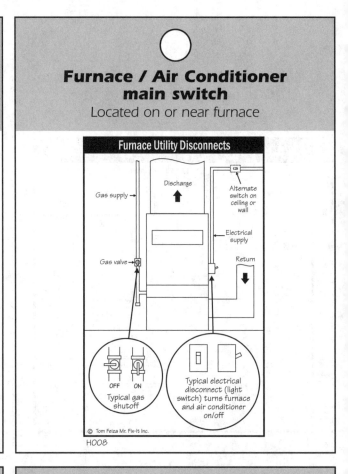

Furnace Utility Disconnects

Gas supply

Discharge

Alternate switch on ceiling or wall

Electrical supply

Gas valve

Return

OFF   ON
Typical gas shutoff

Typical electrical disconnect (light switch) turns furnace and air conditioner on/off

© Tom Feiza Mr. Fix-It Inc.

H008

Propane Gas Shutoff
Located near entrance of pipe to home and/or on tank

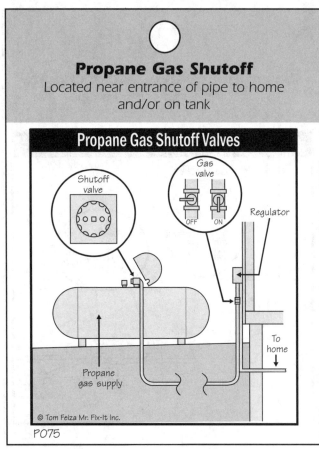

Propane Gas Shutoff Valves

Shutoff valve

Gas valve

OFF   ON

Regulator

To home

Propane gas supply

© Tom Feiza Mr. Fix-It Inc.

P075

Oil Supply Valve
Located at lower end of tank on oil tubing

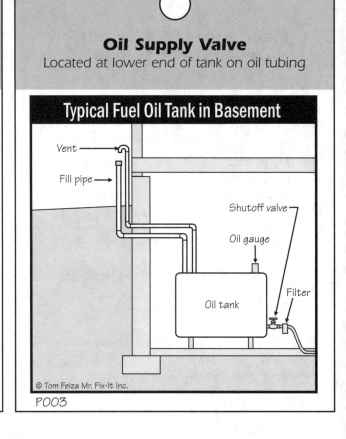

Typical Fuel Oil Tank in Basement

Vent

Fill pipe

Shutoff valve

Oil gauge

Filter

Oil tank

© Tom Feiza Mr. Fix-It Inc.

P003

Dishwasher Supply
Located below the sink or in the crawl space or basement below

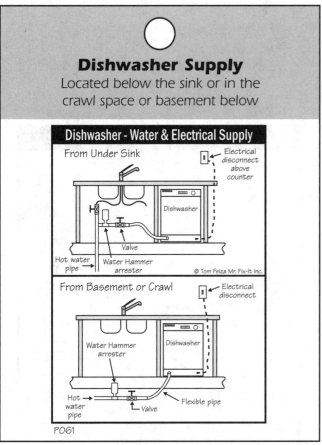

Dishwasher - Water & Electrical Supply

From Under Sink

- Electrical disconnect above counter
- Dishwasher
- Valve
- Hot water pipe
- Water Hammer arrester

© Tom Feiza Mr. Fix-It Inc.

From Basement or Crawl

- Electrical disconnect
- Water Hammer arrester
- Dishwasher
- Hot water pipe
- Valve
- Flexible pipe

P061

Furnace – Outside Air Supply Damper
Located in duct to furnace return

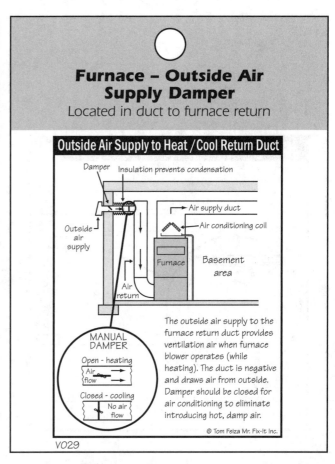

Outside Air Supply to Heat / Cool Return Duct

- Damper
- Insulation prevents condensation
- Air supply duct
- Air conditioning coil
- Outside air supply
- Furnace
- Basement area
- Air return

MANUAL DAMPER

Open - heating
Air flow

Closed - cooling
No air flow

The outside air supply to the furnace return duct provides ventilation air when furnace blower operates (while heating). The duct is negative and draws air from outside. Damper should be closed for air conditioning to eliminate introducing hot, damp air.

© Tom Feiza Mr. Fix-It Inc.

V029

Water heater shutoff
Cold-water valve located at top of water heater

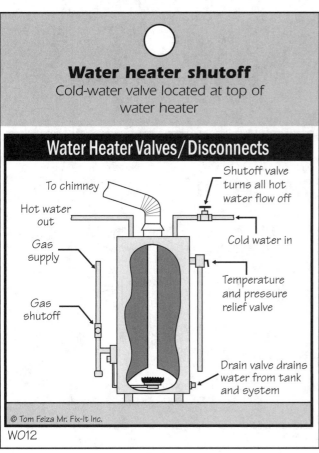

Water Heater Valves / Disconnects

- To chimney
- Hot water out
- Gas supply
- Gas shutoff
- Shutoff valve turns all hot water flow off
- Cold water in
- Temperature and pressure relief valve
- Drain valve drains water from tank and system

© Tom Feiza Mr. Fix-It Inc.

W012

Main electrical disconnect
Located at main fuse box or breaker

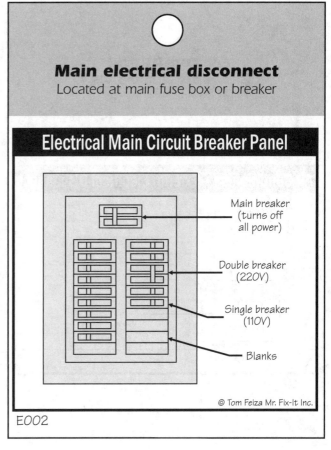

Electrical Main Circuit Breaker Panel

- Main breaker (turns off all power)
- Double breaker (220V)
- Single breaker (110V)
- Blanks

© Tom Feiza Mr. Fix-It Inc.

E002

Emergency release for garage door
Located where door connects to opener track

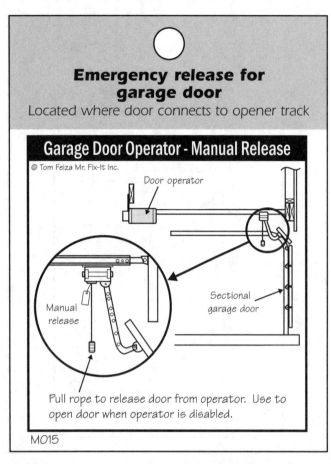

Garage Door Operator - Manual Release

© Tom Feiza Mr. Fix-It Inc.

Door operator

Manual release

Sectional garage door

Pull rope to release door from operator. Use to open door when operator is disabled.

M015

Emergency garage door cable release
Lock located in garage door

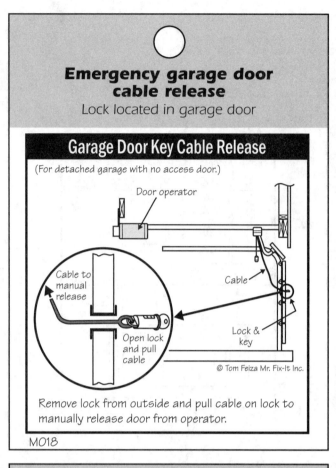

Garage Door Key Cable Release

(For detached garage with no access door.)

Door operator

Cable to manual release

Cable

Open lock and pull cable

Lock & key

© Tom Feiza Mr. Fix-It Inc.

Remove lock from outside and pull cable on lock to manually release door from operator.

M018

Air conditioner 240-volt disconnect
Located near exterior AC unit

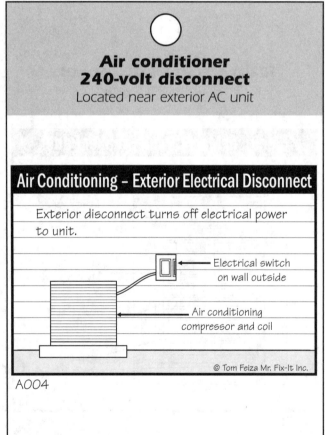

Air Conditioning - Exterior Electrical Disconnect

Exterior disconnect turns off electrical power to unit.

Electrical switch on wall outside

Air conditioning compressor and coil

© Tom Feiza Mr. Fix-It Inc.

A004

Heat Pump Disconnect
Located near exterior heat pump unit

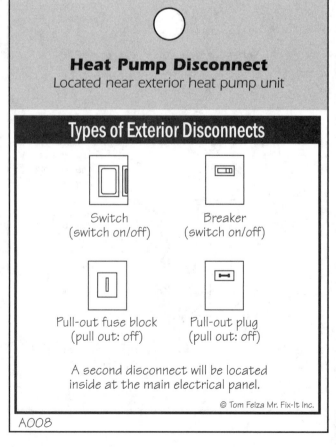

Types of Exterior Disconnects

Switch (switch on/off)

Breaker (switch on/off)

Pull-out fuse block (pull out: off)

Pull-out plug (pull out: off)

A second disconnect will be located inside at the main electrical panel.

© Tom Feiza Mr. Fix-It Inc.

A008

Index

Z

Ordering Information
Books by Tom Feiza, Mr. Fix-It

Mr. Fix-It's books are available through book retailers, from Internet bookstores, and from Tom Feiza – Mr. Fix-It, Inc.
Wholesale discounts are available for quantity purchases through Tom Feiza – Mr. Fix-It, Inc.

How to Operate Your Home – Professional Edition
(ISBN 978-0-9832018-2-3) $29.95

The ultimate guide for operating your home – just like an owner's manual for your car. Answers all those questions about how a home works and how you should be operating your home. Full-color cover, 304 pages, over 600 illustrations.

My Home – Mi Casa: Tips To Operate Your Home in Spanish/English
(ISBN 978-0-9674759-6-7) $19.95

Spanish and English guide to all systems in your home. Over 300 illustrations in Spanish and English. Operate, maintain, and repair your home. Full-color cover, 160 pages.

How to Operate Your Home – Standard Edition
(ISBN 978-0-9832018-3-0) $18.95

A 160-page "systems only" version of How To Operate Your Home with a full-color cover and over 300 illustrations. Includes the first eight chapters of How To Operate Your Home plus a bonus chapter on emergency shutoffs.

My Home – Tips for Operating Your Home
(ISBN 978-0-9674759-8-1) $12.95

A quick guide to help you operate your home. Over 150 illustrations and explanations of how systems work. Full-color cover, 64 pages.

Basic Home Systems
$11.95

A guide to most basic systems found in homes. Designed as a cost-effective attachment to your home inspection report, and three-hole-drilled for easy addition to a binder.

Home Systems Illustrated
(ISBN 978-0-9832018-0-9) $249.95

Includes more than 1,200 line art drawings of home systems, equipment, construction details, operational tips, typical problems and maintenance tips for residential construction. All illustrations are provided in JPEG format on a CD. The 443-page book displays all illustrations.

Mr. Fix-It Quick Tips
$275 for 13 Tips

Do you want to keep in touch with your customers but lack the content? Let Quick Tips do the talking for you. Send as e-mails (including Constant Contact®), use in newsletters and other printed material, and publish on your website. 26 new tips every year. Unlimited use.

Home Tips
$89 for 10 articles

10 Mr. Fix-It Home Tips PDF articles for your website, email, printing, and newsletters. Typical topics: Keep Your Basement Dry, Window Condensation, Replace Your Roof. Delivered electronically. 65 pages full of content.

SEE THE NEXT PAGE FOR A BOOK ORDER FORM

Visit **www.htoyh.com** or **www.HowToOperateYourHome.com** for updated information on all our products, or to order online.

Quantity discounts are available for large orders.
Contact Tom Feiza – Mr. Fix-It, Inc. at (800) 201-3829, tom@misterfix-it.com

Order Form
April 2013

HOW TO OPERATE YOUR HOME

ITEM	QUANTITY	PRICE	QTY	TOTAL
How to Operate Your Home – Professional Edition	1-9 books	$29.95/each		
304 pages, over 600 drawings	10-15 books	$15.00/each		
24 chapters	1 case ($9.50/book)	$152/case		
16 books/case	2 cases ($8.50/book)	$136/case		
Drilled / undrilled (select one)	3 cases ($7.50/book)	$120/case		
	6 cases ($6.50/book)	$104/case		
How to Operate Your Home – Standard Edition	1-9 books	$18.95/each		
160 pages, over 300 drawings	10-27 books	$9.00/each		
9 chapters (bonus chapter included)	1 case ($4.75/book)	$133/case		
28 books/case	2 cases ($4.25/book)	$119/case		
Basic Home Systems	1-9 books	$11.95/each		
80 pages, over 100 drawings	10-59 books	$6.00/each		
60 books/case	1 case ($3.75/book)	$225.00/case		
	2 cases ($3.25/book)	$195.00/case		
My Home - Mi Casa	1-9 books	$19.95/each		
Spanish/English, 160 pages	10-27 books	$11.00/each		
28 books/case	1 case ($6.00/book)	$168.00/case		
	2 cases ($5.00/book)	$140.00/case		
My Home	1-9 books	$12.95/each		
Bullet point format, 64 pages	10-61 books	$8.00/each		
62 books/case	1 case ($3.75/book)	$232.50/case		
	2 cases ($3.25/book)	$201.50/case		
Mr. Fix-It Quick Tips – Tip and Color Illustration	13 issues	$275.00		
Home Systems Illustrated – 2011 Edition	1	$249.95		
Over 1,200 JPEG images on CD and 443-page book	upgrade from 2009 edition	$125.00		
Home Tips	10 PDF articles	$89.00		

Subtotal	
WI residents add 5.1% sales tax	
Shipping (UPS ground – we will calculate)	
TOTAL	

Shipping Information:

❏ Residential   ❏ Commercial

_____
Name

_____
Company

_____
Address

_____
City, State, ZIP

_____
Phone

_____
E-mail

_____
How did you hear about us?

Send form and check payable to:
Tom Feiza, Mr. Fix-It, Inc.
N8 W28892 Shepherds Way
Waukesha, WI 53188

Payment Method / Cardholder Address:

❏ Cash/Money Order   ❏ Check

❏ Visa   ❏ MasterCard

❏ Discover   ❏ American Express

_____
Card Number   Exp. Date

_____
Cardholder Name, Company

_____
Cardholder Address

_____
Cardholder City, State, ZIP

_____
Signature

Credit Card Orders:
Fax Form to: (262) 303-4883
Phone Order: (262) 303-4884
Toll-Free: (800) 201-3829

Thanks for your order!